THE LAST DAYS SERIES

THE FINAL

ANTICHRIST

THE COMING CAESAR

DON STEWART

The Final Antichrist:
The Coming Caesar

By Don Stewart

© 2016 Don Stewart

Published by EOW (Educating Our World)
www.educatingourworld.com
San Dimas, California 91773
All rights reserved

TABLE OF CONTENTS

The Final Antichrist:
The Coming Caesar

Introduction

There are many questions which arise regarding this figure known as "Antichrist." Is it a force, a religious system, or an actual person who is in view?

If it is a person, is he a mere human being, or is he a supernatural character, perhaps even the offspring of the devil himself? Has this person already appeared on the stage of history, or should we expect to see him in the future? What does the Bible have to say about these questions?

These matters have been debated throughout the centuries. Indeed, there is tremendous curiosity and fascination among believers and non-believers alike on this subject of Antichrist. Fortunately, the Bible gives us much detail about the origin, background, evil character, inglorious career and eventual doom of the final Antichrist, the coming Caesar.

This book will look at what Scripture has to say about this personage. Our goal is to discover exactly how we should understand the biblical references to the Antichrist.

OUR FOCUS IS UPON JESUS

The ultimate goal, however, is not to focus on Antichrist, but rather upon Jesus Christ. Antichrist will appear for only a short time while our relationship with Jesus Christ will last forever. Consequently, we should always have this eternal perspective as we study this subject.

With this in mind, let us now look at what the Bible has to say about "The Final Antichrist: The Coming Caesar."

Who or What Is The Antichrist?

In the New Testament we find the term "Antichrist" used. What does it refer to? Is it a person or an impersonal force? If it is a person can we know his identity? What can we learn about Antichrist from the Bible?

THE MEANING OF THE WORD ANTICHRIST

The word "Antichrist" is actually made up of two Greek words. The word "anti" can mean either, "in place of," "instead of," or "in opposition to."

The Greek word "Christos" means the "Messiah," or "Anointed One." He is the "Christ."

Therefore, the term Antichrist indicates someone, or some thing, that attempts to take the place of, usurp the authority of, or be in opposition to, the genuine Messiah, Jesus Christ. In other words, Antichrist is, in many ways, the opposite of Christ.

THE TERM ANTICHRIST IS ONLY FOUND IN THE WRITINGS OF JOHN

The specific word "Antichrist" is only found in the New Testament writings of the Apostle John. He uses the term five different times in two of his letters, First John and Second John. They are as follows.

THERE ARE MANY ANTICHRISTS, A FINAL ANTICHRIST IS STILL TO COME (1 JOHN 2:18)

In this verse, we have two different references to Antichrist. We discover that there are many Antichrists who will come and go, as well as one final Antichrist who is yet to appear. John wrote.

> Dear children, the last hour is here. You have heard that the Antichrist is coming, and already many such Antichrists have appeared. From this we know that the last hour has come (1 John 2:18 NLT).

This first reference in this verse is singular, not plural. It is "the Antichrist" who is coming. This seems to be referring to something or some one very specific who has not yet arrived on the scene.

There is also a plural reference in this verse. At the time of his writing, John reports that "many Antichrists" have already appeared. From this we can conclude that many Antichrists have appeared and will continue to appear until the final Antichrist arrives.

ANTICHRIST DENIES THE TRUE CHRIST (1 JOHN 2:22)

John later said that anyone who denies Jesus is the Messiah, or the Christ, is "an Antichrist." He put it this way.

> And who is a liar? Anyone who says that Jesus is not the Christ. Anyone who denies the Father and the Son is an Antichrist (1 John 2:22 NLT).

If a person denies God the Father and God the Son, then they are considered to be an Antichrist; one who is opposed to the God of the Bible.

THE SPIRIT OF ANTICHRIST WAS ALREADY PRESENT (1 JOHN 4:3)

Though Antichrist was coming, we are also told that the spirit of Antichrist was already present at the time of John. He wrote.

> Every spirit that does not confess Jesus is not from God.
> This is the spirit of the antichrist, which you heard was
> coming and now is in the world already (1 John 4:3 ESV).

There is such a thing as the "spirit of Antichrist," and we are told that this particular spirit was in the world when John wrote.

PRESENT-DAY DECEIVERS ARE LINKED TO ANTICHRIST (2 JOHN 7)

In the Second letter of John, he warned about deceivers, or Antichrists, who are already in the world. He linked them to the final Antichrist. We read the following.

> For many deceivers have gone out into the world, those who
> do not confess the coming of Jesus Christ in the flesh. Such
> a one is the deceiver and the antichrist (2 John 7 ESV).

Anyone who does not confess that Jesus Christ has come in the flesh, that God the Son became a human being in the Person of Jesus Christ, is called the deceiver, the Antichrist.

OBSERVATIONS ABOUT WHAT THE BIBLE SAYS CONCERNING ANTICHRIST

From these writings of John, we learn the following things from the five times that he uses this expression "Antichrist."

1. THE FINAL ANTICHRIST IS YET TO COME

The first use of the term is to designate some person or some thing which will rise up and oppose Christ in the future. At the time John wrote, this final Antichrist had not yet appeared. Therefore, Antichrist was still to come.

What is interesting to note is that the people to whom John was writing had already heard about this coming Antichrist. John himself may have been the one who taught them about this personage. The subject was well-known to the people at that time in the early church.

2. PRESENTLY THERE ARE MANY ANTICHRISTS

Although there will be a final Antichrist, the second usage of the term informs us that many Antichrists have come and will continue to come before the appearance of the final one. In other words, every generation has "an Antichrist." This is what John is emphasizing in his letter. Many types of this future Antichrist, the coming Caesar, have already appeared and are still appearing. Believers need to be aware of this.

These truths about Antichrist are in harmony with what Paul wrote to the Thessalonians about the spirit of lawlessness which was already at work. He wrote.

> For the secret power of lawlessness is already at work; but the one who now holds it back will continue to do so till he is taken out of the way. And then the lawless one will be revealed, whom the Lord Jesus will overthrow with the breath of his mouth and destroy by the splendor of his coming (2 Thessalonians 2:7,8 NIV).

This lawless power of Antichrist has been at work since the beginning of the Christian church through many individual Antichrists which have come and gone. This same spirit of Antichrist will continue until the arrival of the final Antichrist.

3. ANTICHRIST, BY NATURE, IS A LIAR

The third use of the term Antichrist by John points out one of the basic qualities of this adversary of the Lord; Antichrist is a liar. It is one who denies that Jesus is the Christ, the Messiah. Therefore, the Antichrist denies both God the Father and God the Son.

4. THE MESSAGE OF ANTICHRIST IS A DENIAL OF JESUS

The fourth usage informs us of the message of Antichrist. The spirit of Antichrist will not confess that Jesus Christ actually came in human flesh. It is a denial that God became a human being in the Person of

Jesus Christ. This is crucial to understand. Antichrist denies the very reason for which Jesus Christ came into our world.

5. ANTICHRISTS DENY THE CHRIST HAS ACTUALLY COME INTO THE WORLD

The fifth usage of the term Antichrist also emphasizes the denial of this personage that Jesus Christ has come in the flesh.

Some attempt to find a denial of Jesus' Second Coming in this statement. They translate 2 John 7 as a future tense, "Jesus Christ is coming." This would have Antichrist denying the Second Coming of Christ, as well as his First Coming.

While this is possible, it seems more likely that Antichrist is denying the fact that God became a human being in the Person of Jesus Christ. Thus, the specific denial of Antichrist is the denial of the coming of Christ the first time around; a key truth of the New Testament.

This sums up some basic facts we learn about Antichrist from John's use of the term.

IS ANTICHRIST A PERSON, RELIGIOUS SYSTEM, OR INFLUENCE?

The term Antichrist has been subject to a number of different interpretations among Bible believers. Some see it as referring to a false religious system while others believe it refers to an evil influence or spirit that is against Jesus Christ.

There is also the view that Antichrist refers to an actual person, who has already come upon the scene of history, or who will come in the future. We will examine each of these possibilities as we look at what the Scripture has to say about this important topic.

ANTICHRIST IS PROMINENT IN SCRIPTURE

While John is the only biblical writer to use this particular term "Antichrist," we will discover that the subject of the coming "Antichrist" is actually found throughout the entire Scripture. Indeed, one may be surprised to learn that there are over one hundred references to the future Antichrist in the Bible.

Thus, Antichrist is a very important subject. This being the case, the entire scope of biblical teaching on this subject should be thoroughly examined. This is exactly what we plan to do.

SUMMARY TO QUESTION 1
WHO OR WHAT IS ANTICHRIST?

The word Antichrist is made up of two Greek words; *anti* and *Christos*. The word "anti" can mean, "in place of," "instead of," or "in opposition to." The Greek word, "Christos" means "the Messiah," or "Anointed One." It refers to the Christ. Therefore, the term Antichrist indicates something or someone who attempts to take the place of, or be in opposition to, the genuine Messiah, Jesus Christ.

The specific term Antichrist is only found in the New Testament, and only in the writings of the disciple John. It is used in both the singular and in the plural. Four references are in the letter of First John while there is one reference in Second John. These five times in which this term is used tells us much about Antichrist.

For one thing, when John wrote his first letter the final Antichrist had not yet arrived; although many Antichrists had already appeared. This indicates a single final Antichrist will come on the scene. However, before this personage does appear there will be many individuals who will exhibit similar traits to the final Antichrist. They too can be rightfully labeled "Antichrists."

Consequently, we must distinguish between the many Antichrists which have appeared throughout the history of the church, and the final Antichrist who is yet to appear. We also find that Antichrist is a liar who denies Jesus is the Messiah. By denying Jesus Christ, one denies both God the Father and God the Son.

The message of Antichrist is that Jesus was not God in human flesh. In other words, he denies the very central message of the gospel. This is crucial to understand. Antichrist denies the biblical truth that God the Son came to our world in the Person of Jesus Christ.

These are some of the basic facts regarding the subject of Antichrist from the use of the term in John's writings. Much more could be added.

There is a question as to whether Antichrist should be viewed as a person, as an influence, or as a religious system. Believers have debated this through the ages.

As we shall see, it will be obvious that John, as well as the other biblical writers, was writing about an evil individual who will eventually come upon the stage of history, a final Antichrist.

While John is the only biblical writer who uses this specific term "Antichrist," this subject is found over one hundred times in Scripture. Both testaments contain references to this final Antichrist. Therefore, it is not an obscure topic. Antichrist is one of the main characters of the Bible.

Why Is It Important To Study About Antichrist?

Before we engage in a detailed study of the subject of Antichrist, it is important that we understand why we ought to do so. Why should we take our time and study such an evil subject? Shouldn't our time be better spent by studying certain truths about God? Shouldn't we concentrate on the good instead of the evil?

There are, however, a number of reasons as to why the subject of Antichrist should get our attention.

1. THE SUBJECT OF ANTICHRIST IS PART OF HOLY SCRIPTURE

To begin with, the subject of Antichrist is contained in the Bible, the Word of God. Since it is recorded in Holy Scripture it should not be neglected, rather the subject of Antichrist should be thoroughly studied.

In fact, the Bible is clear that *all* Scripture is profitable for our study. Paul wrote to Timothy.

> All Scripture is breathed out by God and profitable for teaching, for reproof, for correction, and for training in righteousness, that the man of God may be competent, equipped for every good work (2 Timothy 3:16,17 ESV).

Since the subject of Antichrist is part of Scripture, it will be profitable for us to study. For this reason alone, it should not be neglected.

Furthermore, as we shall see, there are a number of practical benefits which will result from a look at what the Bible has to say about the coming Antichrist. It is *not* merely an academic exercise.

2. ANTICHRIST IS HIGHLIGHTED IN SCRIPTURE

There is something else. The final Antichrist, this coming Caesar, is not an obscure subject in the Bible. Indeed, as we shall discover there are a number of passages, over one hundred of them in both testaments, which talk about the coming Antichrist. The fact that Scripture gives such attention to this subject is another reason why we should also. Indeed, apart from Jesus Christ, Antichrist is the most written about character in the entire Bible.

3. HE IS PROMINENT IN END-TIME EVENTS

Not only is Antichrist highlighted in Scripture, he is also "the" prominent figure on the earth with respect to end-time events. Paul wrote about this to the Thessalonians.

> Don't let anyone deceive you in any way, for [that day will not come] until the rebellion occurs and the man of lawlessness is revealed, the man doomed to destruction. He will oppose and will exalt himself over everything that is called God or is worshiped, so that he sets himself up in God's temple, proclaiming himself to be God (2 Thessalonians 2:3-4 NIV).

Since Antichrist is the major figure on the earth during the predicted end-time events, we should want to know as much as we can about him.

4. SOME CHRISTIANS THINK WE WILL LIVE TO SEE HIM

There is the perspective, held by many Christians, that the church of Jesus Christ, the true believers, will actually still exist on the earth during the reign of the final Antichrist. We do know that there will be saints, or believers, during this period of time.

In fact, we read in the Book of Revelation that this personage persecutes and actually kills many of the saints of God. Scripture says.

> When he opened the fifth seal, I saw under the altar the souls of those who had been slain for the word of God and for the witness they had borne. They cried out with a loud voice, "O Sovereign Lord, holy and true, how long before you will judge and avenge our blood on those who dwell on the earth?" (Revelation 6:9-10 ESV).

Many think this refers to the believers which are part of the New Testament church. Since the church will be around during the career of a personal Antichrist, then we should do everything that we can to prepare for this difficult period. This includes knowing what we can about this personage.

Even if we will not be around to see Antichrist, at the very least, this man of sin will come shortly before the Lord returns. Either way, we need to know about him.

5. THE SUBJECT IS MORE THAN SOMETHING OF MERE CURIOSITY OR SENSATIONALISM

The study of such a character as Antichrist, therefore, should be more than a mere exercise in curiosity. It has many practical implications. Consequently, if we want to study the entire counsel of God we should not neglect this important subject. This is especially true if we may believe the church will suffer its worse persecution ever through the final Antichrist.

Therefore, it is not a subject merely for the sensationalist or for the curious. It is a subject which every serious student of the Word of God should investigate.

6. ANTICHRIST HAS BEEN A SUBJECT OF STUDY BY BELIEVERS FROM THE BEGINNING

The fact that we are embarking on a study of Antichrist is not something novel. Indeed, from the very beginning of the Christian church there have been those who have been exploring the subject.

For example, the second century church father, Irenaeus, wrote a work titled *Against Heresies*. In this particular volume, this early churchman discussed the person of Antichrist as well as the subject of the "mark of the beast."

One of the immediate disciples of Irenaeus, a man named Hippolytus, wrote a work called *On Christ and Antichrist*. This detailed volume was entirely devoted to the subject of the coming man of sin.

Many other references could be cited. The point is this: Antichrist has been a subject of interest among Bible-believers from the very beginning of the New Testament church.

CONCLUSION: THIS SUBJECT SHOULD BE PROPERLY STUDIED

These are a few of the many reasons as to why this subject should not be neglected. As can readily be seen, it is important that we take the time to understand what the Scripture says about this topic.

Sad to say, it actually promotes the interests of the devil to keep people in ignorance about the coming man of sin. Satan would love people to neglect this subject, or cloud it with unwarranted speculation or sensationalism.

Unfortunately, there has been too much sensationalism on this subject. The tragic fact is that many books have been written which claim to identify the long-awaited Antichrist. These writers believe that they have determined the personage whose name equals the number 666. When these writers are eventually shown to be incorrect, as all of them have been, their misidentification has caused many people to ignore the topic, or assume nothing can be accurately known about it. This is heartbreaking. There is much to learn from a proper study of Scripture on this issue.

Our goal, therefore, should be to get a comprehensive understanding of Antichrist from a study of the Bible and then draw conclusions from what we have learned. In this way, we can do justice to this extremely important subject.

SUMMARY TO QUESTION 2
WHY IS IT IMPORTANT TO STUDY ABOUT ANTICHRIST?

The subject of Antichrist is one in which many believers do not ever undertake. For a variety of reasons, they are not the least bit interested in learning what the Bible says about this topic. However, this is not how we should approach this issue. There are a number of reasons as to why this subject should be thoroughly studied.

For one thing, the biblical teaching about Antichrist is part of Holy Scripture. Since all Scripture is profitable for our personal study, we should discover what the Bible does say about this issue.

Furthermore, there are many things to be learned from a study of Antichrist. Since Antichrist is one who opposes, or attempts to take the place of Christ, we can learn valuable lessons of what we should and should not do as we attempt to imitate the genuine Christ.

In addition, the subject of Antichrist is highlighted in Scripture. As we shall see in our study, there are a number of passages in both testaments which deal with Antichrist. Since it is an important theme in Scripture we should take the time to look into it.

Indeed, the final Antichrist is center-stage for events which are still to come on the face of the earth. The Book of Revelation, which speaks of these coming events, highlights Antichrist and his evil deeds. Because Antichrist is such an important figure on the earth before the Second

Coming of Jesus Christ, it gives us further reason to know as much as we can about this subject.

There may be an extremely practical reason for a study such as this. Many Bible-believing Christians think that the church will be around to personally experience the final Antichrist. We know that many believers will be persecuted and killed by Antichrist. If it is true that Christians will face Antichrist, then we need to know as much as possible about this personage to prepare for this difficult time. Even if the church will not personally experience this coming man of sin, the subject is still of the utmost importance.

Therefore, the study of Antichrist should be more than a mere curiosity for believers. It has many practical benefits. While we should be careful to steer clear of unwarranted sensationalism when looking into the topic of Antichrist, we should not avoid this important focus of Scripture. Indeed, Christians have made a study of Antichrist from the very beginnings of the church. In this same tradition, modern-day believers should also take the time to delve into this issue.

Unfortunately, many have not done this because of the sensationalism attached to the subject. It is regrettable that so many works have been produced identifying the final Antichrist and how a certain person's name equals the number 666. Of course, their claims are eventually refuted. When this occurs it often causes people to step back from the subject since they do not want to be identified with this sort of frivolous behavior. This is why we need a proper understanding of what Scripture says about this topic. Only then can we make informed conclusions.

What Can We Learn From The Way The Subject Of The Antichrist Been Viewed During The History Of The Church?

The subject of Antichrist has been one in which Christians have continually discussed since the time of Jesus. We can learn much by examining how other Bible-believers have historically viewed this subject. Indeed, from a look at how the church has understood the subject of Antichrist we can make the following observations.

1. CHRISTIANS HAVE SOUGHT TO DISCOVER THE IDENTITY OF ANTICHRIST FROM THE BEGINNING

One important thing which we learn is that Christians have been discussing Antichrist from the very beginning, as well as trying to determine the identity of this coming "man of sin." While the apostles of Jesus were still alive there were at least three candidates who had some of the qualifications of the coming Antichrist. Each of them was a Roman Emperor.

CALIGULA

The first candidate for the biblical Antichrist in New Testament times was the crazed Roman Emperor Caligula. Just like what the Bible says will occur with the predicted final Antichrist, Caligula attempted to place an image of himself in the Holy Temple in Jerusalem. His attempts failed for he was assassinated before his imperial order was carried out. Yet for a time, he looked as though he would be the one who would fulfill these biblical predictions.

NERO

Caesar Nero was another individual to whom the final Antichrist was linked. While he did indeed possess a number of traits that the coming man of sin will himself possess, Nero, like Caligula, passed from the scene without fulfilling the Scripture about this evil personage. He was not the predicted one.

DOMITIAN

There was a third candidate for Antichrist among the Roman Emperors, Domitian. He is the man who banished John the Apostle to the Island of Patmos, where John penned the Book of Revelation. Indeed, some interpreters believe Domitian is actually the first "beast" which John wrote about.

Again, it was not to be. All of the Apostles died, and the Emperor Domitian passed from the scene, without fulfilling the predictions of the coming Antichrist. The final Antichrist was still to appear at some time in the future.

2. IN THE EARLY CHURCH THE ANTICHRIST WAS UNIVERSALLY BELIEVED TO BE A GENUINE MAN, NOT AN INSTITUTION

This brings us to an extremely important point. While Christians from the very beginning have attempted to determine the identity of the Antichrist, without exception, they were looking for an *individual man* to fulfill the biblical predictions. Indeed, as far as we can tell, everyone in the early church who wrote about the coming Antichrist, was looking for a particular individual to fulfill the predictions. We never find them merely looking for some type of "spirit of evil" or a certain "evil institution."

In other words, they understood the Scripture predicting that a man will come on the scene of history who will be the final Antichrist, the great "Opposer" of the Lord.

We will provide a number of illustrations.

THE EARLY DOCUMENT "THE TEACHING OF THE APOSTLES"

A document written at an early date called, "The Teaching of the Apostles," had this to say about the coming man of sin.

For in the last days the false prophets and the destroyers shall be multiplied, and the sheep shall be turned into wolves, and love shall be turned into hate. For when lawlessness increases, they shall hate and persecute and deliver up one another; and then shall appear the world-deceiver as the Son of God, who shall do signs and wonders, and the earth shall be delivered into his hands, and he shall do lawless deeds such as have never yet been done since the beginning of the world. Then shall the race of men come into the fire of trial, and many shall be offended and shall perish, but they who have endured in their faith shall be saved under the very curse itself.

This document, which may date back to a period of time shortly after the time of the apostles, makes it clear that in the last days, a miracle-working world-deceiver will come on the scene shortly before the return of Christ. In other words, the believers were expecting a specific person to come and do all these things.

IRENAEUS: BISHOP OF LYON (A.D. 140-202)

Irenaeus, writing in the second century, composed a treatise on the coming Antichrist. He too emphasized that Antichrist was a particular individual who would appear immediately before the coming of Christ. He wrote that Antichrist will sit in a rebuilt Jerusalem temple. He said.

> He will reign a time, times, and half a time (Daniel 7:25) i.e.
> three and a half years and will sit in the temple at Jerusalem;
> then the Lord shall come from heaven and cast him into the
> lake of fire, and shall bring to the saints the time of reign-
> ing, the seventh day of hallowed rest, and give to Abraham
> the promised inheritance (Irenaeus, *Against Heresies*, 30.4).

Irenaeus was obviously looking for a personal Antichrist to come, as
well as a future temple to be built.

THE FIRST COMPLETE WORK ON THE SUBJECT OF ANTICHRIST: HIPPOLYTUS (A.D. 220)

Hippolytus was a disciple of Irenaeus. As far as we can tell, he wrote
the first complete work on the subject of the coming man of sin
called, "On Christ and Antichrist." Among other things, he said the
following.

Which horn (Daniel 7) shows that the one which budded is none
other than the Antichrist who will restore the kingdom of the Jews .
. . Christ Jesus sprung from the Hebrews; He too will be born a Jew.
Christ declared His flesh to be a temple and raised it on the third day,
so he (the Antichrist) will restore at Jerusalem the Temple of Stone . . .

This is a further reference to this coming "man" of sin. Hippolytus
was looking for a specific person to come on the scene. In addition,
he believed that this final Antichrist would restore the temple that had
been destroyed some one hundred and fifty years earlier.

TERTULLIAN OF CARTHAGE A.D. 170: ANTICHRISTS ARE ALREADY HERE

Tertullian, the Bishop of Carthage, also wrote about the coming
Antichrist, as well as other Antichrists who had already arrived. He
seems to be the first of the early Christian writers which recognized
that the spirit of Antichrist was always present in the world. In other
words, there was always someone who was acting as "Antichrist" in

his rebellion against Christ and His church. However, he also realized that a personal Antichrist was still to come.

CYRIL BISHOP OF JERUSALEM (FOURTH CENTURY)

In the fourth century, we have the following words from Cyril, Bishop of Jerusalem, about the coming Antichrist. He put it this way.

This aforementioned Antichrist comes when the times of the sovereignty of the Romans shall be fulfilled, and the concluding events of the world draw nigh. Ten kings of the Romans arise at the same time in different places, perhaps; but reigning at the same period. But after these, the Antichrist is the eleventh, having, by his magic and evil skill, violently possessed himself of the Roman power. Three of those who have reigned before him, he will subdue; the other seven he will hold in subjection to himself. At first he assumes a character of gentleness (as if a wise and understanding person), pretending both to moderation and philanthropy; deceiving, both by lying miracles and prodigies which come from his magical deceptions, the Jews, as if he were the expected Messiah. Afterwards he will addict himself to every kind of evil, cruelty, and excess, so as to surpass all who have been unjust and impious before him; having a bloody and relentless and pitiless mind, and full of wily devices against all, and especially against believers. But having dared such things three years and six months, he will be destroyed by the second glorious coming from heaven of the truly begotten Son of God, who is our Lord and Savior, Jesus the true Messiah; who, having destroyed Antichrist by the Spirit of His mouth, will deliver him to the fire Gehenna.

This is further testimony from another early church leader about this coming man of sin. Indeed, many specific details that are found in the Scripture about this coming world leader are cited by Cyril. He believed that they would be literally fulfilled someday, fulfilled by an individual person.

THE EPISTLE OF BARNABAS: THE ANTICHRIST IS THE BLACK ONE

There was an epistle written early in the history of the church which was attributed to the New Testament character Barnabas, the man who was the traveling companion of Paul. It is universally agreed that the biblical Barnabas did not write this epistle. Still, from this early document we learn about the coming man of sin whom the author calls "the Black One."

We find that this "Black One" will come out of the Roman Empire, which was assumed to be the fourth beast of Daniel's vision of four successive world empires. The writer warned of the following.

> Take heed in these last days. For the whole time of our faith shall profit us nothing unless we now, in the season of law-lessness and in the offenses that shall be, as become sons of God, offer resistance, that the Black One may not effect an entrance.

He wrote that the Black One must be resisted. This is further indication of the belief that the man of sin would be a solitary human being who had not yet made his appearance on the earth.

GREGORY OF TOURS (SIXTH CENTURY)

Gregory of Tours, who wrote at the end of the sixth century, penned the following words about the future Antichrist.

> Concerning the end of the world, I believe what I have learnt from those who have gone before me. Antichrist will assume circumcision, asserting himself to be the Christ. He will then place a statue to be worshipped in the Temple at Jerusalem, as we read that the Lord has said, 'You shall see the abomination of desolation standing in the holy place.'

Although the city of Jerusalem, along with the temple, had been destroyed some six centuries earlier, it was understood that the temple would one day be rebuilt.

Examples such as these, from the writings of the early believers, could be multiplied.

Therefore, the one thing which becomes clear from reading the Christian writers of the early centuries is that they universally believed Antichrist to be a definite human being who was still to come on the scene of history. Furthermore, he would literally fulfill the biblical predictions concerning the man of sin, including claiming to be God in a rebuilt temple in the city of Jerusalem.

(A.D. 1000) THE EXPECTATION OF CHRIST'S COMING (THE PAMPHLET OF ADSO)

The year A.D. 1000 was assumed to be significant by the Christians of that era. Indeed, as the one thousand year mark from the time of Christ approached, there was a certain expectation for the soon return of the Lord. The wife of Louis IV, the King of France, embraced this idea of the near coming of Christ. Since Scripture teaches that Antichrist must appear *before* the Second Coming of Christ, she then asked Adso, her court chaplain, to put together whatever he could compile about the subject of the future man of sin.

Adso eventually put his findings into writing. It was titled, "Little work on Antichrist." He concluded that the spirit of Antichrist had been around in the past in the Roman Emperors Nero and Domitian. However, there was still a final Antichrist to come. This Antichrist would be a real person.

From his understanding of Scripture, Adso assumed this man of sin would be a Jew from the tribe of Dan. Though he would be born in Babylon, Antichrist would be brought up in the land of Israel in two of the cities which Jesus cursed, Chorazin and Bethsaida.

He wrote the following of the final Antichrist.

> [He] will be born of Jewish parents, of the tribe of Dan,
> but his mother will not be a virgin, as many believe. . . .

> [Instead] the devil will enter into the mother of Antichrist, and his evil power will always support him. Babylon will be his birthplace, but he will be brought up and taught in [the cities of] Bethsaida and Chorazin. After his education at the hands of evil spirits he will go to Jerusalem and place his seat in the Temple which he will have rebuilt. . . . He will claim that he is the Son of the All-Powerful God. . . . He will perform many signs and great miracles. Those who believe in him will be marked on the forehead with a sign. For three and a half years he will rule, at the end of that period, he will put to death Enoch and Elijah, who will have previously opposed him by preaching the true faith. Shortly afterwards, Christ will appear, and Antichrist will be killed by Michael the Archangel.

Note that Adso believed that this miracle-working man of sin would come to the temple in Jerusalem and blaspheme the Lord, claiming to be the Son of God. Those who will accept his claim, and follow the man of sin, will receive his mark on their forehead. According to Adso, this final Antichrist would eventually be killed at the Second Coming of Jesus Christ by Michael the Archangel.

This pamphlet of Adso on the subject of Antichrist had enormous influence during the medieval period. As is consistent with what has been written before, the people were looking for a specific man to come onto the scene.

3. IN THE FOURTEENTH CENTURY: ANTICHRIST BEGINS TO BE INTERPRETED IDENTIFIED WITH THE PAPACY

As we have noted, Christians were looking for a specific individual to fulfill what Scripture says about the coming beast of the Book of Revelation, the final Antichrist. While many Antichrists had come, and were still coming, there is going to be one specific individual who will be different from all of the rest. Not only will he be a world ruler, his coming will immediately precede the Second Coming of Christ.

IDEAS ABOUT ANTICHRIST BEGIN TO CHANGE

However, this idea began to change in the fourteenth century. At that time the Antichrist was not equated with a personage who would arrive some time in the future but rather with someone who was presently upon the earth, the pope and the papacy.

About A.D. 1350, group of believers, known as the Waldensians published a pamphlet which equated Antichrist with the head of the Roman Catholic Church. While they were not the first group to do this, their identification struck a responsive chord in the hearts of many people and consequently the idea began to spread.

Since the Roman Church, led by the pope, had a history of persecuting Bible-believers, the idea that the papacy was the predicted Antichrist seemed to fit with what the Scripture had to say about this subject. Indeed, there are many elements of the Roman Church, the pope, and the papacy which were consistent with the biblical description of Antichrist.

Yet, while there are many points of agreement between the practices of the Roman Church with its popes and the coming Antichrist, the Bible clearly predicts that Antichrist will be a man; not an institution such as the Roman Catholic Church and the papacy. Furthermore, this one man must come on the scene immediately prior to the return of Jesus Christ. While the Roman Church and the papacy is in many ways a type of Antichrist, it does not fulfill the specific predictions of Scripture.

4. THE PROTESTANT REFORMERS IDENTIFIED ANTICHRIST WITH THE PAPACY

Unfortunately, most of the Protestant Reformers identified the papal system and the pope as the predicted Antichrist. This idea almost became an article of faith among Protestants during the sixteenth century. Indeed, there was a unified view among Protestant interpreters as to the identity of the beast.

This includes such people as the German reformers Martin Luther and Philip Melanchthon, French reformer John Calvin, the Swiss reformer Zwingli and the biblical translator William Tyndale.

All of these men of God were convinced that the biblical Antichrist was alive and living in the city of Rome with the title the Bishop of Rome, the pope.

5. CERTAIN CONFESSIONAL STATEMENTS REFLECTED THE IDEA THAT THE POPE WAS ANTICHRIST

Furthermore the identification of the pope with the Antichrist was memorialized in a number of confessional statements during that era. These statements summed up the beliefs of a certain specific group of Christians.

For example in 1646, the Westminster Confession stated the following.

> There is no other head of the church but the Lord Jesus Christ: nor can the Pope of Rome in any sense be the head thereof; but is that Antichrist, the man of sin and son of perdition, that exalteth himself in the church against Christ, and all that is called God (*Westminster Confession of Faith*, 25:6).

The accepted view of that particular era among Protestants was that the papacy and the man of sin were one-in-the-same.

6. Through A Literal Interpretation Of Prophecy The Idea Returns That Antichrist Is A Person Who Is Still To Come

While the idea was accepted in many Protestant circles that the papacy was the biblical Antichrist, things began to change. As people began to do a serious study of the prophetic Scripture it became apparent that Antichrist was not limited to a mere evil influence, religious system, or one particular pope ruling at a certain time. Though there were indeed people and institutions in every generation fulfilling the role of Antichrist, there is still a coming man of sin who must appear immediately before the return of Jesus Christ.

Consequently, a literal understanding of the predictions of Holy Scripture has led Bible students to this conclusion: a final Antichrist will appear on the scene of history at some unknown time in the future.

This briefly sums up some of the highlights of the understanding of Antichrist among Bible-believing Christians throughout the history of the church. To this, much more could be added.

SUMMARY TO QUESTION 3
WHAT CAN WE LEARN FROM THE WAY THE SUBJECT OF THE ANTICHRIST BEEN VIEWED DURING THE HISTORY OF THE CHURCH?

The subject of Antichrist has been one of interest for Bible believers from the very beginning of the Christian church. Consequently, there are a number of lessons which can be learned from what has occurred in the past.

We find that the Christians have always had a keen interest in the topic of Antichrist. For example, those living in the early years of the church were paying close attention to what Scriptures said about the identity of the man of sin. Indeed three Roman Emperors, Caligula, Nero, and Domitian fulfilled many of the requirements of this evil personage. However, none of these men was the evil beast which the Scripture spoke about.

One thing which does become clear from the writings of the early Christians on the subject of Antichrist is that the coming man of sin is viewed as a person, not an evil institution or an evil force. This was seemingly a universal belief among those in the early church.

Church fathers such as Irenaeus of Lyon, Tertullian of Carthage, Cyril of Jerusalem, and Gregory of Tours all testified to a personal Antichrist which was still to come. The Epistle of Barnabas, though not written by the Apostle Barnabas, spoke of the coming of the "Black Man." Again, they were looking for a person.

As the year A.D. 1000 approached there was an eager expectation of the return of Christ to the earth. The wife of the King of France, believing this to be true, asked her court chaplain, Adso, to compile everything he could find on the subject of Antichrist; seeing that the man of sin must appear before Jesus comes back. From his research, Adso concluded that Antichrist would be Jew who would come to the temple in Jerusalem and defile it by claiming to be the Son of God. His reign would be shortened by the Second Coming of Christ where he would be killed by Michael the Archangel. The pamphlet of Adso had enormous influence during this historical period. Once more we find that the people were looking for an individual man to fulfill the predictions of Antichrist.

In fact, it seems that it was commonly held by Christians until about the fourteen century that the biblical description of Antichrist was the description of a person who was still to come on the stage of history. However, in the fourteen century the idea became popular that the Antichrist was not a personage to come in the future but rather was already on the earth in the person of the pope and the papacy.

Indeed, once a number of Protestant groups labeled the pope and the papacy as the biblical Antichrist, the idea spread quickly. Soon it became the accepted interpretation among Protestants. The Protestant Reformers, seemingly to a man, made it clear that they believed the papacy was the predicted "first beast" of the Book of Revelation.

This was also reflected in certain of the confessions of faith of that era. For example, the Westminster Confession of Faith, in 1646, made it clear that the signers of this confession believed the pope was the biblical Antichrist.

It was only after Bible students returned to a literal interpretation of all Scripture, including Bible prophecy, that the idea was once again upheld of a personal Antichrist who was still to come at some unknown time in the future.

We find this to be true in our present day. Indeed, among those who believe Bible prophecy should be interpreted in a literal manner, the understanding of Antichrist is the same as what was universally held by the early church; the coming Antichrist is an evil individual who is yet to appear on the stage of history.

What Are The Various Views Of The Book Of Revelation With Respect To The Coming Antichrist?

One issue which must be dealt with before we engage in our detailed study of the biblical Antichrist concerns how we will look at what Scripture in general, and the Book of Revelation in particular, says about this subject. To do this we need a basic understanding of how Revelation has been interpreted.

Generally speaking, there are four basic ways in which the words contained in the Book of Revelation are interpreted. We can simply state them as follows.

1. THE PRETERIST VIEW

The word "preterist" is Latin for "past." There are some Bible commentators who believe the events listed in the Book of Revelation have, for the most part, already been fulfilled. Therefore, a study of Antichrist is a study of past historical events, not future events. While there are many lessons to be learned from the study of Antichrist, we should not look forward to a personal Antichrist because anything written about him has already been fulfilled. The biblical Antichrist has already come. This is the preterist position.

2. THE IDEALIST VIEW

Another way of looking at the events in Revelation is the idealist perspective. Contrary to the preterist view, which sees Revelation dealing with actual historical events, the idealist view does not understand these things in a literal manner. Revelation idealizes the struggle between good and evil. It is a mistake according to the idealist view, to interpret these passages literally. What is written in Revelation illustrates timeless truths.

3. THE HISTORICIST VIEW

Some interpreters see the Book of Revelation as being continually fulfilled in history. This is known as the historicist interpretation. Thus, the predictions of the Antichrist have a present application in every generation throughout this age. Many Protestant interpreters believe the predictions about the Antichrist have its ongoing fulfillment in the papacy. They point out the many similarities between the practices of the Roman Church and the biblical teaching about Antichrist.

Others see the fulfillment in the rise of Muhammad and Islam. Thus, historicists see a literal fulfillment of the predictions in the Book of Revelation which are constantly occurring.

4. THE FUTURIST VIEW

Finally there is the futurist view which sees the bulk of Revelation as describing events still to come. This includes references to Antichrist. Those who hold this particular point of view believe that a personal Antichrist, also called the "beast" or "first beast," will come on the scene of history immediately before the Second Coming of Christ.

Therefore, according to the futurist, Scripture speaks of a particular individual known as the man of sin, or Antichrist, who is still to come.

This gives a brief summation of the various ways in which the references to the beast, or Antichrist, as described in the Book of Revelation and elsewhere, are interpreted.

SUMMARY TO QUESTION 4
WHAT ARE THE VARIOUS VIEWS OF THE BOOK OF REVELATION WITH RESPECT TO THE COMING ANTICHRIST?

It is important that we have a basic understanding of the various views that Bible students have of the Book of Revelation with respect to the subject of Antichrist. Four main views have been put forth by Bible-believing Christians. They can be briefly states as follows.

The preterist view sees most things written in the Book of Revelation as having already taken place in history. Therefore, any predicted Antichrist has come and gone from the scene. Hence, any study of Antichrist is one of a past historical figure, it is not of a personage who is still to come.

The idealist view holds that the events described in Revelation are not to be understood literally but rather are symbolic of the struggle between good and evil, right and wrong. Consequently, we should not look for a personal Antichrist, either in the past or in the future. Antichrist represents the timeless struggles believers face.

The historicist view holds that the events recorded in Revelation are literal events and have had a continual fulfillment throughout church history. Often this has led Protestant commentators to view the Roman Catholic Church and the pope as the predicted Antichrist. Others believe Muhammad is the predicted beast of Revelation.

The futuristic view believes most of the things written in the Book of Revelation will take place in the future. Therefore, we should expect a personal Antichrist, the beast of Revelation, to come on the scene of history at some future moment. This will take place immediately before the Second Coming of Jesus Christ.

This briefly sums up the four major perspectives of the Book of Revelation. Within each of these perspectives there is a wide variety of interpretation.

Have The Events In The Book Of Revelation, Including Those Dealing With Antichrist, Been Fulfilled In History? (Preterist View)

Some Bible commentators believe the events in the Book of Revelation, were for the most part fulfilled in the first century. Therefore, any reference to a personal Antichrist would have been long-fulfilled. Those holding this viewpoint are known as "preterists" which is Latin for "past." This being the case there is no need to find any future fulfillment of the predictions regarding the coming beast, the Antichrist. The biblical Antichrist has come and gone from the pages of history.

We can briefly sum up the arguments for preterism as follows.

1. THE BOOK OF REVELATION WAS WRITTEN AT AN EARLY DATE

One of the necessary ingredients for those who hold the preterist position is an *early* date of the Book of Revelation. If Revelation was written before the middle of the year A.D. 66, then the events which are written as predictions could tie in to the destruction of the city of Jerusalem. Therefore, the events listed could now be considered as having taken place in the past.

2. MOST PREDICTED EVENTS ARE NOW PAST

This brings us to our next point. Preterism holds that the great judgments found in the Book of the Revelation have already been fulfilled.

Consequently, Revelation is interpreted exclusively as dealing with the difficult first-century situations which the believers were facing. According to the preterist position, there is no attempt to predict future events beyond that first generation.

Usually preterists say that any future understanding of Revelation removes the relevance for John's original audience. To be relevant to these people, God must be speaking of issues which directly affected them; not matters which would be fulfilled at some time in the distant future. While there are timeless lessons we learn from the Book of Revelation, there is nothing in the Book that gives us any roadmap for future events. Everything has been fulfilled in the past.

3. JESUS' COMING HAS ALREADY OCCURRED

Jesus' Olivet Discourse, Matthew 24-25, is also seen as having first-century fulfillment. Instead of the events Jesus spoke about as being still in the future, preterism argues that everything has already been fulfilled in the past. Their key verse is Jesus' words to His disciples shortly before His betrayal.

> Truly I tell you, this generation will certainly not pass away
> until all these things have happened (Matthew 24:34 NIV).

To the preterist, "all these things" means "everything." This includes references to His "coming." All the things which Jesus predicted would happen did indeed happen in that first generation.

4. THIS POSITION RESCUES SCRIPTURE FROM ERROR

Preterism insists that their interpretation actually rescues the Bible from the charge of being in error, or mistaken in its predictions. Unless we insist that Jesus' statements about His return in one generation were fulfilled in the first century at the destruction of Jerusalem, then His words are seen to be in error.

In other words, Jesus would have been mistaken about the time of His coming because He did not return visibly in A.D. 70. Not wishing to attribute any mistake to Jesus' predictions, preterists say that everything Jesus predicted was fulfilled in that first generation. However, though the timing is understood to be literal, one generation, the fulfillment of His predictions was anything but literal.

5. THERE IS NO NEED TO LOOK FOR A FINAL ANTICHRIST

Preterists conclude that all the predicted events have been fulfilled. This includes the "abomination of desolation" which Jesus spoke about. This defiling of the temple occurred when the Roman legions entered the temple area at the time Jerusalem was destroyed. Consequently, there is no need to insist that a temple will be rebuilt in the future where a coming Antichrist must sit and proclaim himself to be God. All of that has symbolically happened in the past.

This being the case, Antichrist is a figure from the past, he is not going to arrive in the future. Therefore, all attempts to determine what a future Antichrist may or may not do are futile. Antichrist is not coming.

RESPONSE

Preterism has not been widely accepted among Bible students. There are a number of reasons as to why this is so.

1. THE EARLY DATE OF REVELATION IS DIFFICULT TO MAINTAIN

To begin with, dating Revelation before the middle of the year A.D. 66 is difficult, if not impossible, to maintain. Indeed, there are numerous reasons as to why the traditional date of the book is accepted; somewhere in the 90's of the first century. The evidence is just not there for the early date.

2. PRETERISM IS INCONSISTENT IN BIBLICAL INTERPRETATION

Preterism has been accused of being inconsistent in its biblical inter-pretation. While attempting to be as literal as possible, especially with time references, when a passage contradicts the system, the passage is made to say something non-literal, or symbolic. In other words, the system determines the meaning ahead of time. Of course, it should be the other way around. We should allow the Scripture determine our system of interpretation.

3. PRETERISM SELECTIVELY QUOTES SCRIPTURE

In addition, preterism is accused of selectively quoting Scripture. Passages that contradict their system are passed over and ignored. Indeed, Jesus specifically talked about the people "seeing Him" at the time of His return. Matthew records Him saying.

> For I tell you, you will not see me again until you say, 'Blessed is he who comes in the name of the Lord.' (Matthew 23:39 NIV).

However, the people in A.D. 70 certainly did not "see Jesus again" when the city of Jerusalem was destroyed.

4. JESUS DID NOT RETURN IN ANY SENSE IN A.D. 70

This leads us to the main complaint raised against preterism; the idea that Jesus' predicted Second Coming occurred with the destruction of Jerusalem in A.D. 70. The thought that Jesus' coming refers to the destruction of Jerusalem, rather than a literal visible return as Scripture so plainly predicts, has been a major point of contention.

Indeed, while attempting to find a fulfillment of Jesus' words in first century events, the obvious sense of what He is teaching is ignored. Jesus clearly spoke of a literal, visible coming back to the world. This is clearly taught in the first chapter of the Book of Revelation. It says.

> Behold, he is coming with the clouds, and every eye will see him, even those who pierced him, and all tribes of the earth will wail on account of him. Even so. Amen (Revelation 1:7 ESV).

Every eye will see Jesus when He personally returns. This is not the sort of coming which preterists maintain occurred.

5. PRETERISM DOES NOT RESCUE JESUS FROM ERROR

Finally, we do not have to resort to preterism to rescue Jesus' words from error. Indeed, a literal consistent understanding of what Christ said will occur does not have to lead one to believe Jesus was in error. For one thing, the phrase "this generation" does not have to be understood in the sense which preterists maintain.

Indeed, there are some eighteen different views of exactly what Jesus meant when He spoke of "this generation not passing away until all these things are fulfilled." Seemingly, the simplest way to understand His words is that they refer to the future generation which sees the predicted signs taking place. It is "that" generation which will not pass away until everything is fulfilled. It was not the generation He was addressing.

ANTICHRIST IS COMING

Therefore, contrary to the preterist outlook, Antichrist, the beast of the Book of Revelation, is coming. Consequently, we should do a serious study of the Word of God to determine exactly what believers should expect to happen when he does arrive on the scene. We should not assume that the references to him were all fulfilled in the past.

SUMMARY TO QUESTION 5
HAVE THE EVENTS IN THE BOOK OF REVELATION, INCLUDING THOSE DEALING WITH ANTICHRIST, BEEN FULFILLED IN HISTORY? (PRETERIST VIEW)

There is the view held by some Bible students that the events predicted by Jesus in His Olivet Discourse, recorded in the Gospel of Matthew, as well as those predictions recorded in the Book of Revelation, have already received their fulfillment. This is the position of "preterism." The approach can be briefly summed up as follows.

Preterists must argue for an early date of the composition of the Book of Revelation. This way they are able to tie in certain predictions in the Book with the destruction of Jerusalem in the year A.D. 70. Consequently, these predictions found in the Book of Revelation have already been fulfilled in the first century.

It is also contended that these passages in the Book of Revelation were directed at a first-century audience. According to preterists, if we assume they were speaking of events far off into the future, then it would be meaningless for those living at the time the Book was composed.

The preterist position understands Jesus' statement, "This generation shall not pass until all these things are fulfilled" in a literal fashion. Everything in that passage which Jesus said about future events was fulfilled in that same generation. Nothing remains to be fulfilled. They understand Jesus' predictions of His "coming again" to refer to the destruction of Jerusalem. The Book of Revelation is also interpreted in that manner. Hence, everything predicted has already been fulfilled.

Preterists also believe that this position rescues Scripture from the possible charge of error; since not everything Jesus predicted was literally fulfilled by A.D. 70. Therefore, much of what Jesus said has to be understood symbolically.

Therefore, the predicted Antichrist has already appeared in the first-century. Consequently, we do not need to look for him in the future. There is no "man of sin" who is still to come.

The position of preterism has been widely criticized. First, it is difficult to place the writing of the Book of Revelation at least three and one half years before the destruction of the city of Jerusalem in A.D.

70. There are too many obstacles to date it this early. Since this is the case, one cannot point to the destruction of Jerusalem as fulfilling these predictions in Revelation. They remain unfulfilled to this day.

Preterists are also inconsistent in their interpretation. While they understand Jesus' statement "this generation that will not pass away" in a literal manner, they symbolically interpret other passages which contradict their theory. Scripture is thus quoted selectively, not consistently.

In addition, preterism does not do justice to Jesus' words. To say that Jesus returned in A.D. 70 does not fit what the Bible predicts. He did not. The return of Jesus Christ which the New Testament proclaims is personal and visible. The destruction of Jerusalem was not that predicted return.

Furthermore, Jesus' predictions of His Second Coming do not have to be rescued by preterism. One can have a consistent view of Jesus' predictions as infallible without insisting His Second Coming happened in some sense in the year A.D. 70.

In sum, the Antichrist has not yet come because Jesus Himself did not come back in A.D. 70. Preterism does not give us the answer as to how we should view the subject of Antichrist. Another solution needs to be found.

Should We Actually Be Looking For A Personal Antichrist?
(The Idealist View, The Timeless View)

One way of looking at the predicted events in Scripture is to interpret them in a non-literal manner. Many have applied this interpretive technique to the Book of Revelation. This is known as the "Idealist View," or the "Timeless View."

THE ISSUE: INTERPRET LITERALLY OR NOT?

The key issue in answering this question concerning the subject of the beast, the Antichrist, as well as other events contained in the Book of Revelation, is whether or not we should interpret the Bible literally. Literal interpretation will lead one to believe the Antichrist is a person who is still to come on the scene of history.

On the other hand, spiritualizing or interpreting the persons and events in a non-literal manner will cause one to see Antichrist as something non-personal.

Those who have an idealized view of the Book of Revelation basically see the entire book as a simple description of the ongoing fight of good versus evil. The Book of Revelation teaches we are going to win in the end but there are no time markers to tell us when the victory will be won.

It is a timeless struggle. Indeed, according to idealism Scripture gives us no time references whatsoever with respect to the future. Consequently they see it as a mistake to attempt to understand the various references as literal events about a literal person who either has already arrived in history, or will come at some time in the future.

Therefore, they will usually assume the Antichrist is an evil force, or some evil system. The references to the beast and his actions will be interpreted in a non-literal, symbolic manner. Everything is symbolic.

THERE IS NO PERSONAL ANTICHRIST IN THE IDEALISTIC SYSTEM

This being the case, should we understand Antichrist as an evil influence or an evil religious system? There are those who argue for either of these. However, they insist that we should not be looking for an actual historical person, or historical religious system to fulfill what is written about the Antichrist, the beast. The Book of Revelation is not meant to be understood in that manner.

SOME PROBLEMS WITH THE IDEALIST VIEW

There are a number of objections which are raised against the idealist view. The main ones can be summed up as follows.

1. IDEALISTS INTERPRET INCONSISTENTLY

For one thing, they are not consistent in their interpretation. Idealists will interpret most of the Book of Revelation symbolically. Yet they will literally accept the passages which speak of the Second Coming of Jesus Christ to the earth. They do believe that He will literally return. However, once it is admitted that some of the passages are not symbolic, but are meant to be interpreted literally, then one must give explicit reasons as to why these other passages should be understood in a non-literal manner. Idealists have never done this in a convincing manner.

2. WORDS DO NOT MEAN WHAT THEY SAY

Furthermore, it becomes difficult to hold to the position that words do not really mean what they clearly seem to mean. According to idealism, "days" do not mean days, the "twelve tribes of Israel" do not mean the twelve tribes of Israel, the number "one thousand" does not mean one thousand, the "temple" does mean the temple, the "two periods of three and one half years" do not really mean three and one half years, the "two witnesses" are not really two people and the "beast, the Antichrist" is not really a person, etc..

Idealists do not believe these can be seen as actual places, times and persons in history. These references are viewed as symbols that may refer to various places, persons and events throughout history, but they do not refer exclusively to any particular place, person or event in history.

The problem with this is determining what they do mean. This is the fatal problem with idealism. Nobody can agree what these symbols actually represent. Instead of coming to some consensus about the meaning of these symbols, commentators contradict one another. This reveals how meaningless such a method of interpretation is. If a symbol can be used to mean anything and everything, then ultimately it means nothing! This is what one ends up with in the idealistic system.

Therefore, God's communication, the Bible, is now left in the hands of each reader to provide their own meaning to the text. It is no wonder that no consensus can be reached among interpreters who view Bible prophecy in an idealistic manner.

3. THERE IS A LITERAL OBJECT BEHIND EVERY SYMBOL

Nobody discounts the fact that there are symbols in Scripture. However, when someone says that a passage is symbolic, the question which should be asked of them is, "Symbolic of what?" The symbol has to mean something.

The issue of course is this: what does it mean? The fact that those who hold the idealist view cannot come to any consensus on the meaning of these symbols makes their method of interpretation highly suspect.

ANTICHRIST SHOULD BE UNDERSTOOD AS A LITERAL PERSON WHO IS STILL TO COME

The conclusion is that idealism is not the way to interpret the New Testament references to the beast, the Antichrist. We are dealing with a coming person, not a symbol or idea.

Therefore, idealism provides no real answer as to the question of Antichrist.

SUMMARY TO QUESTION 6
SHOULD WE ACTUALLY BE LOOKING FOR A PERSONAL ANTICHRIST? (IDEALIST VIEW)

Those who hold the idealist view of the Book of Revelation do not believe that a personal Antichrist has come in the past, or will even come on the scene of history in the future. They view Revelation as a timeless struggle. The terms used in the book such as the beast, 144,000, two witnesses, false prophet, Armageddon, etc. are not to be understood in a literal manner, but rather symbolically. They are symbols of the timeless struggle of good versus evil. Hardly anything in the Book of Revelation is to be understood literally.

Consequently idealists believe that it is wrong to see the events in Revelation as having been fulfilled in the past or that they will be fulfilled in the future. Therefore, there is no such thing as a personal Antichrist who has come, or who is to come. Antichrist is a symbol.

Idealism has been criticized on a number of fronts. For one thing, it does not take seriously the many literal references in the Book of Revelation. In other words, things do not mean what they clearly appear to mean. To say days do not mean days, persons do not mean persons, and specific places do not specific places, does injustice to the words of the Lord. The fact that idealists cannot agree among themselves, as to what these symbols are symbolic of, further shows the meaninglessness of their comments.

There is a better answer as to the way the subject of the Antichrist should be viewed. The better way is to assume a personal Antichrist is still to come.

What Are The Arguments That The Predictions About Antichrist Are Being Fulfilled In History? (Historicist View)

In the first century, the Apostle John wrote that Antichrist is coming. But what was he referring to? Some believe that it was not speaking of one human being coming at one particular time but rather the fulfillments are taking place throughout the course of church history.

THE HISTORICIST VIEW

We must understand the historicist view of the Book of Revelation. Instead of seeing the events fulfilled in the past as the preterist position, or events which will be fulfilled at a future time, the futurist view, the historicist sees the events taking place throughout the entire course of this age. In other words, each generation of believers sees the fulfillment of these predictions.

Some historicists have taught that the various popes who have led the Roman Catholic Church have been the predicted Antichrist. Thus, rather than one particular person at one particular time fulfilling the predictions of Antichrist, there is a continual fulfillment in history of these predictions. Each generation has their own Antichrist.

PROPHECIES ARE BEING FULFILLED TODAY

Historicism also believes that prophecies are being fulfilled today as they have been throughout the history of the church. Interpreters from this perspective have found such events in the Book of Revelation as the rise of the Roman Catholic Church, the rise of Islam, and the World Wars.

Therefore, from the historicist perspective, the predictions in the Book of Revelation are not something that has been fulfilled, or not something which will be fulfilled in the future, the fulfillments have continually been occurring and are still taking place.

RESPONSE TO THE HISTORICIST VIEW

The historicist view suffers from a number of problems. For one thing, interpreters cannot agree on whom or what continually fulfills the predictions of the Book of Revelation. Indeed, from the historicist school of interpretation we find a wide variety of so-called fulfillments to the various predicted events. This alone should cause one to be careful about accepting any interpretation concerning what these passages truly mean.

HISTORICISM LEADS TO DATE-SETTING

One of the problems with the historicist view is the practice of setting dates for events the predicted in Scripture. Jesus said nobody knows the day or hour of His return.

> But about that day or hour no one knows, not even the angels in heaven, nor the Son, but only the Father (Matthew 24:36 NIV).

However, this has not stopped some historicists from claiming that they do know when Jesus Christ will return. Many dates have been set in the past for the return of Christ at some *exact* future time. Complicated systems were worked out from Scripture to show the precise moment of the appearing of Christ.

EACH PREDICTION HAS BEEN WRONG

Of course, the proof that this does not work is that the date-setters have all been wrong! Each time the date of the coming of Christ has been predicted the fulfillment has not come to pass. Indeed, examples of these mistaken predictions could fill volumes. Certainly this should make it clear that such a method of interpretation is wrong. Not only is it wrong, it contradicts what Jesus said about knowing the day and hour of His return.

THERE IS A SINGLE PERSONAL ANTICHRIST WHO IS STILL TO COME

Contrary to the historicist view, Scripture teaches that there will come a day when a personal Antichrist, a coming Caesar, arrives on the scene. That day has not happened yet. While many Antichrists have indeed come, and have had many of the traits of the predicted man of sin, the final Antichrist is yet to appear.

SUMMARY TO QUESTION 7
WHAT ARE THE ARGUMENTS THAT THE PREDICTIONS ABOUT ANTICHRIST ARE BEING FULFILLED IN HISTORY? (HISTORICIST VIEW)

There are those who reject the idea that Antichrist will be an actual person who has appeared once in the past, or who will appear in the future. The historicist view holds this position. Instead of speaking of past events, or predicting the future, the Book of Revelation is viewed as having continuous fulfillment throughout this present age. The text is understood to be symbolic of literal historical events. Therefore, the Book of Revelation is symbolic of two thousand years of the history of the Christian Church.

Consequently, the historicist view is that Antichrist represents not just one individual but rather an evil system which has been with the church from the beginning. Usually, the beast, the Antichrist of Revelation, is assumed to be the Roman Catholic Church. Others assume it to be Muhammad and the rise of Islam. Accordingly, we should not look for one person to fulfill the predictions of Antichrist at any one time in history.

Numerous problems plague the historicist position. To begin with, there is no unanimous opinion among historicists interpreters as to when these predictions were fulfilled, how they were fulfilled, or how they will be fulfilled. Each and every prediction made by the historicist interpreters with respect to the return of Jesus Christ has been wrong. This should cause us to challenge whether the Scriptures are meant to be interpreted in this manner. The evidence says that they should not be.

Are The Predictions About The Antichrist Fulfilled InRoman Catholic Church And The Papacy?

Since the time of the Protestant Reformation it has been customary to link the Antichrist and the Roman Catholic Church. Indeed, many works have been written which have attempted to show that the predictions in Scripture of the coming Antichrist have been fulfilled in the Roman Catholic Church and the papacy.

However, the evidence is clear that this is *not* the case. While many of the practices of the Roman Church do line up with what is said of the predicted Antichrist, a thorough study of Scripture will demonstrate that the Antichrist is a person, *not* a religious institution. We can make the following observations.

ANTICHRIST IS A HUMAN BEING: NOT A RELIGIOUS SYSTEM

We can offer a number of reasons as to why the Antichrist is a man, not a system, as well as provide further reasons as to why the description of Antichrist does not fit with the history or practices of the Roman Catholic Church. The evidence is as follows.

1. ANTICHRIST IS A SINGULAR INDIVIDUAL

To begin with, whenever we find the word "Antichrist" in Scripture, either in the singular form or in the plural form, it always refers to a person or to persons, it never denotes a system.

As the Christ, the Messiah, is the title of a single person, Jesus of Nazareth, the Son of God, in the same manner the Antichrist will be a title of a single person. Consequently, there is no indication whatsoever that Antichrist refers to an evil spirit or an apostate religious system. None.

2. THE TRUE MESSIAH IS A HUMAN BEING, NOT A SYSTEM, THE FALSE MESSIAH WILL BE ALSO

Furthermore, Jesus made it clear that Antichrist will be an individual person. Indeed the Lord contrasted Himself with the coming man of sin. Jesus said that the final Antichrist will be a person who is received by the Jews. John records Him saying.

> I have come in my Father's name, and you do not accept me; but if someone else comes in his own name, you will accept him (John 5:43 NIV).

The Jews believed that the predictions of the coming Messiah were always referring to a person, never to a system. They were looking for a man who would deliver them.

Indeed when the magi, the wise men, came to Jerusalem to seek the newborn King of the Jews, the Christ, they were seeking the birth of a person. The Bible says.

> Now after Jesus was born in Bethlehem of Judea in the days of Herod the king, behold, wise men from the east came to Jerusalem, saying, "Where is he who has been born king of the Jews? For we saw his star when it rose and have come to worship him" (Matthew 2:1-2 ESV).

The Christ, or Messiah, is a person. In the same manner, Antichrist will be a person. Therefore, the Roman Catholic system is not in view here when Jesus spoke of another "coming in his own name."

Furthermore, nobody from the nation of Israel has ever occupied the position as Bishop of Rome, or pope. And there is something else: the Jews would never accept any Gentile pope as their promised Messiah.

3. THE MAN OF SIN SITS IN GOD'S TEMPLE IN JERUSALEM

We are also told that the coming man of sin, the final Antichrist, sits in the temple of God. Paul explained it this way.

> Don't let anyone deceive you in any way. For that day will not come unless the apostasy comes first and the man of lawlessness is revealed, the son of destruction. He opposes and exalts himself above every so-called god or object of worship, so that he sits in God's sanctuary, publicizing that he himself is God (2 Thessalonians 2:3-4 HCSB).

The wicked one, the Antichrist, will come to the temple in the city of Jerusalem. No pope has ever done this.

4. ANTICHRIST WILL PERSONALLY MAKE OR CONFIRM A COVENANT WITH THE JEWS

The Antichrist, an individual person, will make, or confirm, a covenant with the Jews. We read about this in the Book of Daniel.

> He will confirm a covenant with many for one 'seven.' In the middle of the 'seven' he will put an end to sacrifice and offering. And at the temple he will set up an abomination that causes desolation, until the end that is decreed is poured out on him (Daniel 9:27 NIV).

There is no historical record of any pope having ever made, or confirmed, a seven-year agreement with the Jews. Yet this passage in Daniel calls for a person, not an institution, making a covenant with the Jewish nation. Again, *a single individual* is in view.

These are a few of the passages which make it clear that Antichrist will be an individual rather than some religious institution.

OTHER PROBLEMS WITH THE PAPACY BEING ANTICHRIST

There are a number of other problems if one insists the Roman Catholic Church is to be equated with the Antichrist. They are as follows.

PROBLEM 1: THE SEAT OF HIS POWER WILL NOT BE IN ROME

The geography does not fit the Roman Catholic Church. Daniel wrote that the Antichrist will have the seat of his power between the seas and the beautiful holy mountain. We read.

> He will pitch his royal tents between the seas at the beautiful holy mountain. Yet he will come to his end, and no one will help him (Daniel 11:45 NIV).

"Between the seas" means it will be somewhere between the Mediterranean Sea and the Red Sea. The mention of the "beautiful holy mountain" refers to Jerusalem.

Therefore, it seems that Antichrist will set up his headquarters on the Temple Mount in Jerusalem or somewhere north of the city. It is not possible to locate this place with the city of Rome and the Vatican. The geography does not allow it.

PROBLEM 2: ANTICHRIST DOES NOT APPEAR UNTIL THE TIME OF THE END

The Bible also makes it clear that Antichrist is a personage who appears at the end of this age. Daniel the prophet stated that the Antichrist, the "little horn," will embark on his career immediately before God's kingdom comes to the earth. He wrote.

> As I watched, this horn was waging war against the holy people and defeating them, until the Ancient of Days came

and pronounced judgment in favor of the holy people of the Most High, and the time came when they possessed the kingdom. "He gave me this explanation: 'The fourth beast is a fourth kingdom that will appear on earth. It will be different from all the other kingdoms and will devour the whole earth, trampling it down and crushing it'" (Daniel 7:21-23 NIV).

We read later in Daniel that the time of wrath is at "the time of the end." The Bible says.

He said: "I am going to tell you what will happen later in the time of wrath, because the vision concerns the appointed time of the end" (Daniel 8:19 NIV).

This places the coming of Antichrist at the time of the end of this age.

We further read in Daniel.

In the latter part of their reign, when rebels have become completely wicked, a fierce-looking king, a master of intrigue, will arise. He will become very strong, but not by his own power. He will cause astounding devastation and will succeed in whatever he does. He will destroy the mighty warriors, the holy people. He will cause deceit to prosper, and he will consider himself superior. When they feel secure, he will destroy many and take his stand against the Prince of princes. Yet he will be destroyed, but not by human power (Daniel 8:23-25 NIV).

The king will be destroyed by the prince of princes, the Messiah. This occurs at the Second Coming of Jesus Christ to the earth.

In Daniel 9, we discover that the agreement Antichrist makes with the Jews will soon thereafter bring "to an end" Israel's sins and to bring in everlasting righteousness. Daniel wrote.

> Seventy weeks are decreed about your people and your holy city, to finish the transgression, to put an end to sin, and to atone for iniquity, to bring in everlasting righteousness, to seal both vision and prophet, and to anoint a most holy place (Daniel 9:24 ESV).

The seven-year agreement that the final Antichrist makes with the Jews will bring all these predicted things to an end. Since the time when Antichrist will appear is still in the future, then it necessarily follows that the Roman Catholic Church and the papacy cannot be the Antichrist.

PROBLEM 3: ANTICHRIST RULES FOR ONLY FORTY-TWO MONTHS

The Bible also says that the coming man of sin, the beast, the Antichrist, has a limited time to rule. Scripture is clear that his rule over the earth will only last for forty-two months. In fact, there are six separate passages which teach this. For example, we read in the Book of Revelation.

> Then the beast was allowed to speak great blasphemies against God. And he was given authority to do whatever he wanted for forty-two months (Revelation 13:5 NLT).

Daniel tells us the same thing but uses a different method of explaining the time. He puts it in the following way.

> He will defy the Most High and oppress the holy people of the Most High. He will try to change their sacred festivals and laws, and they will be placed under his control for a time, times, and half a time (Daniel 7:25 NLT).

A time, two times and a half a time equals three and one half years. This is the allotted time Antichrist is allowed to rule.

It is not possible to harmonize these statements about the rule of Antichrist with the history of the Roman Church.

PROBLEM 4: ANTICHRIST FORMALLY DENIES GOD THE FATHER AND GOD THE SON

The Antichrist will also formally deny the doctrine of the Trinity, in particular, God the Father and God the Son. John wrote.

> Who is the liar but he who denies that Jesus is the Christ? This is the Antichrist, he who denies the Father and the Son (1 John 2:22 ESV).

The formal denial of the doctrine of the Trinity rules out the Roman Catholic Church from being the predicted Antichrist. In all of the councils and creeds, their symbols of faith and worship, the Roman Church has always maintained that there are three distinct Persons, or centers of consciousness, in the Godhead; God the Father, God the Son, and God the Holy Spirit. This is the doctrine of the Trinity.

While there have been many areas in which Rome has departed from the teaching of Holy Scripture, the doctrine of the Trinity is not one of them. Indeed, the Bishop of Rome, the pope, acknowledges both God the Father and God the Son.

He also confesses himself to be both the servant of God and His worshipper. When the pope blesses the people he does not bless them in his own name, but rather in the name of the Holy Trinity.

In addition, since the time of the Council of Trent (A.D. 1563) every Roman Catholic has had to confess the following:

> I believe in God the Father . . . and in the Lord Jesus Christ....and in the Holy Ghost, the Lord and Giver of life, which proceedeth from the Father and the Son.

Protestants rightly find many faults in the Roman system. However, their formal view of the Trinity is not one of them.

PROBLEM 5: IF ROME IS ANTICHRIST THEN WHO IS THE FALSE PROPHET?

There is also the problem of identifying the second beast, the false prophet. This second beast is a miracle worker who aids the first beast. The Book of Revelation says.

> Then I saw another beast coming up out of the earth; he had two horns like a lamb, but he sounded like a dragon. He exercises all the authority of the first beast on his behalf and compels the earth and those who live on it to worship the first beast, whose fatal wound was healed (Revelation 13:11-12 HCSB).

If the first beast is the Roman Church, the papacy, then who is the second beast, the false prophet who aids the first beast?

PROBLEM 6: THERE HAS NEVER BEEN A SPEAKING IMAGE

We are informed that the false prophet causes an image of the beast to speak. Scripture says the following will happen.

> And by the signs that it is allowed to work in the presence of the beast it deceives those who dwell on earth, telling them to make an image for the beast that was wounded by the sword and yet lived. And it was allowed to give breath to the image of the beast, so that the image of the beast might even speak and might cause those who would not worship the image of the beast to be slain (Revelation 13:14,15 ESV).

Nothing in the history of the Roman Church, or the actions of any pope, remotely fulfills this prediction in the Book of Revelation.

PROBLEM 7: THE SACRIFICES HAVE NOT CEASED UNDER ROMANISM

Scriptures says that, among other things, the Antichrist will cause the sacrifices in the temple to cease. Daniel wrote the following about this.

In the middle of the 'seven' he will put an end to sacrifice and offering. And at the temple he will set up an abomination that causes desolation, until the end that is decreed is poured out on him (Daniel 9:27 NIV).

We also read elsewhere about the ceasing of temple sacrifices in the Book of Daniel. Scripture says.

He even exalted himself as high as the Prince of the host; and by him the daily sacrifices were taken away, and the place of His sanctuary was cast down (Daniel 8:11 NKJV).

The Antichrist will take away the daily sacrifice. If Roman Church is the Antichrist, then how can these verses be made to fit with the continuous repeated sacrifice of the Mass? The simple answer is that it cannot.

In addition, these passages in Daniel are speaking of sacrifices in a future temple which has not been built yet. Obviously the Roman Church has not caused them to cease because they have not been re-started.

PROBLEM 8: ANTICHRIST SHALL HAVE WORLDWIDE DOMINION

The dominion of the Antichrist will stretch across the entire world. The Bible says everyone will marvel at him.

One of its heads seemed to have a mortal wound, but its mortal wound was healed, and the whole earth marveled as they followed the beast (Revelation 13:3 ESV).

He will be given authority over everything. The Bible explains the dominion of the coming man of sin as follows.

It was granted to him to make war with the saints and to overcome them. And authority was given him over every tribe, tongue, and nation (Revelation 13:7 NKJV).

This has never been fulfilled in the history of the Roman Church. It has not even come close.

Furthermore, we read of what the beast will do when he does arrive; he will brand the entire world with his mark. Scriptures predicts the following.

> So that no one can buy or sell unless he has the mark, that is, the name of the beast or the number of its name (Revelation 13:17 ESV).

Neither the Roman Catholic Church, nor any of the popes, have ever attempted something like this act, let alone fulfill it. The Roman Church is not in view here.

PROBLEM 9: EVERYONE BUT ROMAN CATHOLICS WOULD BE SAVED!

There is something else which must be considered. John wrote that the ones whose names are written in the Book of Life are those who have not worshipped the beast. He said.

> And the beast was allowed to wage war against God's holy people and to conquer them. And he was given authority to rule over every tribe and people and language and nation. And all the people who belong to this world worshiped the beast. They are the ones whose names were not written in the Book of Life before the world was made— the Book that belongs to the Lamb who was slaughtered (Revelation 13:7,8 NLT).

If we assume that the pope is the beast, the Antichrist, then this will lead us to absurd conclusions. John says that all who do not worship the beast will have their names written in the Lamb's book of life. This means every person who has *not* been aligned with the Roman Catholic Church for the last one thousand seven hundred years has their names written in the Book of Life.

This would include every atheist, agnostic, and those who have embraced other religions! These are the saved! This, of course, is ludicrous.

We conclude that the coming Antichrist cannot be equated with the Roman Catholic Church and the papacy. Those who attempt to do this do so contrary to the evidence.

SUMMARY TO QUESTION 8
ARE THE PREDICTIONS ABOUT THE ANTICHRIST FULFILLED IN ROMAN CATHOLIC CHURCH AND THE PAPACY?

Since the fourteenth century it has been popular to equate the Roman Catholic Church with the predicted Antichrist of Scripture. However, the facts say otherwise. We can make the following observations on this important question.

For one thing, Antichrist is not a system, he is a man. Every reference in Scripture to Antichrist is a reference to a human being. There are no exceptions to this.

Indeed, Jesus made it clear that the same Jewish nation who rejected Him, will one day accept another person who comes in his own name. They rejected a Man, they will receive a man. When they were looking for the Messiah, they were looking for a man. In the same way, the Anti-Messiah, or Antichrist, will also be a man.

We are also told that the man of sin will place himself in the Holy of Holies in the Jerusalem temple. This is impossible for an institution to do something like this. Furthermore, no pope has ever attempted to do this.

Also it is a person which makes a covenant or agreement with the Jewish people. It is not an institution which does this.

These facts, to which many others could be added, make it clear that the Antichrist is a human being, not an institution or merely a spirit of evil.

Furthermore, there are other problems with equating the biblical Antichrist with the Roman Catholic Church. Indeed, we can list at least nine problems with attempting to equate the coming Antichrist with Rome.

First, Antichrist has his headquarters somewhere in the Promised Land, not in Rome. The specific location of his headquarters is provided for us in Scripture and it rules out Rome or the Vatican as being the site of his reign.

In addition, Antichrist does not appear until the end of history. Therefore, we should not look for him at anytime during this present age. He coming will take place immediately before the return of Christ to the earth.

When he does appear, it will only be for a specific period of time, forty-two months. This also rules out Rome as being the predicted man of sin.

We also find a formal denial of the Trinity by the coming Antichrist. The Roman Catholic Church has never done this. Indeed, in all of its formal creeds it publicly acknowledges the Trinity. In contrast, Antichrist openly blasphemes the Triune God.

Scripture also says that a second beast, the false prophet, will promote Antichrist. If one argues that Antichrist is Roman Catholicism, then who is this false prophet which promotes the church? There is nothing that fits this description if we assume that the Roman Catholic Church is the predicted Antichrist.

In addition, this false prophet makes an image of the beast which is able to speak. Again, we have never seen anything like this happen in history, certainly not in the history of the Roman Church.

Scripture says that Antichrist will stop the sacrifices from occurring. Roman Catholicism has continually offered the sacrifice of the Mass to this day. These sacrifices have never ceased.

Also, the beast is said to have worldwide rule and authority. In fact, nobody will be able to buy or sell without his mark. Nothing in the history of Roman Catholicism remotely suggests this has ever taken place.

Finally, the saved or redeemed are those who do not receive the mark of the beast. If the Roman Church is the beast, then everyone who is not a Roman Catholic must be part of the group of the saved! This, of course, is absurd since it would mean that every unbeliever in the last two thousand years would have their name written in the Book of Life because they have rejected the Roman Church.

Many more things could be added to this. However, it is clear from the evidence that the biblical Antichrist cannot be equated with the Roman Catholic Church. While the Roman Church may have a number of practices which characterize the Antichrist, the biblical predictions of Antichrist are the predictions of a man, not an institution. The Roman Catholic Church is not the final Antichrist.

What Are The Arguments For The Final Antichrist Being A Literal Human Being Who Is Still To Come? (Futurist View)

While there are those who see Antichrist as an impersonal force, or some evil religious system, many commentators believe that when the Bible speaks of Antichrist, an actual person is in view. This being the case, the question is whether this person has already come in history, the preterist view, or whether he is still to come, the futurist view.

The idea that there will be a final Antichrist which is an actual person, who is still to come on world's stage, is based upon a number of things. We can highlight them as follows.

THE BOOK OF REVELATION SPEAKS OF FUTURE EVENTS

The futurist view is based on a literal understanding of the Book of Revelation. While the first three chapters are dealing with issues of that particular time, from chapter four forward the subject is the future.

God has given us the Book of Revelation for a number of reasons and one of them is the explanation of "things to come." Therefore, when Revelation is read in a *normal* sense, the events spoken about must take place in the future. Indeed, there is no possible way to find their fulfillment in the first century, or at some other time in church history.

This is especially true of what Scripture says about the coming "beast," the "Antichrist." The biblical description of who he is, as well as what he will do, remains unfulfilled. Nobody has come upon the scene of history and fulfilled what is written about this biblical "beast," the "man of sin."

In fact, Scripture says that this coming man of sin will only be stopped when Jesus Christ comes again.

We read the following in the Book of Revelation.

> Then I saw the beast and the kings of the world and their armies gathered together to fight against the one sitting on the horse and his army. And the beast was captured, and with him the false prophet who did mighty miracles on behalf of the beast—miracles that deceived all who had accepted the mark of the beast and who worshiped his statue. Both the beast and his false prophet were thrown alive into the fiery lake of burning sulfur (Revelation 19:19-20 NLT).

Any attempt to say this passage has already been fulfilled is futile. The coming of Antichrist, as well as his eventual doom, is still a future event.

Therefore, all things considered, the futurist view of Revelation is the most consistent with the facts.

THE TESTIMONY OF THE BOOK OF DANIEL

The idea that the appearance of the final Antichrist is still future is confirmed by the Book of Daniel.

The wars of final Antichrist are described in Daniel 11:40-45. The time of this conflict is declared to be "the time of the end."

> At the time of the end the king of the south will attack him (Daniel 11:40 NET).

There is nothing in the context that would restrict the force of the word 'end.' Consequently, the end of all things must be the meaning.

> Furthermore, this battle concludes with the destruction of Antichrist in the Holy Land followed by the resurrection of the Old Testament believers (Daniel 12:2).

Since these predicted events have not yet occurred, therefore the "end" in view here must be the final days of this present age.

THE EVIDENCE THAT HE IS A HUMAN BEING

As for Antichrist being an actual person who is still to come on the stage of history, the following observations should be made.

1. HE IS A MEMBER OF A SATANIC GROUP OF INDIVIDUALS

As we look at the text of Revelation, we find that Antichrist is a member of a satanic group of three individuals. We read the following in the Book of Revelation.

> Then I saw three evil spirits that looked like frogs; they came out of the mouth of the dragon, out of the mouth of the beast and out of the mouth of the false prophet (Revelation 16:13 NIV).

Here the Antichrist, the beast, is compared to the dragon, Satan, and the false prophet. Since Satan is clearly portrayed in Scripture as an actual personage, we should also view the beast and the false prophet in the same manner. It would be inconsistent to interpret one or two of these references literally while the others figuratively. It is important to be consistent in our interpretation.

2. HE IS COMMISSIONED BY THE DEVIL

This personage is commissioned of the devil himself. John explained how the dragon, the devil, gave power to the beast.

> The beast I saw resembled a leopard, but had feet like those of a bear and a mouth like that of a lion. The dragon gave the beast his power and his throne and great authority (Revelation 13:2 NIV).

This is another indication that we are dealing with a human being.

3. THIS PERSON IS ENERGIZED AND EQUIPPED BY SATAN

We are also told that this man of sin is energized and equipped by Satan. We read the following in Thessalonians.

> The coming of the lawless one is by the activity of Satan with all power and false signs and wonders (2 Thessalonians 2:9 ESV).

The fact that he is called "the lawless one" indicates that we are dealing with a single person. It is not an institution.

4. ANTICHRIST IS A STILL HUMAN BEING

With all these traits, Antichrist is still a human being. John made this very clear when he wrote the following.

> This calls for wisdom: let the one who has understanding calculate the number of the beast, for it is the number of a man, and his number is 666 (Revelation 13:18 ESV).

Here we find that his number is that of a man. This seems to make his identity clear. Antichrist is a human being.

5. HE WILL SELL HIS SOUL TO THE DEVIL

It seems that the final Antichrist will be a human being who personally gives his soul over to the devil. When the devil tempted Jesus, he offered the Lord all the kingdoms of the world. The only requirement is that Jesus would have to bow down to him. Matthew records the following.

Again, the devil took him to a very high mountain and showed him all the kingdoms of the world and their glory. And he said to him, "All these I will give you, if you will fall down and worship me" (Matthew 4:8–9 ESV).

The Lord would not bow. We read what happened next.

Jesus said to him, "Away from me, Satan! For it is written: 'Worship the Lord your God, and serve him only'" (Matthew 4:10 NIV).

When the devil tempted the Lord Jesus, and offered him the kingdoms of the world, he did not receive the response from the Lord which he was after.

Rather he only received a rebuke. However in the final Antichrist, Satan finds a human being who is willing to sell his soul for the chance to rule the world.

CONCLUSION: THE FINAL ANTICHRIST IS COMING

Therefore, when all the evidence is in, we can conclude the following. The Bible, when interpreted in a normal literal sense, says that there will be a personal final Antichrist who comes on the scene of history shortly before the return of Jesus Christ. This Antichrist will not be an evil influence, or an ungodly system, but rather he will be an actual human being who does the bidding of Satan. His coming is still in the future. This is the consistent biblical view of the subject of Antichrist.

SUMMARY TO QUESTION 9
WHAT ARE THE ARGUMENTS FOR THE FINAL ANTICHRIST BEING A LITERAL HUMAN BEING WHO IS STILL TO COME? (FUTURIST VIEW)

While some believe Antichrist is a person who has already appeared on the stage of history, a normal or literal reading of the Book of Revelation will show that this is not possible. The description of the character and exploits of Antichrist makes it clear that we are dealing with a person who has yet to appear on this earth. Indeed, the Bible is clear that Antichrist will only be stopped when Jesus Christ literally returns to the earth with the armies of heaven. Obviously, this has not happened yet.

As for Antichrist being more than an impersonal force or some religious system, we find that the career of Antichrist, as given in Scripture is indeed the career of a person. The way he is described is more in keeping with a human being rather than some religious institution, or some ungodly force. In fact, Revelation 13 specifically describes him as a man. This settles the issue.

Not only is the Antichrist a person, he is a person who has not yet appeared in history. As noted, the Bible is extremely clear that this personage will appear a few short years before the Second Coming of Christ. In fact, his coming and actions trigger events which will lead to the return of Jesus Christ.

Therefore, the most consistent view is to see Antichrist as a human being who will appear on the earth immediately before Christ returns. Antichrist is still to come.

What Is The Case For The Final Antichrist Being A Literal Offspring Of The Devil?

The evidence seems clear that the final Antichrist will be a human being. However, there is some question as to whether he will actually be more than a mere human being. There have been those who have proposed that he is an actual physical offspring of Satan. In other words, he will be the son of the devil. This would make him half human and half demon.

HE IS THE IMITATOR OF CHRIST IN ALL WAYS

We must remember that Antichrist is a personage who attempts to take the place of Jesus Christ. The word "anti" has the meaning of "against" as well as "instead of." He also imitates Christ in all areas.

As the God the Father sent His Son into the world, Satan, the father of lies, will also have his son who attempts to rob the Son of God of all which is rightfully His.

The main reasons for this theory are as follows.

REASON 1: HE IS THE SEED OR OFFSPRING OF THE SERPENT

We begin at the very beginning. The Book of Genesis speaks of a constant struggle between the seed, or the offspring of the woman, and the offspring of the serpent. The prediction of God is as follows.

> And I will cause hostility between you and the woman, and between your offspring and her offspring. He will strike your head, and you will strike his heel (Genesis 3:15 NLT).

Two seeds, or offsprings, are in view here. We find the offspring of the serpent and the offspring of the woman. From the Book of Revelation we find the true identity of the serpent. He is the devil. The Bible explains.

> The great dragon was hurled down—that ancient serpent called the devil, or Satan, who leads the whole world astray. He was hurled to the earth, and his angels with him (Revelation 12:9 NIV).

Therefore, the struggle will be between the devil and his offspring, and the woman and her offspring. In the same chapter of Revelation, the nation Israel is described as a woman clothed in the sun.

> A great and wondrous sign appeared in heaven: a woman clothed with the sun, with the moon under her feet and a crown of twelve stars on her head (Revelation 12:1 NIV).

Israel is called the woman who gave birth to the Messiah, the Christ. Therefore, the woman is identified as Israel while the serpent represents the devil.

According to this prediction in Genesis, there will be hostility between Satan and the woman's spiritual seed, Israel, as well as hostility between the woman's physical seed, Christ, and Satan's physical seed, the Antichrist.

Furthermore the words, "your seed" refers to a specific individual. The seed of the woman is Jesus Christ while the seed of the serpent is the Antichrist. The conclusion is that Antichrist will be more than a man, he will be an actual literal offspring of the devil.

REASON 2: THE DESCRIPTION OF ANTICHRIST IN ISAIAH

We find further evidence of this in the words of Isaiah the prophet. He wrote about what will occur immediately before the coming of the Lord. The Lord Himself said.

> Come, my people, enter your chambers, and shut your doors behind you; hide yourselves for a little while until the fury has passed by. For behold, the LORD is coming out from his place to punish the inhabitants of the earth for their iniquity, and the earth will disclose the blood shed on it, and will no more cover its slain . . . In that day the LORD with his hard and great and strong sword will punish Leviathan the fleeing serpent, Leviathan the twisting serpent, and he will slay the dragon that is in the sea (Isaiah 26;20,21, 27:1 ESV).

This passage describes the future time of Jacob's trouble, also known as the "great tribulation," which will come upon the inhabitants of the earth. It is the time of the Lord's wrath. Daniel explained it this way.

> He said: "I am going to tell you what will happen later in the time of wrath, because the vision concerns the appointed time of the end" (Daniel 8:19 NIV).

These words in the Book of Isaiah are addressed to the people of Israel who are alive at this time of wrath. The Lord is going to punish those on the earth for their "iniquity." This word iniquity is singular, not plural.

It is suggested that the iniquity for which these people of Israel are going to be punished is their worshipping of Satan's man. Indeed, we find a specific reference to this personage. He is called the Leviathan, the piercing, or twisting serpent.

The connection indicates that just before the Millennium, the thousand year reign of Christ upon the earth, God shall punish the twisting or crooked serpent, the Antichrist. The fact that the man of sin is named "the crooked serpent" or "the twisting serpent" may provide further indication that he is the literal son of "that old serpent, the devil."

REASON 3: EZEKIEL 28: THE ANTICHRIST IS THE PRINCE OF TYRE

There seems to be a further reference to Antichrist in Ezekiel 28. It is contended that we are introduced to two characters in this chapter, the King of Tyre, and the Prince, or Ruler, of Tyre. Many Bible students see the reference to the King of Tyre as a direct reference to the created being who became Satan, the adversary of God. What is said about the King of Tyre can only be said of the devil, nobody else.

Yet there is another character in this passage who some see as distinct from the King of Tyre, Satan. This is the Prince, or Ruler, of Tyre.

The parallels between this personage and the coming Antichrist are striking. He is described in this manner.

> The word of the LORD came to me: "Son of man, say to the prince of Tyre, Thus says the Lord GOD: Because your heart is proud, and you have said, 'I am a god, I sit in the seat of the gods, in the heart of the seas,' yet you are but a man, and no god, though you make your heart like the heart of a god—you are indeed wiser than Daniel; no secret is hidden from you; by your wisdom and your understanding you have made wealth for yourself, and have gathered gold and silver into your treasuries; by your great wisdom in your trade you have increased your wealth, and your heart has become proud in your wealth—therefore thus says the Lord GOD: Because you make your heart like the heart of a god, therefore, behold, I will bring foreigners upon you, the most ruthless of the nations; and they shall draw their swords against the beauty of your wisdom and defile

your splendor. They shall thrust you down into the pit, and you shall die the death of the slain in the heart of the seas. Will you still say, 'I am a god,' in the presence of those who kill you, though you are but a man, and no god, in the hands of those who slay you? You shall die the death of the uncircumcised by the hand of foreigners; for I have spoken, declares the Lord GOD" (Ezekiel 28:1-10 ESV).

There are a number of ways in which this personage is linked with the final Antichrist. They can be summed up as follows.

HE TRIES TO TAKE THE PLACE OF GOD

First, we find that the Lord God says to this personage "You have said I am a god, I sit in the seat of the gods." This description is significant.

Indeed, it fits well with what Paul wrote to the Thessalonians about the actions of the coming Antichrist. Paul stated Antichrist will attempt to take the place of God, by sitting in the temple in Jerusalem, and claiming to be God. He wrote.

Who opposes and exalts himself against every so-called god or object of worship, so that he takes his seat in the temple of God, proclaiming himself to be God (Second Thessalonians 2:4 ESV).

Therefore, each of these characters attempts to take the place of the true God in that they each sit in the seat, or place, of God.

THIS PERSONAGE HAS GREAT WISDOM

Second, this person is said to be "wiser than Daniel." This speaks of the extraordinary intelligence of this personage. This is consistent with what is said of Antichrist. Daniel wrote.

I considered the horns, and behold, there came up among them another horn, a little one, before which three of the first horns were plucked up by the roots. And behold, in this horn were eyes like the eyes of a man, and a mouth speaking great things (Daniel 7:8 ESV).

Elsewhere in the writings of Daniel, we are told that this person is a "master of intrigue." Scripture says.

At the end of their rule, when their sin is at its height, a fierce king, a master of intrigue, will rise to power (Daniel 8:23 NLT).

The final Antichrist will be possessed of extraordinary intelligence. Seemingly, he has the answer to all of the problems which the world faces.

HE ACCUMULATES GREAT WEALTH

Third, it is said of this character, "you have gotten wealth for yourself, and have gathered gold and silver into your treasuries; by your great wisdom in trade you have increased your wealth." Again, this is consistent with what we know of the coming Antichrist. The psalmist wrote the description of a person who has these characteristics.

Here now is the one who did not make God his stronghold but trusted in his great wealth and grew strong by destroying others! (Psalm 52:7 NIV).

We find that he will honor "the god of fortresses." Scripture says.

Instead of them, he will honor a god of fortresses; a god unknown to his ancestors he will honor with gold and silver, with precious stones and costly gifts (Daniel 11:38 NIV).

The figure of this Leader, or Prince, of Tyre has unmistakable features which belong to the coming Antichrist.

Therefore, the argument goes like this. If the devil is labeled as the "King of Tyre" in the second part of this chapter, then it is logical to assume that the personage mentioned in the first part, the Prince of Tyre, is the son of the king, the Antichrist. Antichrist, then, is related to Satan as a "prince" is to a "king," as a son is related to his own father.

REASON 4: THE DEVIL IS THE FATHER OF THE LIE

A further indication that Antichrist is actually a superhuman character is found in a statement of Jesus. He said to the religious leaders of His day.

> For you are the children of your father the devil, and you love to do the evil things he does. He was a murderer from the beginning. He has always hated the truth, because there is no truth in him. When he lies, it is consistent with his character; for he is a liar and the father of lies (John 8:44 NLT).

The Greek text has the article before the word "lie." In other words, Satan is the father of the lie, the Antichrist.

There is another passage in the New Testament where "the lie" is mentioned. Paul wrote the following words to the church at Thessalonica.

> For this reason God sends them a powerful delusion so that they will believe the lie (2 Thessalonians 2:11 NIV).

Again the article "the" is found in the Greek text. It is "the" lie.

WHY THE ANTICHRIST IS "THE LIE"

Three reasons have been put forward as to why the Antichrist should be termed "the lie.'

To begin with, he is called "the lie" because his deceitful claim to be the real Christ will be the greatest falsehood ever foisted upon the human race.

In addition, in many ways, he is the direct opposite of the genuine Christ. Jesus is "the Truth." The gospel of John records Jesus making this claim.

> Jesus told him, "I am the way, the truth, and the life. No one can come to the Father except through me" (John 14:6 NLT).

While Jesus is "the Truth," Antichrist is "the lie" to whom Jesus was referring.

Finally, he is the direct descendent of Satan, the arch liar.

These reasons are given to show why Antichrist can rightfully be called "the lie."

REASON 5: HE IS CALLED THE SON OF PERDITION, THE SON OF SATAN

The final Antichrist, while he will be a man, it seems that he may be more than a mere man. Just as Jesus Christ, God the Son, was a true Man and yet He was more than man, the Antichrist will also be more than a simple human.

The Antichrist will be more like a superman for whom the world is looking. In fact, some believe that he will be a supernatural character, the son of Satan.

Indeed, there are those who contend that this is directly stated by Paul in his second letter to the Thessalonians. He specifically called this coming world leader the "son of perdition," or the "son of destruction."

> Let no one deceive you in any way. For that day will not come, unless the rebellion comes first, and the man of lawlessness is revealed, the son of destruction (2 Thessalonians 2:4 ESV).

He is the "son" of perdition, or "son" of destruction; a literal child of the devil. Here the Antichrist is explicitly declared to be superhuman;

"the son of destruction." Just as the Jesus Christ is the Son of God, so the final Antichrist will be the son of Satan.

However, this is not the only way to read this verse. It could also be translated in this manner.

> Don't let anyone deceive you in any way, for [that day will not come] until the rebellion occurs and the man of lawlessness is revealed, the man doomed to destruction (2 Thessalonians 2:3 NIV).

Translating it like this means that the Antichrist is one who is "doomed to destruction" rather than being an actual offspring of the devil.

What we do know is that in Jesus Christ we find that all the fullness of the Godhead dwells or lives in bodily form. Paul wrote to the Colossians.

> For in Christ all the fullness of the Deity lives in bodily form (Colossians 2:9 NIV).

Jesus also could make this statement about Himself. John records Jesus saying.

> Jesus answered: "Don't you know me, Philip, even after I have been among you such a long time? Anyone who has seen me has seen the Father. How can you say, 'Show us the Father'? (John 14:9 NIV).

In the same manner, the Antichrist will be the full and final embodiment of the devil. He will not only be the incarnation of the devil, but the consummation of his wickedness and power.

REASON 6: THE COMING OF THE BEAST IS INTIMATELY CONNECTED WITH THE DEVIL

In the Book of Revelation we find that this beast, the Antichrist, is intimately connected with the devil himself. We read the following in the Book of Revelation.

> The dragon stood on the shore of the sea. And I saw a beast coming out of the sea. It had ten horns and seven heads, with ten crowns on its horns, and on each head a blasphemous name (Revelation 13:1 NIV).

We find a link between the two. Note that the coming forth of the beast, the Antichrist, is immediately connected with the dragon! But this is not all. He is described the exact same way as the devil; he has ten horns and seven heads. This is exactly how Satan himself is previously described by the same author, John, in the Book of Revelation. He wrote.

> Then another sign appeared in heaven: an enormous red dragon with seven heads and ten horns and seven crowns on its heads (Revelation 12:3 NIV).

To sum up, these passages have caused a number of people to see the final Antichrist as a literal offspring of the devil himself.

SUMMARY TO QUESTION 10
WHAT IS THE CASE FOR THE FINAL ANTICHRIST BEING A LITERAL OFFSPRING OF THE DEVIL?

Those who reject the idea that the Antichrist is an evil force or religious system believe the Bible describes a human being when it describes this personage. Furthermore, it is a human being who is still to come in history.

However, there are some people who do not think that the coming Antichrist is a mere human being. Instead they believe that he will actually be the literal offspring of the devil. There are a number of reasons as to why this is argued.

In Genesis, we are told of a war between the offspring of the serpent and the offspring of the woman. From the Book of Revelation, we find that the serpent represents the devil, while the woman represents

Israel. This prediction also looked forward to one individual offspring, a singular one coming from the serpent and from Israel. The offspring of the woman is Jesus Christ, the Messiah of Israel. He is the one who will crush the offspring of the serpent. The literal offspring of the serpent is assumed to be Antichrist. The Bible tells us that the coming of Christ will destroy this personage. Therefore, from the very beginning we are introduced to serpent and his offspring.

In the Book of Isaiah, Antichrist is called the "twisting serpent." The fact that he is somehow related to the serpent is another indication that we are dealing with an actual offspring of Satan himself.

The prophet Ezekiel describes two personages: the prince of Tyre and the King of Tyre. While the King of Tyre is seen to represent Satan, the prince of Tyre is viewed by some to represent of Antichrist. Indeed, the description of this prince fits well with what it said of the coming Antichrist. The fact that he is intimately associated with the devil in this passage is a further reason why many view Antichrist as his actual offspring.

Jesus Himself called the devil the father of "the lie." The lie is assumed by some interpreters to be a reference to the coming Antichrist. As Jesus is the truth, Antichrist is the lie.

To many, the identity of Antichrist is confirmed by a statement of Paul. He is called the son of perdition, that is, the son of Satan. This settles the issue for some people. The fact that he is given this particular designation points out his true origin, Antichrist is the son of the devil.

Finally, the coming of the beast in the Book of Revelation is connected with the devil himself. His origin is said to be from beneath. This also fits the idea that Antichrist is the actual offspring of Satan.

These passages support the idea that the coming man of sin will be more than a mere human being. In some mysterious way, he will be physically connected to the old serpent, the devil.

Should We Assume The Coming Antichrist Will Be The Literal Child Of The Devil?

There are many people who assume that the future man of sin, the final Antichrist, is more than a mere human being. While he is fully human, they also believe that he is supernatural in his character. His supernatural nature is attributed to him as being an actual offspring of the devil.

Not everyone agrees with this assessment. In fact, there are a number of reasons as to why this idea of the supernatural character of Antichrist is rejected. They are as follows.

1. THE PASSAGES DO NOT HAVE TO BE INTERPRETED IN THAT MANNER

The passages which are used to show that Antichrist is an actual offspring of Satan do not necessarily have to be interpreted that way. Indeed, all of them have alternative interpretations which are just as good, if not better, than the ones which see Antichrist as physically related to the devil. Therefore, we are not forced to this conclusion from a study of Scripture.

Indeed, the idea that Antichrist is called "the son of perdition" does not mean that he is a literal offspring of the devil. The words "son of" are used in the Bible in a number of different ways. It does not necessarily mean an actual or literal offspring of someone else.

2. THESE CREATED BEINGS DO NOT REPRODUCE

There is also the issue of the nature of the various beings which beings God has created. From Scripture, it seems that the angels, seraphim, cherubim, and living creatures are all sexless deathless creatures. The devil is a member of this created order. Scripture seems to indicate that they do not, and cannot, reproduce.

In addition, the Book of Genesis also says that each type of creature which God made reproduces only after "its own kind." For, example, we read the following about the sea creatures and the birds.

> So God created the great sea creatures and every living crea-
> ture that moves, with which the waters swarm, according
> to their kinds, and every winged bird according to its kind
> (Genesis 1:21 ESV).

The fact each is made "according to its kind" limits who can procreate with whom. Since humans are a unique "kind," in that they are only able to procreate within their own group, it seems that any type of mating with these specially created beings is out of the question.

3. HOW WOULD SATAN KNOW WHEN TO CONCEIVE ANTICHRIST?

The one thing which seemingly contradicts this idea of Antichrist being an actual child of the devil concerns the timing of his birth. According to the Scripture, the beginning of the seventieth week of Daniel, the great tribulation, occurs when a peace treaty is signed between the beast, the Antichrist, and the nation of Israel. Antichrist must be a full-grown adult at this time, as well as in a position of leadership to be able to accomplish this. The question then becomes, "How will Satan know when this is going to occur?"

If there is a time when Satan unleashes Antichrist onto the world, then it is he who is controlling history. God, instead being the One who controls all things, would be reacting to Satan's timing.

However, if there is anything clear from the Scripture it is that the Lord is in control of all things! Therefore, it is not possible to accept the idea that the Lord is waiting for Satan to make his move with the coming Antichrist.

Indeed, Jesus said the time of His Coming is in the hands of God the Father. In the Book of Acts, we read the following.

> So when they met together, they asked him, "Lord, are you at this time going to restore the kingdom to Israel?" He said to them: "It is not for you to know the times or dates the Father has set by his own authority (Acts 1:6-7 NIV).

God the Father has set the time periods by means of His own authority. It is the Lord who sets all of these events in motion, including the signing of the peace treaty that begins the last seven years before the return of Jesus Christ. Since the Lord does not reveal His plans to the devil, it would not be possible for him to know the timing of this future event, or any other event for that matter.

It is for these good reasons that people reject the idea that the final Antichrist will be a literal child of the devil.

SUMMARY TO QUESTION 11
SHOULD WE ASSUME THE COMING ANTICHRIST WILL BE THE LITERAL CHILD OF THE DEVIL?

The coming Antichrist is seen by some interpreters as a literal child of the devil. Therefore, he is supernatural, as well as human, in his nature.

This view has rightly been challenged. The case against Antichrist being a supernatural being can be summed up as follows.

While it is true that the seed of the woman is ultimately fulfilled in the person of Christ, an individual, this does not mean that the offspring of the serpent must also be literally fulfilled in a human being. In other words, it is not necessary.

The passages used to support this contention do not have to be interpreted in such a way as to demand that the final Antichrist has some physical relationship to the devil. The fact that the man of sin is called "the son of perdition" does not mean he is a literal child of Satan.

In fact, the phrase "son of" has a number of possible meanings. Indeed, in both testaments, we find the term "son" used in a variety of ways. A literal offspring is only one of the ways in which the word is used.

This leads to the problem of equating the Antichrist with Satan in some physical sense. Satan is a spirit-being, seemingly a member of the cherubim. Consequently he has no physical or corporeal form. Furthermore, as an created being, like the angels, seraphim, and living creatures, he does not have the capability to reproduce. Indeed, as far as we know from Scripture, these specially created beings such as angels, seraphim, cherubim, etc. are sexless, deathless creatures. They cannot bear offspring, they cannot cease to exist.

This being the case it is difficult to see how Antichrist could be the literal offspring of the devil since these spirit-beings cannot reproduce.

The special nature of humans and these created beings also has to be taken into consideration. Indeed, humans and these specially created spirit-creatures are different orders of beings. There is no indication from Scripture whatsoever that they are able to have offspring with each other.

Furthermore, Genesis says that God created different types of creatures to reproduce "after their own kind." This limits who can mate with whom. Consequently the idea that Satan could somehow conceive a child through uniting with a human mother does not seem biblically possible.

There is one thing which seems to clearly refute the idea of Antichrist being the actual offspring of the devil, the timing of his coming. Jesus made it clear that nobody knows the time which He Himself will return to the earth. This includes the angels, as well as all of the other specially created beings.

Since Satan is one of these beings, he does not know the time of the Lord's return. This being the case, how would he know when to have Antichrist conceived?

Indeed, the final Antichrist must be a grown man at the time he signs the peace treaty with Israel, rules the world for three and one half years, and is finally judged by the Lord when He returns with His church, the true believers, at the Second Coming.

Yet there is no indication whatsoever that Satan would know the time when these things will occur. This fact seems to refute the idea that Antichrist will be an actual offspring of the devil.

Consequently, when all the evidence is in, we do know the coming Antichrist will be an evil personage but we should not assume that he will be the literal son of the devil.

Was Caesar Nero The Predicted Antichrist?

When of the Letter of First John was written, Antichrist had not yet come.

> Children, it is the last hour. And as you have heard, "Antichrist is coming," even now many antichrists have come. We know from this that it is the last hour (1 John 2:18 HCSB).

Some believe that Antichrist has come since that time. There have been a number of candidates who have been put forward as fulfilling John's prediction. One of the most popular has been Caesar Nero, the crazed Roman Emperor.

THE CASE FOR CAESAR NERO BEING ANTICHRIST

There are those Bible interpreters who hold the view that the Book of Revelation, the last Book of Scripture, mainly addresses contemporary problems for the first century Christians. This is called the "preterist interpretation," or "preterism."

According to this perspective, when John addressed the churches the beast, the Antichrist, was a reference to the present Roman Emperor, Caesar Nero.

1. THERE ARE MANY RESEMBLANCES

To begin with, there are many remarkable resemblances between the historical character of Caesar Nero and the biblical description of the Antichrist. Nero was an enormously egotistical individual, vicious in nature, who persecuted God's people. These all fit the person of Antichrist. Antichrist is predicted to be an incredible proud individual, who kills indiscriminately, and, in particular, persecutes God's people. Nero certainly fit that description.

2. NERO CLAIMED TO BE DIVINE

Furthermore, the Roman emperors were called in Latin *divus* or *sebastos*. These words indicate deity or divinity. Nero claimed this for himself. Indeed, on coins minted in his reign, he is called the "Savior of the world." This also fits what Paul wrote about the Antichrist.

> Let no one deceive you in any way. For that day will not come, unless the rebellion comes first, and the man of lawlessness is revealed, the son of destruction, who opposes and exalts himself against every so-called god or object of worship, so that he takes his seat in the temple of God, proclaiming himself to be God (2 Thessalonians 2:3-4 ESV).

Consequently, we find Nero claiming deity for himself, just as Paul predicted he would.

3. HIS NAMES ADDS UP TO 666

The Book of Revelation says the identity of the beast, or Antichrist, can be determined by adding up the numbers in his name. John wrote.

> Here is wisdom. Let him who has understanding calculate the number of the beast, for it is the number of a man: His number is 666 (Revelation 13:18 NKJV).

It is claimed that it can be shown that the number of Nero is the number of the Antichrist, 666. If one adds up the letters of the name Caesar Nero in Hebrew it will come to 666.

This is done as follows. Neither the Hebrew language nor the Greek language used a system of numbers. Instead the letters of the alphabet stood for numbers. For example, A=1, B=2, etc. Therefore the name of a person could be converted into its corresponding letters.

It is argued that when the letters of the name of Nero are added up in Hebrew the total comes to 666. This is further evidence that John had Nero in mind when he wrote of the coming Antichrist.

There is also the fact that Nero's name in Latin adds up to 616. This is significant because some manuscripts of the Book of Revelation have the number of Antichrist as 616, rather than 666. Either way, Nero's name fits the number of Antichrist.

CONCLUSION: THERE IS NO COMING ANTICHRIST: NERO WAS THE PREDICTED ONE

These reasons have been put forward to demonstrate the coming Antichrist was Caesar Nero. The predictions of Scripture have been fulfilled some two thousand years ago.

Since Antichrist has already come in the past in the person of Caesar Nero, there is no need to look for a future Antichrist. He is an historical character, not a personage who will appear in the future.

RESPONSE

While Nero and Antichrist had certain features in common, it is better to understand him as a type or foreshadow of the one which the Bible says is to come. We can make the following observations.

1. NERO DID NOT HAVE ALL THE TRAITS OF ANTICHRIST

While Nero did share in some of the traits of the future Antichrist, he did not have all of them. Indeed, it is not possible to fit the deeds of Nero with what the Bible says about the future man of sin. Many examples could be given.

For one thing, there is no evidence whatsoever that the mark of Nero's name, 666, was placed on the forehead or right hand of anyone. This did not happen. The people in the Roman Empire in that day could still buy and sell without the mark of Nero because there was no mark of Nero!

2. NERO NEVER CAME TO THE TEMPLE IN JERUSALEM

While Nero may have taken upon himself titles of deity, he never came to the temple in the city of Jerusalem and claimed to be God, as will be true with the predicted Antichrist. In fact, Nero never came to Israel at all.

Many other unfilled predictions could be noted. The point is this: the life of Nero cannot be equated with the life of the predicted Antichrist.

3. NERO'S NAME DOES NOT EQUAL 666

There are more problems. While there have been those who insist that the name of Caesar Nero adds up to the number 666, to do so takes some creativity. Nero's name in Greek, *Neron Kaisar*, does not equal 666 but rather 1005! Some attempt to solve this by putting *Neron Kaisar* into Hebrew which can equal 666. However, to do this there has to be a slight variation in the spelling of the word for Caesar.

Yet doing this presents a real problem. Why would John, writing to a group of individuals, who read Greek and not Hebrew, use a system of numbers with a Hebrew form of his name rather than a Greek form? Interestingly, we also discover that none of the ancient interpreters of the Book of Revelation came up with this Hebrew solution.

The fact that Nero's name adds up to 616 in Latin should not be conclusive either. Again, why should Latin be used as the language to confirm the identity of the mysterious Antichrist?

Furthermore, the 616 reading has not accepted by the majority of textual scholars as the correct one to identity the beast of Revelation.

There is something else which should be noted. Almost anything can be done with numbers and letters if one wishes. Through clever manipulation one can get the letters of a person's name to add up to whatever total they wish. When the future Antichrist does come, it will be plain how the 666 fits his name. Until that time comes, attempting to figure out the identity of this character is just worthless speculation.

4. NERO WAS DEAD WHEN JOHN WROTE

There is another problem, a big problem. Another reason for denying that Nero was not the Antichrist is to be found in the fact that he was deceased *before* John wrote about the beast he described in Revelation chapter thirteen! Nero died in A.D. 68 while John wrote the Book of Revelation some thirty years after the death of Nero. Thus, Nero could not have fulfilled John's predictions because Nero was long dead.

5. CHRIST DID NOT RETURN TO SEND NERO IN THE LAKE OF FIRE

Finally, the fact that we have not yet seen the return of Christ demonstrates the Antichrist has yet to appear. According to the Book of Revelation, Jesus Christ will return to this earth, capture the Antichrist, and thrust him into the lake of fire. The Bible says.

> Then I saw the beast and the kings of the earth and their armies gathered together to make war against the rider on the horse and his army. But the beast was captured, and with him the false prophet who had performed the signs on his behalf. With these signs he had deluded those who had

received the mark of the beast and worshiped his image. The two of them were thrown alive into the fiery lake of burning sulfur (Revelation 19:19-20 NIV).

Certainly nobody is attempting to say that this as already happened. Therefore, Caesar Nero was not the predicted Antichrist. This being the case, we need to expect the appearance of a personal Antichrist at some time in the future. Antichrist has not yet appeared.

SUMMARY TO QUESTION 12
WAS CAESAR NERO THE PREDICTED ANTICHRIST?

Many Antichrists have arisen throughout the history of the church claiming to be the promised Messiah. Others while not personally claiming to be the Messiah have been identified as the biblical Antichrist.

One of the most popular choices in the past has been Caesar Nero. Those who hold this view believe the events in the Book of Revelation were fulfilled in the first century. Nero was the beast, the Antichrist, which John wrote about.

Caesar Nero did indeed have many traits or qualities of the Antichrist which is depicted in Scripture. He was an arrogant murderous individual, a man who specifically targeted Christians for persecution. This is what Scripture says of Antichrist.

Moreover, like the predicted Antichrist, Nero took upon himself titles that belong to deity. This is another indication that he was the beast of Revelation.

Furthermore, the letters in his name, when converted into the Hebrew language, add up to the number 666, the number of the beast. In addition, the alternative number for the beast, 616, is the sum total of adding up the numbers of Nero's name in Latin.

Thus, it is argued that Nero seems like the likely candidate for the man of sin.

However, for a number of reasons, the idea that John was writing about Nero as the beast, the Antichrist, is not convincing. Indeed, there are several things that are predicted in Scripture about Antichrist that preclude Nero from being that character.

While Nero may have possessed many qualities of the coming Antichrist, he certainly did have all of them. He did not enter the temple of Jerusalem and claim to be God as Paul says the coming man of sin will do. Nero was never even in Israel.

In addition, there is nothing in his reign that remotely resembles what John says the beast will do with respect to his mark, branding all the people with a 666. There was no restriction concerning buying and selling in the Roman Empire with respect to Nero's name, or brand. None.

Moreover, it takes some real creativity to make 666 out of the spelling his name. Nero's name does not equal this number in Greek. In addition, to make it equal 666 in Hebrew there has to be a variation in the spelling of his name. In other words, the letters in his name do not add up to 666 no matter how you add them up.

As far as the number 616 goes, it is questionable whether the writer of Revelation expected his readers to use Latin to come up with the number of the name of the beast. In addition, 616 is still a variant reading in Revelation 13. Indeed, there is no clear consensus that it should be used instead of 666.

Furthermore, when John described the beast of Revelation he did this some thirty years after the death of Nero! Since Nero was dead when John wrote Revelation, it is highly unlikely Nero was the beast to which John referred; unless we assume accepted the myth that Nero was raised from the dead! However, there is no evidence that John believed this.

However, the main problem is that Scripture says that the appearance of Antichrist will be immediately before the Second Coming of Jesus Christ. The Bible says that Christ will return to the earth, capture the Antichrist, and thrust him into the Lake of fire. This, of course, has not yet happened and hence rules out Nero as that predicted character.

Nero can rightfully be included among those characters who are a type of Antichrist. In other words, he has traits which the final Antichrist will possess. He was "an" Antichrist. However, he is not the predicted one in Scripture, the final Antichrist. That person is still to come.

Does The Bible Depict Many Different Types Or Illustrations Of The Coming Antichrist?

There are a number of personages in Scripture which give us an idea of the character of the coming Antichrist. They are called "types." These types illustrate certain aspects of the nature or attributes of the future man of sin. Consequently, we can gain an excellent idea of what to expect from this "beast" from the various types listed in Scripture.

THE MAJOR TYPES OR PREFIGUREMENTS OF ANTICHRIST

While exactly who belongs in this category of the "major types" of Antichrist can be debated, it is clear that three main individuals in Scripture typify the coming Antichrist. They are as follows.

1. NIMROD

Nimrod was called a mighty hunter in opposition to the Lord. He was the person who first built the city of Babylon; the center of rebellion against the things of God. He had many things in common with the coming Antichrist.

2. NEBUCHADNEZZAR

The Book of Daniel tells us of King Nebuchadnezzar of Babylon, a person who foreshadows the deeds of Antichrist. As the King of Babylon, his armies sieged the city of Jerusalem and destroyed the holy temple.

We find that he built a golden image of himself, possibly with the gold from the temple. Nebuchadnezzar forced the people under his rule, upon the threat of death, to worship that pagan image. There are many parallels between this King of Babylon and the final Antichrist.

3. ANTIOCHUS IV

The one character which is most like the coming Antichrist is an individual whose coming was predicted in Scripture but not recorded, Antiochus IV. He came as predicted but he lived at the time between the testaments. Many of the events in his life mirror what the Bible says of the coming Antichrist.

MANY MINOR TYPES OF ANTICHRIST ARE FOUND IN SCRIPTURE

Apart from these three, Scripture gives us a number of examples of types of the coming man of sin. For our purposes, we will call them "minor types" of Antichrist; though some may want to place certain of them in the "major type" category. They include the following.

MINOR TYPE 1: THE SERPENT IN EDEN

To find our initial type of Antichrist, we go all the way back to the beginning, to the Garden of Eden. Adam and Eve, the first two human beings, encountered the serpent in paradise. As a type of the coming Antichrist, the serpent cast doubt about God's Word and His character.

THE SERPENT CASTS DOUBTS ABOUT GOD'S WORD

The serpent began his dialogue with Eve by casting doubts about the truthfulness of what God had told Adam and Eve. The Bible says.

> Now the serpent was more crafty than any other beast of the field that the LORD God had made. He said to the woman, "Did God actually say, You shall not eat of any tree in the garden?" (Genesis 3:1-2 ESV).

The honesty of what God had said is questioned. In the same manner, Antichrist will speak out against God's Word. Scripture says.

> The beast was given a mouth to utter proud words and blasphemies and to exercise its authority for forty-two months (Revelation 13:5 NIV).

The truthfulness of the words of the God of the Bible is doubted by the beast, the Antichrist. Instead, this personage actually claims to be God.

GOD'S CHARACTER IS QUESTIONED BY THE SERPENT

The character of God is also questioned by the lying serpent. In response to the woman, the serpent said the following.

> God knows that your eyes will be opened as soon as you eat it, and you will be like God, knowing both good and evil (Genesis 3:5 NLT).

The serpent was calling God a liar.

Antichrist will also say horrible things about the true God. Scripture says.

> He began to speak blasphemies against God: to blaspheme His name and His dwelling—those who dwell in heaven (Revelation 13:6 HCSB).

This is another instance where the serpent is similar to Antichrist.

THE JUDGMENT PRONOUNCED AGAINST THE SERPENT

The serpent was judged for its actions. The Lord said to this creature.

> And I will cause hostility between you and the woman, and between your offspring and her offspring. He will strike your head, and you will strike his heel (Genesis 3:15 NLT).

Hatred between the serpent and its offspring would be directed against the woman and her offspring. It seems that the ultimate offspring of the woman is Christ Himself, while the ultimate offspring of the serpent is Antichrist, the man of sin. The hatred that started in the Garden of Eden will continue throughout the time human beings are here upon the earth.

From the Book of Revelation we find that the power or force behind the serpent in Eden was the devil himself. Scripture says.

> And the great dragon was thrown down, that ancient serpent, who is called the devil and Satan, the deceiver of the whole world—he was thrown down to the earth, and his angels were thrown down with him (Revelation 12:9 ESV).

In the same way, the devil will be the one energizing the coming Antichrist. We also read in the Book of Revelation.

> This beast looked like a leopard, but it had the feet of a bear and the mouth of a lion! And the dragon gave the beast his own power and throne and great authority (Revelation 13:2 NLT).

Therefore, in a number of ways, the serpent in Eden reflects the words and deeds of the coming Antichrist.

MINOR TYPE 2: AMALEK: SON OF ESAU

The Book of Genesis gives us another type of Antichrist, Amalek the son of Esau. While Esau, the son of Isaac, was the older brother of Jacob, or Israel, he was not the son of promise. Scripture not only says the older son would serve the younger son, we also find that Esau despised his birthright. This despising of the things of the Lord carried over to his son Amalek. Indeed, we find that the Amalekites were the constant enemies of God's chosen people, Israel.

On their way to the Promised Land, Israel was attacked by the Amalekites. The Bible says.

> While the people of Israel were still at Rephidim, the warriors of Amalek attacked them (Exodus 17:8 NLT).

The Bible says that Amalek will be perpetually at war with God's people, Israel. We also read in Exodus.

> He said, "They have raised their fist against the LORD's throne, so now the LORD will be at war with Amalek generation after generation" (Exodus 17:16 NLT).

Because of their constant attacks against God's people, the Lord said that the memory of Amalek will be blotted out. We read the following words of Moses.

> When the LORD your God gives you rest from all the enemies around you in the land he is giving you to possess as an inheritance, you shall blot out the name of Amalek from under heaven. Do not forget! (Deuteronomy 25:19 NIV).

Therefore, the nation that came from Amalek, the Amalekites, was a type of Antichrist; people constantly at war with God's people.

There is also the possibility that an Amalekite actually killed the first king of Israel, Saul. After Saul's death, an Amalekite told David the following story.

> By chance I happened to be on Mount Gilboa, and there was Saul leaning on his spear, and behold, the chariots and the horsemen were close upon him. And when he looked behind him, he saw me, and called to me. And I answered, 'Here I am.' And he said to me, 'Who are you?' I answered him, 'I am an Amalekite.' And he said to me 'Stand beside me and kill me, for anguish has seized me, and yet my life still lingers' (2 Samuel 1:6-9 ESV).

The Amalekites were indeed a constant source of trouble for the people of God. The same will be the situation for the coming Antichrist. He too will be an arch-enemy of Israel.

MINOR TYPE 3: THE PHARAOH OF THE EXODUS

When the children of Israel were settled in Egypt a Pharaoh arose who feared the growing numbers of the people. Consequently, to protect his nation, he put the people of Israel into slavery. The Lord then raised up a prophet named Moses who would eventually deliver the people out of Egypt to the Promised Land.

However, this did not happen easily. Pharaoh did everything which he could to keep God's people out of the Land of Promise. In doing so, Pharaoh became a type of the final Antichrist.

Indeed, we find that Pharaoh is a foreshadowing of the Antichrist in numerous ways. They include the following.

1. HE CAME FROM EGYPT WHICH REPRESENTS THE UNBELIEVING WORLD SYSTEM IN SCRIPTURE

First, Pharaoh was king of Egypt. In Scripture, Egypt is the enduring symbol of the godless world-system which will one day be overthrown. Pharaoh prefigured the leader of the final world-kingdom.

2. HE PERSECUTED THE CHOSEN PEOPLE

We also find that the Pharaoh of the Exodus was the heartless tormenter of the chosen people. The Bible says.

> So the Egyptians made the Israelites their slaves. They appointed brutal slave drivers over them, hoping to wear them down with crushing labor. They forced them to build the cities of Pithom and Rameses as supply centers for the king (Exodus 1:11-12 NLT).

In the same way, the coming Antichrist will persecute the Jews in a special way. The Bible says.

> And when the dragon saw that he had been thrown down to the earth, he pursued the woman who had given birth to the male child (Revelation 12:13 ESV).

The woman, who gave birth to the male child, represents the nation of Israel. Satan, the dragon, persecutes the chosen people through his representative, the Antichrist.

3. HE ATTEMPTED TO ERADICATE THE ENTIRE NATION

The Bible also says that Pharaoh tried to wipe out the entire nation. Scripture records that he gave orders that all the male children should be slain in infancy. The Bible puts it this way.

> Then Pharaoh, the king of Egypt, gave this order to the Hebrew midwives, Shiphrah and Puah: "When you help the Hebrew women as they give birth, watch as they deliver. If the baby is a boy, kill him; if it is a girl, let her live" (Exodus 1:15-16 NLT).

In a similar manner, the Antichrist will desire to destroy the entire nation of Israel. We read in Revelation.

> Then the dragon became furious with the woman and went off to make war on the rest of her offspring, on those who keep the commandments of God and hold to the testimony of Jesus. And he stood on the sand of the sea (Revelation 12:17 ESV).

From its very beginning, the nation of Israel has been the subject of the intense hatred of the devil. While many have attempted to eliminate the people of Israel from the planet, all attempts have miserably failed. The God of Israel has promised to protect His people. From the Book of Revelation, we realize that He will keep them safe until the very end.

4. HE OPENLY DEFIED THE LORD, THE GOD OF ISRAEL

The Pharaoh of the Exodus openly defied the Lord God. When Moses and Aaron appeared before him, he would not let God's people go. The Bible describes it this way.

> Afterward Moses and Aaron went and said to Pharaoh, "Thus says the LORD, the God of Israel, 'Let my people go, that they may hold a feast to me in the wilderness.'" But Pharaoh said, "Who is the LORD, that I should obey his voice and let Israel go? I do not know the LORD, and moreover, I will not let Israel go" (Exodus 5:1,2 ESV).

He would not let the people go because he had no respect for the God of Israel, the Living God.

We find that the final Antichrist will also defy the living God. The Bible says.

> He began to speak blasphemies against God: to blaspheme His name and His dwelling—those who dwell in heaven (Revelation 13:6 HCSB).

The pattern is certainly consistent. Those who have the spirit of Antichrist, like the Pharaoh of Egypt, openly defy God.

5. TWO WITNESSES PERFORMED MIRACLES IN HIS PRESENCE

We also find that the two witnesses of the Lord, Moses and Aaron, performed miracles in the presence of the Pharaoh. We read of this in the Book of Exodus.

> So Moses and Aaron went to Pharaoh and did just as the LORD commanded. Aaron cast down his staff

before Pharaoh and his servants, and it became a serpent (Exodus 7:10 ESV).

In the same manner, the Lord will have His two witnesses in the great tribulation period which will perform miracles before the Beast, the Antichrist.

> They have the power to shut the sky, that no rain may fall during the days of their prophesying, and they have power over the waters to turn them into blood and to strike the earth with every kind of plague, as often as they desire. And when they have finished their testimony, the beast that rises from the bottomless pit will make war on them and conquer them and kill them (Revelation 11:6,7 ESV).

We find that in neither case were the miracles by the "two witnesses" heeded by the evil personage.

6. HIS ASSOCIATES SEEMINGLY HAD MIRACULOUS POWERS

Pharaoh had magical resources at his disposal. We read of the powers which his wise men, sorcerers, and magicians demonstrated. The Bible says.

> Then Pharaoh summoned the wise men and the sorcerers, and they, the magicians of Egypt, also did the same by their secret arts (Exodus 7:11 ESV).

The man of sin will also have his miracles to show the people. Paul wrote the following about the powers of this coming Antichrist in his letter to the Thessalonians.

> The coming of the lawless one is by the activity of Satan with all power and false signs and wonders (2 Thessalonians 2:9 ESV).

Miracles are also associated with the one who promotes this final Antichrist. They will be performed by his cohort, the false prophet. Scripture says.

> And it performed great signs, even causing fire to come down from heaven to the earth in full view of everyone. Because of the signs it was given power to perform on behalf of the first beast, it deceived the inhabitants of the earth. It ordered them to set up an image in honor of the beast who was wounded by the sword and yet lived. It was given power to give breath to the image of the first beast, so that it could speak and cause all who refused to worship the image to be killed (Revelation 13:13-15 NIV).

Therefore, Pharaoh and Antichrist are each associated with miracles.

7. HE BROKE HIS PROMISE TO ISRAEL

The ungodly Pharaoh made promises to the Hebrew people. However, he did not keep his word. The Bible says.

> Pharaoh summoned Moses and Aaron and said, "Pray to the LORD to take the frogs away from me and my people, and I will let your people go to offer sacrifices to the LORD." . . . But when Pharaoh saw that there was relief, he hardened his heart and would not listen to Moses and Aaron, just as the LORD had said (Exodus 8:8,15 NIV).

This illustrates what the final Antichrist will also do toward the people of Israel. He will make, or confirm, an agreement with them but he will eventually break it. We read of this in the Book of Daniel. The Bible says.

> He will confirm a covenant with many for one 'seven.' In the middle of the 'seven' he will put an end to sacrifice and offering. And at the temple he will set up an abomination

that causes desolation, until the end that is decreed is poured out on him (Daniel 9:27 NIV).

The covenant, or agreement, will be broken after three and one half years. He will not keep the promises which he made to them.

8. HE EXPERIENCED A TERRIBLE DEATH

This evil Pharaoh met a harsh end of his life. His demise took place at the hands of the very God whom he defied. The psalmist wrote about the death of Pharaoh.

He [the Lord] hurled Pharaoh and his army into the Red Sea (Psalm 136:15 NLT).

Pharaoh died with his army at the Red Sea when the Lord commanded the water to engulf them.

In the same way, the final Antichrist will be captured by the Lord and hurled into the lake of fire.

And the beast was captured, and with it the false prophet who in its presence had done the signs by which he deceived those who had received the mark of the beast and those who worshiped its image. These two were thrown alive into the lake of fire that burns with sulfur (Revelation 19:20 ESV).

The end of each of these individuals is horrific.

9. ISRAEL ENTERED A NEW BEGINNING AT HIS DEATH

When the Pharaoh of the Exodus and his army was defeated, the nation of Israel started out for the Promised Land, and a new beginning. The Bible says.

And Pharaoh rose up in the night, he and all his servants and all the Egyptians. And there was a great cry in Egypt,

> for there was not a house where someone was not dead.
> Then he summoned Moses and Aaron by night and said,
> "Up, go out from among my people, both you and the
> people of Israel; and go, serve the LORD, as you have said.
> Take your flocks and your herds, as you have said, and be
> gone, and bless me also!" (Exodus 12:30-32 ESV).

The chosen people eventually arrived and settled in the land that the Lord had promised them.

In the same way, after the final Antichrist will be thrown into the Lake of Fire, the nation Israel will receive an everlasting possession, the Land of Promise. The kingdom of God will come to the earth!

Therefore, when all these things are considered, we find that the Pharaoh of the Exodus is clearly a type of the coming Antichrist.

MINOR TYPE 4: GOLIATH OF GATH

One of the most familiar characters in the entire Bible is the Philistine giant Goliath. Interestingly, we find that this giant can be compared to the coming Antichrist in a number of ways.

1. HE WAS A PHYSICAL GIANT

To begin with, we find that Goliath was a giant among men. Like King Saul, he stood head and shoulders above everyone else. In this, Goliath prefigured the Antichrist, who it seems will also be striking in his appearance.

2. HE WAS THE ARCHENEMY OF ISRAEL

Goliath was the enemy of Israel. He is "the" one person who represented the enemies of the Lord. In the same manner, the coming Antichrist will be the greatest enemy the nation has ever faced.

3. HE CHALLENGED THE ARMIES OF THE LORD

Goliath, the enemy of the Lord, challenged the armies of the God of Israel. Scripture relates how he taunted God's chosen people. He said.

> I defy the armies of Israel today! Send me a man who will fight me! (1 Samuel 17:10 NLT).

The future "man of sin" will also attempt to challenge the armies of the Lord. Indeed, he will actually gather his armies together to fight against Jesus Christ Himself.

> And I saw the beast and the kings of the earth with their armies gathered to make war against him who was sitting on the horse and against his army (Revelation 19:19 ESV).

As in the case of Goliath, the army of the Lord will prevail.

4. THE NUMBER 666 IS CONNECTED WITH HIM

Interestingly, the number 666 is connected with the giant Goliath. Note how the Scripture reveals these three sixes in describing this giant.

A. HE WAS SIX CUBITS TALL

To begin with, his height is listed at six cubits. We read about this in the Book of 1 Samuel. It says.

> A champion named Goliath, who was from Gath, came out of the Philistine camp. His height was six cubits and a span (1 Samuel 17:4 NIV).

This makes him about nine feet tall!

B. SIX PIECES OF ARMOR ARE MENTIONED

Six pieces of armor are listed for Goliath: a bronze helmet, bronze armor on his shins, a bronze sword, a spear shaft, an iron point of his spear, and a shield-bearer.

He had a bronze helmet on his head and wore a coat of scale armor of bronze weighing five thousand shekels on his legs he wore bronze greaves, and a bronze javelin was slung on his back. His spear shaft was like a weaver's rod, and its iron point weighed six hundred shekels. His shield bearer went ahead of him (1 Samuel 17:5-7 NIV).

The number six keeps reoccurring.

C. THE HEAD OF HIS SPEAR WEIGHED SIX HUNDRED SHEKELS

There is still more. The head of his spear weighed six hundred shekels of iron, about fifteen pounds. The Bible says.

The shaft of his spear was as heavy and thick as a weaver's beam, tipped with an iron spearhead that weighed 15 pounds. His armor bearer walked ahead of him carrying a shield (1 Samuel 17:7 NLT).

Goliath was six cubits in height, with six specific pieces of armor, and the head of his spear weighed six hundred shekels of iron. It is no coincidence that this giant is described with three sixes.

5. THE ONE WHO KILLED HIM WAS DAVID, A TYPE OF CHRIST

Finally, Goliath was killed by David who is a type, or foreshadowing, of Jesus Christ. The Bible says.

So David triumphed over the Philistine with only a sling and a stone, for he had no sword (1 Samuel 17:50 NLT).

As we have noted, Antichrist meets his demise at the coming of Christ to the earth. Jesus captures him alive and throws him and the false prophet into the lake of fire.

In each of these respects, the giant Goliath of Gath foreshadowed the coming Antichrist.

MINOR TYPE 5: KING SAUL OF ISRAEL

Next we come to a type, or foreshadow, of Christ who was a member of the chosen people of God, the nation of Israel. The first king of Israel, Saul, prefigures the coming man of sin in a number of ways. We can make the following observations.

1. HE WAS A LARGER THAN LIFE FIGURE

When we are first introduced to Saul his striking physical stature is emphasized. The Bible says.

> His son Saul was the most handsome man in Israel—head and shoulders taller than anyone else in the land (1 Samuel 9:2 NLT).

This physical description is repeated later (1 Samuel 10:23). Obviously Saul had a presence about him which intimidated people.

This being the case, we can readily see how Saul prefigures the coming man of sin, who has no peers. The Book of Revelation says the following about him.

> People worshiped the dragon because he had given authority to the beast, and they also worshiped the beast and asked, "Who is like the beast? Who can make war against it?" (Revelation 13:4 NIV).

This lawless one will so tower above all his contemporaries that all people shall cry out, "Who is like unto the beast?" The answer is, "Nobody."

2. HE RULED OVER ISRAEL BUT NOT AS GOD'S MAN

Saul was chosen by the people to rule over Israel. The Bible explains what happened in this manner.

> Samuel said to all the people, "Do you see the man the LORD has chosen? There is no one like him among all the

people." Then the people shouted, "Long live the king!"
(1 Samuel 10:24 NIV).

Saul was first king of Israel but he was *not* the rightful king. The people mistakenly thought that he was God's man. He was not.

Not only was Saul the people's choice rather than God's choice, Saul was not a descendent of the rightful line for the kingship, the tribe of Judah. Saul was from the tribe of Benjamin. In other words, he did not have the proper credentials.

In the same manner, the people of Israel will choose Antichrist to rule over them even though he does not possess the proper biblical credentials. Among other things, it may mean that the final Antichrist will actually be a Gentile rather than a Jew.

3. HE BLASPHEMOUSLY PERFORMED THE DUTIES OF A PRIEST

The Bible is clear about the responsibilities of the various God-given offices. Kings had their duties, and priests had their own responsibilities. They were not to perform the duties outside of their office. Saul was a king, not a priest. However, he deliberately performed duties which belonged to the priestly class. Scripture records the following.

> So he demanded, "Bring me the burnt offering and the peace offerings!" And Saul sacrificed the burnt offering himself (1 Samuel 13:9 NLT).

The coming Antichrist will also perform an action which is limited to the Great High Priest. Indeed, he will go into the Holy of Holies in the temple in Jerusalem. This is a place where the king was never allowed to go.

4. HIS REIGN WAS IMMEDIATELY BEFORE THE TRUE ANOINTED ONE

The timing of the reign of Saul is foreshadowing the coming Antichrist. He ruled immediately before God's man, David, assumed the throne. The final Antichrist will rule immediately before the One whom David prefigured, Jesus Christ, God the Son, will reign.

5. HE WAS A GREAT WARRIOR WHO REBELLED AGAINST GOD

While King Saul was a great warrior, he rebelled against the commands of God. The Lord made this clear when he said the following to Samuel the prophet.

> I regret that I have made Saul king, because he has turned away from me and has not carried out my instructions. Samuel was angry, and he cried out to the LORD all that night (1 Samuel 15:11 NIV).

Antichrist, likewise, will be a great man of war who also will rebel against the living God.

6. SAUL ORDERED GOD'S SERVANTS KILLED

Saul was not God's man for the job, David was. The Bible says this caused Saul to fear David. The Bible says.

> Saul was afraid of David, because the LORD was with David but had departed from Saul (1 Samuel 18:12 NIV).

This eventually led the evil King Saul to attempt to kill David. The Bible says.

> The next day an evil spirit from God came forcefully on Saul. He was prophesying in his house, while David was playing the lyre, as he usually did. Saul had a spear in his hand and he hurled it, saying to himself, "I'll pin David to the wall." But David eluded him twice (1 Samuel 18:10,11 NIV).

Though he was not able to kill God's man, Saul ordered the murder of the servants of the true God. Scripture describes the event in this manner.

> And the king said to the guard who stood about him, "Turn
> and kill the priests of the LORD, because their hand also is
> with David, and they knew that he fled and did not disclose
> it to me." But the servants of the king would not put out
> their hand to strike the priests of the LORD. Then the king
> said to Doeg, "You turn and strike the priests." And Doeg
> the Edomite turned and struck down the priests, and he
> killed on that day eighty-five persons who wore the linen
> ephod (1 Samuel 22:17,18 ESV).

The future Antichrist will also go about killing the Lord's own people.
The Bible says.

> Also it was allowed to make war on the saints and to con-
> quer them. And authority was given it over every tribe and
> people and language and nation (Revelation 13:7 ESV).

Therefore, the coming Antichrist, like Saul, will cause the murder of
the people of God.

7. HE USED FORBIDDEN SPIRITUAL POWERS

Saul's life came to a tragic end after he defied the Lord's command
and inquired of an evil spirit (1 Samuel 29). This type of practice was
strictly forbidden by the Lord. Indeed, even before Israel entered the
Land of Promise, the Lord gave the following warning.

> When you come into the land that the LORD your God
> is giving you, you shall not learn to follow the abominable
> practices of those nations. There shall not be found among
> you anyone who burns his son or his daughter as an offer-
> ing, anyone who practices divination or tells fortunes or
> interprets omens, or a sorcerer or a charmer or a medium or
> a wizard or a necromancer, for whoever does these things is
> an abomination to the LORD. And because of these abom-
> inations the LORD your God is driving them out before

you. You shall be blameless before the LORD your God, for these nations, which you are about to dispossess, listen to fortune-tellers and to diviners. But as for you, the LORD your God has not allowed you to do this (Deuteronomy 18:9-14 ESV).

Because of his disobedience to this command, the Lord pronounced that Saul would die the next day, which he did.

The coming Antichrist is also associated with the powers of spiritual darkness. Indeed, it is the devil himself who gives him power. The Bible says the following.

And the beast that I saw was like a leopard; its feet were like a bear's, and its mouth was like a lion's mouth. And to it the dragon gave his power and his throne and great authority (Revelation 13:2 ESV).

King Saul forfeited his life by trying to call upon the powers of darkness. In the same manner, it seems that the final Antichrist actually turns his soul over to the devil.

It is truly tragic that the first king of the nation of Israel, Saul, is a type of the coming Antichrist in so many different ways.

MINOR TYPE 6: ALEXANDER THE GREAT

Alexander of Macedon, Alexander the Great, the man who conquered the world and died at the age of thirty-two, was a type of the coming Antichrist. Although the exploits of Alexander are not chronicled in Scripture, they are predicted.

A LITTLE HORN: HE CAME OUT OF NOWHERE

Alexander, like the coming Antichrist, is called a "little horn." He is the male goat mentioned in the Book of Daniel. Scripture says the following about him.

> While I was watching, suddenly a male goat appeared from the west, crossing the land so swiftly that he didn't even touch the ground. This goat, which had one very large horn between its eyes, headed toward the two-horned ram that I had seen standing beside the river, rushing at him in a rage. The goat charged furiously at the ram and struck him, breaking off both his horns. Now the ram was helpless, and the goat knocked him down and trampled him. No one could rescue the ram from the goat's power. The goat became very powerful. But at the height of his power, his large horn was broken off. In the large horn's place grew four prominent horns pointing in the four directions of the earth (Daniel 8:5-8 NLT).

We learn several things about the conquests of Alexander from this Scripture.

HIS CONQUEST WAS SWIFT

The goat is described as moving across the earth without touching the ground. This indicates lightning speed. This accurately describes the conquest of Alexander. Indeed, he conquered the known world with lightning speed.

In the same manner, Antichrist will rise quickly to a place of prominence in the end times. From relative obscurity the coming man of sin will soon become the world leader.

HE SPREAD A NON-CHRISTIAN CULTURE WHICH INCLUDED THE WORSHIP OF FALSE GODS

Alexander spread the Hellenic, or Greek, culture wherever he went. This non-biblical culture, among other things, taught the worship of many different gods; instead of the one God who is revealed in Scripture.

In the same manner, Antichrist will also reject the worship of the one true God. Scripture says of him.

> He will have no respect for the gods of his ancestors, or for the god loved by women, or for any other god, for he will boast that he is greater than them all. Instead of these, he will worship the god of fortresses—a god his ancestors never knew—and lavish on him gold, silver, precious stones, and expensive gifts (Daniel 11:37-38 NLT).

The God of the Bible was rejected by Alexander, and will be rejected by the final Antichrist.

The coming Antichrist will also spread a culture which is opposed to the God of the Bible. Scripture says.

> And he was given a mouth speaking great things and blasphemies, and he was given authority to continue for forty-two months. Then he opened his mouth in blasphemy against God, to blaspheme His name, His tabernacle, and those who dwell in heaven (Revelation 13:5-6 NKJV).

Like the era of Alexander the Great, the mindset of this future age will be one which openly rejects God's truth.

ALEXANDER DEMANDED WORSHIP AS A GOD

Under the leadership of Alexander, Greece became the most powerful nation on the earth. Because of his incredible success on the battlefield Alexander became extremely proud and arrogant. Furthermore, he believed that the Greek gods, Hercules and Achilles, were his ancestors. It was seemingly these things that led him to compel the people of the provinces to worship him as a god.

The coming Antichrist will also demand worship from the people. Scripture says this will be promoted through his evil cohort, the false prophet.

The Bible says that an image or statue of the beast, the Antichrist, will be created. Those who refuse to worship the beast and his image will be put to death.

> He was then permitted to give life to this statue so that it could speak. Then the statue of the beast commanded that anyone refusing to worship it must die (Revelation 13:15 ESV).

This is another way in which Alexander pre-figured the coming Antichrist, the demand for personal worship.

HE MET HIS DOOM QUICKLY

As fast as was his rise to the top, Alexander did not stay there for very long. At the peak of his power, the mighty horn, died. As the prophecy stated, his kingdom was divided into four parts with each of his four generals taking a certain portion. No single person took the place of Alexander the Great.

In the same way, soon after Antichrist will consolidate the entire world under his rule, Jesus Christ will come back to the earth. Like Alexander, the rule of this future beast, the man of lawlessness, will only be for a small amount of time.

These are some of the reasons as to why Alexander the Great is an obvious type of the coming man of sin, the Antichrist.

MINOR TYPE 7: HEROD THE GREAT

King Herod, also called "Herod the Great," can unquestionably be seen as a type of Antichrist in a number of ways. They include the following.

1. HE WAS AN EVIL KING WHO RULED BEFORE THE KING OF KINGS

To begin with, the Gospel of Matthew emphasizes that Herod was "king" at the time of the birth of Jesus. Matthew wrote the following description of him.

Jesus was born in Bethlehem in Judea, during the reign of King Herod. About that time some wise men from eastern lands arrived in Jerusalem, asking (Matthew 2:1 NLT).

Two other times in this chapter, the position of Herod as "king" is emphasized (verses 3 and 9).

Of course, this is in contrast to the real King, Jesus. The One who was born in the stable is the "King of kings." Thus, we have a tale of two kings. One of them is evil, and the other is good.

In this manner, Herod prefigured the last evil king who would rule before the appearing of the King of kings.

Indeed, Jesus' kingly role is emphasized in His return to the earth. The Book of Revelation says the following of Him at His Second Coming.

On his robe at his thigh was written this title: King of all kings and Lord of all lords (Revelation 19:16 NLT).

While Herod was the evil king who was ruling before the First Coming of Christ, Antichrist will rule as king or ruler immediately before the Second Coming. In this manner, the life of Herod parallels that of the final Antichrist.

2. HE WAS A HYPOCRITICAL LIAR

We also find that Herod was a shameless liar. When the magi, or wise men, appeared in Jerusalem they wanted to know where the Christ was to born. Herod was concerned about what he had heard from these visitors. Matthew writes.

Now after Jesus was born in Bethlehem of Judea in the days of Herod the king, behold, wise men from the east came to Jerusalem, saying, "Where is he who has been born king of the Jews? For we saw his star when it rose and have come to worship him." When Herod the king heard this, he was troubled, and all Jerusalem with him (Matthew 2:1-3 ESV).

Herod then lied about his intent to the wise men. He pretended that he wanted to worship the newborn King when he really intended to kill him. Scripture explains Herod's lie to the magi.

> And he sent them to Bethlehem, saying, "Go and search diligently for the child, and when you have found him, bring me word, that I too may come and worship him" (Matthew 2:8 ESV).

Such is the role that the final Antichrist will play in the future. At first, he will appear to be a friend to the Jews. He will make, or confirm, a covenant, or agreement, with them that seemingly puts the nation at peace.

3. HIS TRUE CHARACTER WAS SOON REVEALED

Though pretending to be on the side of the newborn king, Herod's true nature soon became apparent. Scripture records his reaction when he realized he had been tricked.

> Then Herod, when he saw that he had been tricked by the wise men, became furious, and he sent and killed all the male children in Bethlehem and in all that region who were two years old or under, according to the time that he had ascertained from the wise men (Matthew 2:16 NLT).

We find that the Antichrist will act the same way, and in the same city, Jerusalem. Three and one half years after he makes an agreement with the Jews, he will break that same covenant.

> He will make a firm covenant with many for one week, but in the middle of the week he will put a stop to sacrifice and offering. And the abomination of desolation will be on a wing of the temple until the decreed destruction is poured out on the desolator (Daniel 9:27 NLT).

The genuine character of these leaders, Herod and Antichrist, will eventually be revealed.

4. HE ATTEMPTED TO THWART GOD'S PROPHETIC WORD

In Herod's decree to murder the babies in Bethlehem and in the surrounding region, he was attempting to kill Christ Himself. In doing this, he was trying to thwart God's prophetic word.

Previously the angel of the Lord had told Joseph, the husband of Mary, the following destiny about the baby who was to be born.

> And she will have a son, and you are to name him Jesus, for he will save his people from their sins (Matthew 1:21 NLT).

The baby Jesus came into the world for a specific purpose. He was to grow to be a man and save His people from their sins. While Jesus also did come into the world to die, it would only be at the proper time and place. Paul wrote.

> But when the fullness of time had come, God sent forth his Son, born of woman, born under the law (Galatians 4:4 ESV).

Herod tried to defeat God's plan. He wanted to kill the Lord Jesus before God's plan could take place.

We find that Herod's murdering of the children of Bethlehem pictures the horrific assaults which the Antichrist will make upon the entire nation. As has been the case with so many others in the past, Antichrist will make a futile attempt of removing the entire Jewish nation from the face of the earth.

Therefore, these cruel acts of Herod will be repeated in the future. The gospel of Matthew records the fulfillment of Jeremiah's prophecy in what Herod ordered.

> A voice was heard in Ramah, weeping and loud lamentation, Rachel weeping for her children; she refused to be comforted, because they are no more (Matthew 2:18 HCSB).

This is a quotation from the prophet Jeremiah. Six hundred years earlier the prophet had written.

> Thus says the LORD: "A voice is heard in Ramah, lamentation and bitter weeping. Rachel is weeping for her children; she refuses to be comforted for her children, because they are no more" (Jeremiah 31:15 ESV).

What is interesting is that this prediction of Jeremiah will receive another and final fulfillment at the close of the "great tribulation" period. It is clear from the context in the Book of Jeremiah that the "bitter weeping and lamentation" will again be heard in Ramah just before Jesus Christ returns and restores Israel. Consequently, the final fulfillment of the weeping for the children is still in the future.

However, the weeping will turn into joy. As Herod failed to destroy the Christ-child, the coming man of sin will also fail in his attempt to obliterate the Jewish people. As always, the Lord will prevail!

CONCLUSION: THERE ARE MANY PRE-FIGUREMENTS OF THE COMING ANTICHRIST

This sums up some of the pre-figurements of Antichrist which are found in the Scripture. Certain of them such as Nimrod, Nebuchadnezzar and Antiochus IV, can be considered major types of the coming 'man of sin' while others are minor types. Some may want to place these "lesser" figures of Antichrist into the major type category. There is no problem doing this because these categories, major and minor types, are only for convenience sake.

Whatever way in which we eventually decide to categorize these pre-figurements of Antichrist, one thing is clear; Scripture is full of allusions to the coming man of sin.

SUMMARY TO QUESTION 13
DOES THE BIBLE DEPICT MANY DIFFERENT TYPES OR ILLUSTRATIONS OF THE COMING ANTICHRIST?

On the pages of Scripture we find a number of people who are types or pre-figurements of the coming Antichrist. Some are obvious while others are not so obvious.

Seemingly, the most obvious ones are Nimrod, Nebuchadnezzar, and Antiochus IV. Nimrod was the first king of Babylon. He was called a mighty hunter in opposition to the Lord. It was likely that the tower of Babel was built under his leadership. His defiant behavior against the Lord is typical of the coming Antichrist.

Nebuchadnezzar the King of Babylon destroyed the Holy temple in Jerusalem. Later, he built a golden statue of himself, sixty cubits by six cubits, possibly with the gold from the temple. The people were forced to worship this golden image. If not, they would face immediate death. A similar episode will occur with the final Antichrist and an image of his likeness.

Antiochus IV defiled the Holy temple in Jerusalem and proclaimed himself to be a god. This too will be part of the actions of the future man of sin.

While these three characters can easily be seen as types of Antichrist, there are many more biblical characters who also show some of the traits of the coming man of sin. The following also prefigure the final Antichrist.

The first type of Antichrist is not a real person; it is the serpent in the Garden of Eden. We are told that the serpent somehow had the ability to speak. In doing so, it questioned God's Word and His character. The serpent tempted the woman, Eve, to sin. The consequence for the serpent was the pronunciation of punishment. The serpent's actions, in many ways, prefigure the career of Antichrist.

The Book of Genesis provides another example of the coming Antichrist in the son of Esau, Amalek. The people of Amalek were a perpetual enemy of Israel. On the way to the Promised Land, the Amalekites attempted to eradicate the nation of Israel. It was to the point that the Lord said that He would blot out the memory of Amalek. Amalek, and his descendants, are a type of Antichrist.

The Pharaoh of the Exodus is also a type of Antichrist. He was from Egypt; a place which the Bible consistently illustrates as an example of the evil-world system. Furthermore, he is called an Assyrian. This is one of the many titles of Antichrist. We also find Pharaoh persecuting the chosen people as well as attempting to eradicate them. This will also be in the program of Antichrist. Pharaoh publicly defied the Lord, as will the coming Antichrist.

Though two witnesses performed miracles in his presence, he still did not change his evil ways. The same thing will occur with the coming beast, the Antichrist.

Pharaoh also made an agreement with the chosen people but then broke the agreement. He met a horrific end to his life, as will the beast of the Book of Revelation, the Antichrist. Finally, after the demise of Pharaoh, the nation of Israel was able to enter the land of promise. After the demise of Antichrist, the remnant of believing Jews will enter into the promised kingdom age. In each of these ways, the Pharaoh of the Exodus mimics the coming Antichrist.

Goliath of Gath, the giant who was defeated by the shepherd boy David, has many traits in common with the future Antichrist. For one thing, the number six is prominent in his description. Like the coming Antichrist, Goliath openly defied the Lord, the God of Israel. Goliath was killed by the sword by God's man, David. Antichrist will be killed by the Lord Jesus Himself.

Sadly, Saul, the first king of Israel, exhibited many attributes which will be found in the future Antichrist. His physical appearance was stunning but he was weighed down with moral weakness. He showed his disdain for the things of God in performing the forbidden duties of a priest. Though he ruled over Israel, it was not as God's chosen man. In fact, Saul attempted to kill God's man, David. Furthermore, Saul ordered the godly priests of Israel to be killed. Like the fate which awaits the final Antichrist, Saul was killed with the sword.

Alexander the Great, whose rise is predicted in the Book of Daniel, can also be compared to the coming Antichrist. He rose up out of obscurity and conquered the entire world in a few short years. In doing so, he spread the Greek, or Hellenic culture to the known world. However, his fall was as fast as his ascension. Indeed, for he died after ruling for a short period of time. Such will be the case with the final Antichrist.

Herod the Great, the king, who ordered the babes in Bethlehem murdered, is also a type of Antichrist. At first, Herod pretended to be a follower of the God of Israel but his true intentions were eventually revealed. This is similar to the career of the future man of sin. The friend of the people turns into their worst enemy. This evil king also attempted to thwart the plan of God. However, his attempt to destroy the Christ-child failed, as will the attempt of the coming Antichrist to destroy the chosen people, the Jews.

To sum up, from the Bible we thus find an incredible amount of information about the coming man of sin by examining certain characters whose behavior pre-figures who he is, and what he will do.

What Was Nimrod? Why Is He Considered To Be A Type Of Antichrist?

The Scripture contains illustrations which prefigure the person and deeds of the coming Antichrist. These types foreshadow the *character* of the "man of sin," as well as his actions when he arrives on the earth. One of these types of the final Antichrist was a man called Nimrod.

We discover some details about him in Genesis 10. It says the following.

> He was a mighty hunter before the LORD; that is why it is said, "Like Nimrod, a mighty hunter before the LORD." The first centers of his kingdom were Babylon, Uruk, Akkad and Kalneh, in Shinar. From that land he went to Assyria, where he built Nineveh, Rehoboth Ir, Calah and Resen, which is between Nineveh and Calah—which is the great city (Genesis 10:9-12 NIV).

From what Scripture has to say about this personage we can make the following observations.

1. NIMROD'S NAME INDICATES HIS REBELLIOUS NATURE

First, the meaning of Nimrod's name or description seems to indicate his evil character. The word Nimrod possibly means, "The Rebel." There are a number of commentators which believe Nimrod, or "the

Rebel," is not actually the name of this individual, but rather a derisive characterization of this person. He was a rebellious person whose name is not recorded in Scripture.

2. HE MAY HAVE BEEN THE HISTORICAL CHARACTER GILGAMESH

Some believe Nimrod is none other than the historical character known as "Gilgamesh." If this is his true identity, then we know much about him. Indeed, there is an ancient document which still exists known as the "Epic of Gilgamesh." This work is one of the earliest written documents known to humanity. It records the deeds of an extremely evil man, Gilgamesh. The story of Gilgamesh says he was one third man but two thirds god. This description seems to fit the deeds of the biblical character known as Nimrod. Indeed, the parallels between Nimrod and Gilgamesh are many.

ANTICHRIST WILL REBEL AGAINST EVERYTHING HOLY

This rebellious depiction of Nimrod is consistent with what we know of the coming man of sin. He is described in this manner by Paul.

> Who opposes and exalts himself against every so-called god or object of worship, so that he takes his seat in the temple of God, proclaiming himself to be God (2 Thessalonians 2:4 ESV).

The Antichrist will certainly rebel against the Lord. Daniel gave this picture of the coming man of lawlessness.

> By his cunning he shall make deceit prosper under his hand, and in his own mind he shall become great. Without warning he shall destroy many. And he shall even rise up against the Prince of princes, and he shall be broken—but by no human hand (Daniel 8:25 ESV).

The comparisons are obvious.

3. NIMROD IS DESCRIBED AS A MIGHTY WARRIOR IN OPPOSITION TO THE LORD

It is also emphasized that Nimrod was a "mighty" warrior. Scripture says.

> Cush was the father of Nimrod, who became a mighty warrior on the earth (Genesis 10:8 NIV).

We find that four times the word *mighty* is connected with Nimrod. Furthermore, some translations read, "He began to be mighty." This may suggest that Nimrod fought his way to become the leader of that era.

This corresponds with the biblical depiction of the final Antichrist. He first appears as "the little horn." He eventually attains his great power by means of conquest.

> Out of one of them came a little horn, which grew exceedingly great toward the south, toward the east, and toward the glorious land (Daniel 8:9 ESV).

Therefore, we have another comparison between Nimrod and Antichrist.

4. HE ACTED IN DEFIANCE OF THE LORD

In consecutive verses, Nimrod is called a mighty hunter "before the Lord." However, this does not mean Nimrod was before the Lord in some type of servant position. To the contrary, the idea is that he was a mighty hunter "in opposition to the Lord." In other words, he was a defiant individual.

Defiance will also characterize the coming Antichrist. Daniel describes him in this manner.

> The king will do as he pleases, exalting himself and claiming to be greater than every god there is, even blaspheming the

God of gods. He will succeed—until the time of wrath is completed. For what has been determined will surely take place (Daniel 11:36 NLT).

Nimrod, and the coming Antichrist, each have in common this trait of defiance.

5. HE WAS THE FIRST KING OF BABYLON

Another important fact is that Nimrod was the first king of Babylon. Scripture says.

> The first centers of his kingdom were Babylon, Uruk, Akkad and Kalneh, in Shinar (Genesis 10:10 NIV).

Babylon became the center for all things opposed to God. Indeed, in the Book of Revelation, Babylon is highlighted as that system which is anti-God in everything which it does.

The fact that Nimrod founded the city of Babylon certainly adds to his likeness to the coming Antichrist. From the Book of Revelation we also find that Antichrist and Babylon work together in opposition to the Lord.

The King of Babylon also seems to be one of the many titles of the Antichrist. We read of this in Isaiah. It says.

> You will taunt the king of Babylon. You will say, "The mighty man has been destroyed. Yes, your insolence is ended" (Isaiah 14:4 NLT).

The fact that Nimrod built a number of cities gives the impression that he wished to establish a world empire in the early days after the flood.

6. HE DESIRED FAME WHEN BUILDING THE TOWER OF BABEL

Nimrod is usually equated with the construction of the Tower of Babel as recorded in Genesis 11. While Nimrod is not directly named in that chapter, we can probably assume that he is the person who organized and headed the movement and rebellion which is described in Genesis 11. This rebellion is described as follows.

> Then they said, "Come, let us build ourselves a city, with a tower that reaches to the heavens, so that we may make a name for ourselves and not be scattered over the face of the whole earth" (Genesis 11:4 NIV).

This act was a direct refusal to obey the command which the Lord had previously given humanity to Noah after the flood.

> Then God blessed Noah and his sons, saying to them, "Be fruitful and increase in number and fill the earth" (Genesis 9:1 NIV).

Nimrod seemingly wished to establish a world-empire with Babylon as its headquarters.

First century Jewish writer, Flavius Josephus, in his work, *Antiquities of the Jews*, had the following to say about Nimrod.

> Now it was Nimrod who excited them to such an affront and contempt of God. He was the grandson of Ham, the son of Noah—a bold man, and of great strength of hand. He persuaded them not to ascribe it to God, as if it were through his means they were happy, but to believe that it was their own courage which procured that happiness. He also gradually changed the government into tyranny—seeing no other way of turning men from the fear of God, but to bring them into a constant dependence upon his own power. He also said he would get revenge on God, if he should have a mind to drown the world again; for that he would build a tower too high for the waters to be able to reach! And that he would avenge himself on God for destroying their forefathers (Josephus, *Antiquities Of The Jews*, 1:4:2).

Therefore, we discover that Josephus equates Nimrod with the construction of the Tower of Babel.

A COMPARISON BETWEEN NIMROD AND ANTICHRIST

Nimrod is the first individual named in the Bible who attempted to build some sort of worldwide empire. This rebel did so in direct defiance to the commandments of the Lord. The center of his defiance was Babylon. All of these things accord well with the career of the coming Antichrist. Therefore, in Nimrod, we find an obvious pre-figurement of the coming beast, the man of sin.

SUMMARY TO QUESTION 14
WHAT WAS NIMROD? WHY IS HE CONSIDERED TO BE A TYPE OF ANTICHRIST?

Scripture contains what is known as "types." These are pre-figurements of people and events which will take place at some time in the future. The Old Testament is filled with many types or pre-figurements of Jesus Christ.

In addition, there are a number of biblical figures which are types or pre-figurements of the coming Antichrist. One of the primary ones is Nimrod. This can be seen in a number of ways.

To begin with, Nimrod's name seems to indicate his defiant nature. It is possible that the word Nimrod means "the rebel." In fact, it has been suggested that Nimrod is not actually the name of this particular individual but rather a derisive title. He is "the rebel;" an unnamed person who rebelled against the true God after the world had been destroyed by the flood.

In fact, it has been suggested that Nimrod is the historical character "Gilgamesh." If this is the case, then we know much more about him. From one of the earliest writings known to humanity, the "Epic of Gilgamesh," we discover that Gilgamesh thought himself to be more of a god than a human being. His vile exploits are recorded in this ancient work.

The Antichrist, who is also called "the beast," is characterized by his rebellion against everything which is holy. Nimrod is certainly a fitting type of Antichrist in this respect. Not only is his name indicative of the future man of sin, we also discover he is called a "mighty warrior before the Lord." Rather than meaning "in the presence" of the Lord, this is understood by many commentators to mean "in the opposition" of the Lord. His infamy is due to his antagonism to the things of God.

We also find that Nimrod was the first king of Babylon. Babylon figures prominently throughout Scripture as a center of opposition to the Lord. Before the return of the Jesus Christ, Babylon will again be center-stage in opposing the Lord.

If we assume Nimrod was the driving force behind the building of the tower of Babel, then this adds to his likeness to the coming Antichrist. The tower was built because the people wanted to make a "name" for themselves.

The final Antichrist is a personage which exalts his name above everything else. These factors indicate that Nimrod, this mighty warrior in opposition to the Lord, is truly a type of the coming man of sin.

In What Sense Is King Nebuchadnezzar Of Babylon Like The Future Antichrist?

Another clear type, or pre-figurement, of the final Antichrist is found in the life of the Babylonian King Nebuchadnezzar. We can note the following ways in which this ancient king was similar in actions to the coming Antichrist.

1. NEBUCHADNEZZAR DESTROYED THE TEMPLE IN JERUSALEM

To begin with, this Babylonian king was responsible for the destruction of the First temple built in the city of Jerusalem. The Book of Chronicles explains what happened.

> The LORD, the God of their ancestors, sent word to them through his messengers again and again, because he had pity on his people and on his dwelling place. But they mocked God's messengers, despised his words and scoffed at his prophets until the wrath of the LORD was aroused against his people and there was no remedy. He brought up against them the king of the Babylonians, who killed their young men with the sword in the sanctuary, and spared neither young man nor young woman, the elderly or the aged. God gave them all into the hands of Nebuchadnezzar. He carried to Babylon all the articles from the temple of God, both large and small, and the treasures of the LORD's temple and the

> treasures of the king and his officials. They set fire to God's temple and broke down the wall of Jerusalem; they burned all the palaces and destroyed everything of value there (2 Chronicles 36:15-19 NIV).

Hence, we are introduced to Nebuchadnezzar in the fact that he defiled the Holy Temple of the Lord.

2. NEBUCHADNEZZAR RULED WITH ABSOLUTE AUTHORITY

Next, we consider the scope of the rule of this king. Nebuchadnezzar, the ruler of the Babylonian Empire, ruled the known world with an absolute authority. The Babylonian system was set up in such a way that his word was law. Indeed, he was answerable to "nobody."

In fact, in a dream that Nebuchadnezzar had which the prophet Daniel interpreted, Nebuchadnezzar was called the "head of gold." Daniel explained it to the king as follows.

> This was the dream, and now we will interpret it to the king. Your Majesty, you are the king of kings. The God of heaven has given you dominion and power and might and glory; in your hands he has placed all people everywhere and the beasts of the field and the birds in the sky. Wherever they live, he has made you ruler over them all. You are that head of gold (Daniel 2:36-38 NIV).

Nebuchadnezzar was a ruler like no other.

3. NEBUCHADNEZZAR BUILT AN IMAGE OF HIMSELF

Since Nebuchadnezzar could not be challenged, in his arrogance as the supreme ruler, he ordered a golden image of himself constructed. The Bible explains it this way.

> King Nebuchadnezzar made an image of gold, whose height was sixty cubits and its breadth six cubits. He set it up on the plain of Dura, in the province of Babylon (Daniel 3:1 ESV).

Not only did he construct this image of gold, the size of this idol is significant; sixty cubits by six cubits, or ninety feet high by about nine feet wide.

4. HE DEMANDED UNIVERSAL WORSHIP OF THE IMAGE

Nebuchadnezzar then decreed universal worship of that golden image of himself. The Book of Daniel informs us what occurred.

> Then the herald loudly proclaimed, "Nations and peoples of every language, this is what you are commanded to do: As soon as you hear the sound of the horn, flute, zither, lyre, harp, pipe and all kinds of music, you must fall down and worship the image of gold that King Nebuchadnezzar has set up" (Daniel 3:4-5 NIV).

Everyone was ordered to worship this image. Indeed, the following command was given.

> And whoever does not fall down and worship shall immediately be cast into a burning fiery furnace (Daniel 3:6 ESV).

Those who did not bow down were sentenced to an immediate horrible death.

5. THERE WERE SOME JEWS WHO DID NOT WORSHIP

Though the leaders of Babylon were commanded to worship this golden image, not everyone obeyed. Three of the Jewish captives, Hananiah, Azariah, and Mishael, or as they are more well-known by their Babylonian names, Shadrach, Meshach, and Abednego, refused the command of the king. Nebuchadnezzar was informed that these three Jewish men did not obey his command. He was told the following.

> But there are some Jews whom you have set over the affairs of the province of Babylon—Shadrach, Meshach and

Abednego—who pay no attention to you, Your Majesty. They neither serve your gods nor worship the image of gold you have set up (Daniel 3:12 NIV).

Nebuchadnezzar became infuriated with these Jews. When they were brought before him, he gave them a second chance, but they would not bow.

Shadrach, Meshach, and Abednego replied, "O Nebuchadnezzar, we do not need to defend ourselves before you. If we are thrown into the blazing furnace, the God whom we serve is able to save us. He will rescue us from your power, Your Majesty. But even if he doesn't, we want to make it clear to you, Your Majesty, that we will never serve your gods or worship the gold statue you have set up (Daniel 3:16-18 NLT).

The king commanded them to be immediately put to death. The Bible says.

The king's command was so urgent and the furnace so hot that the flames of the fire killed the soldiers who took up Shadrach, Meshach and Abednego, and these three men, firmly tied, fell into the blazing furnace (Daniel 3:22-23 NIV).

There would be no chance of these men escaping the flames. Death, it seemed, was inevitable for these Jews who would not bow.

6. THESE JEWS WERE SUPERNATURALLY PROTECTED BY GOD

Yet, the Bible says that the Lord protected them in the midst of the fire. When they came out of the furnace the Bible says the following miracle was observed.

So Shadrach, Meshach, and Abednego stepped out of the fire. Then the high officers, officials, governors, and advisers crowded around them and saw that the fire had not touched them. Not a hair on their heads was singed, and their clothing was not scorched. They didn't even smell of smoke! (Daniel 3:26-27 NLT).

God supernaturally protected these Jewish people in the midst of a fiery furnace. There was no evidence whatsoever they had even been in the fire! Truly, a great miracle had taken place.

THERE ARE MANY SIMILARITIES TO THE CAREER OF THE FINAL ANTICHRIST

King Nebuchadnezzar has many striking similarities to the final Antichrist. They can be summed up as follows.

1. ANTICHRIST WILL DEFILE THE TEMPLE IN JERUSALEM

The act which will identify the true character of the Antichrist is the defiling of the temple. While Nebuchadnezzar ordered the destruction of the temple, Antichrist will do something which is much worse. Indeed, he will personally defile it and blaspheme the God whom it represents. Paul wrote of this dastardly act.

> Don't let anyone deceive you in any way, for [that day will not come] until the rebellion occurs and the man of lawlessness is revealed, the man doomed to destruction. He will oppose and will exalt himself over everything that is called God or is worshiped, so that he sets himself up in God's temple, proclaiming himself to be God (2 Thessalonians 2:3-4 NIV).

This act will begin the final three and one half years of this age which will culminate in the return of the Lord Jesus Christ to the earth.

2. ANTICHRIST WILL RULE THE WORLD WITH ABSOLUTE AUTHORITY

Like Nebuchadnezzar, who was called the head of gold, the coming Antichrist will rule the world. As Nebuchadnezzar was the sole ruler, whose word could not be contradicted, the man of sin will have similar powers. However, his rule will extend throughout the world.

3. AN IMAGE OF ANTICHRIST WILL BE CONSTRUCTED

In addition, Scripture says an image of Antichrist will be constructed. This will come about through a second personage, or second beast, which appears on the scene. The Bible describes what will occur in the following manner.

> Then I saw another beast come up out of the earth. He had two horns like those of a lamb, but he spoke with the voice of a dragon. He exercised all the authority of the first beast. And he required all the earth and its people to worship the first beast, whose fatal wound had been healed. He did astounding miracles, even making fire flash down to earth from the sky while everyone was watching. And with all the miracles he was allowed to perform on behalf of the first beast, he deceived all the people who belong to this world. He ordered the people to make a great statue of the first beast, who was fatally wounded and then came back to life. He was then permitted to give life to this statue so that it could speak. Then the statue of the beast commanded that anyone refusing to worship it must die (Revelation 13:11-15 NLT).

The parallels here are not exact. For one thing, it is the second beast which orders the statue constructed, not the first beast, the Antichrist himself. We discover that there is no second person in Daniel's account. Nebuchadnezzar himself is the one who ordered the statue built.

In addition, the statue is given life so that it can speak. It gives the decree that everyone who does not worship it must die. In the Book of Daniel we find no such miraculous qualities given to the statute. Yet even without the exact parallels, the comparisons are obvious.

4. THE SIZE OF THE STATUE REFLECT ANTICHRIST

Although the parallels are not exact they are certainly present. Indeed, the size of Nebuchadnezzar's image, sixty by six, is indicative of the number of the man of sin. The Bible says it is 666.

> Wisdom is needed here. Let the one with understanding solve the meaning of the number of the beast, for it is the number of a man. His number is 666 (Revelation 13:18 NLT).

This is another obvious parallel.

5. GOD WILL SUPERNATURALLY PROTECT A REMNANT OF JEWS WHO REFUSE TO BOW

But there is still more. We also find that, as was in the case with Nebuchadnezzar, the Lord will protect the lives of a certain number of Jews. Scripture speaks of the supernatural protection of the woman, Israel, which gave birth to the male child, Christ.

> She gave birth to a son, a male child, who "will rule all the nations with an iron scepter." And her child was snatched up to God and to his throne. The woman fled into the wilderness to a place prepared for her by God, where she might be taken care of for 1,260 days (Revelation 12:5-6 NIV).

As God supernaturally protected the three friends of Daniel from Nebuchadnezzar, He also will supernaturally protect a remnant from the nation Israel from the beast, the final Antichrist.

CONCLUSION: NEBUCHADNEZZAR PROVIDES MANY PARALLELS

Therefore, we have in Nebuchadnezzar a pre-figurement of the arrogance of the coming man of sin. Yet, these proud rulers, though ruling the world with absolute authority, will find themselves humbled before the mighty hand of the Lord.

SUMMARY TO QUESTION 15
IN WHAT SENSE IS KING NEBUCHADNEZZAR OF BABYLON LIKE THE FUTURE ANTICHRIST?

Nebuchadnezzar, King of Babylon, the ruler of the world in the 6th century B.C., is another type of the final Antichrist, the coming Caesar. Indeed, there are many ways his character and deeds mirror the future man of sin.

First, the King of Babylon is the personage who was responsible for the destruction of God's Holy Temple in Jerusalem. In fact, we are introduced to him in Scripture as the one who carried out the Lord's judgment upon the Jews by destroying the city and the temple.

In a similar manner, the one specific act that identifies the coming man of sin will be the defiling of the future temple in the city of Jerusalem. He will openly defy the God of Scripture. Therefore, a turning point in the lives of each of these characters, Nebuchadnezzar and Antichrist, occurs at exactly the same place, the temple in Jerusalem.

Nebuchadnezzar was also a unique ruler. He was an absolute monarch whose word was law. In a dream of his which the prophet Daniel interpreted, Nebuchadnezzar is called the head of gold, a king of kings.

In the same manner, the coming Antichrist will rule the world with an iron fist. He will get whatever he wishes. His rule will be one-of-a-kind.

Nebuchadnezzar could do whatever he wished without any interference. In fact, Scripture records that in his arrogance he built a huge golden image of himself. The dimensions of this gigantic statue were also significant, sixty cubits by six cubits, ninety feet by nine feet. All the leaders in his kingdom were commanded to worship this statue of Nebuchadnezzar. Those who did not worship this image were to be put to death.

However, everyone did not worship the statue of Nebuchadnezzar. We are told that three Hebrews refused to bow down to the statue of the King. An enraged Nebuchadnezzar ordered the three young Hebrew men to be immediately thrown into a fiery furnace.

Yet the Lord supernaturally protected these men from death. The King and his men saw a fourth figure in the fire with the three Hebrews; one who was like the Son of God. When the three men came out of the furnace they were not harmed in the least, and their clothing did not even smell like smoke. They were miraculously preserved from harm.

In the same manner, there will be a future image erected of the beast, the Antichrist, which all people of the entire world will be forced to worship. The number six will also play a prominent role in the worship of this individual since 666 is the number of Antichrist. As in the days of Nebuchadnezzar, those who do not worship the image will be sentenced to die.

Yet there will be those Jews who refuse to worship the image of the beast. As in Daniel's day, God will supernaturally protect these Jewish people who refuse to worship the image of the beast. The Son of God, who protected Daniel's three friends, will also protect these Jews from harm.

Nebuchadnezzar in his pride and arrogance gives us an historical picture of the coming Antichrist. Though he attempted to destroy those Jews which did not worship him, his efforts at this failed. The same will be true of the coming Antichrist. He will not be able to eliminate God's people.

Therefore, we have an obvious pre-figuration to the deeds of Antichrist from this personage King Nebuchadnezzar.

QUESTION 16

Who Was Antiochus IV? (Epiphanes) Why Is He Considered To Be The Clearest Example Of A Person Who Foreshadows The Coming Antichrist?

Of all the individuals which are predicted in Scripture, or recorded in biblical history, there is none which gives us a greater picture of the coming Antichrist than a 2nd century B.C. Seleucid King named Antiochus IV.

WHO WAS ANTIOCHUS IV?

It is helpful if we get some sort of understanding of the life and career of Antiochus before we examine how he became the clearest type of the final Antichrist, the coming Caesar. While there is no exact one-to-one correspondence with any of the types of this coming world ruler, Antiochus, as we will see, certainly comes the closest.

Born around 215 B.C., Antiochus IV was the son of King Antiochus III, (also known as "The Great"). Though his original name was Mithradates, this son of the king took the name Antiochus after he ascended to the throne.

He was the eighth in succession of twenty kings of the Seleucid Empire, one of the four empires in which Alexander's empire was divided. Antiochus IV ruled from 175 B.C. until his death in 164 B.C.

HE GAVE HIMSELF DIVINE TITLES

Antiochus was the first Seleucid king to give himself divine titles. This evil king originally had coins minted that simply said. "of King Antiochus." Later, however, the coins read "of King Antiochus, God Manifest, Victory Bringer."

Interestingly, his often eccentric behavior led some of his contemporaries to call him *Epimanes*, "The Mad One." This is a play on words of the title he gave himself, *Epiphanes*.

THE PROPHECIES ABOUT ANTIOCHUS HAVE A DOUBLE FULFILLMENT

Before we look at what the Bible has to say about this person, it is important that we understand that some of the prophecies concerning Antiochus IV in the Book of Daniel have both an historical fulfillment, as well as a fulfillment that is still in the future. Indeed, they will be fulfilled in the "end times" by the final Antichrist.

Prophecies such as these are often called either "dual reference prophecy" or "double reference prophecy." The passages that seem to have this double reference include Daniel 8:9-14; 23-25; and 11:21-35.

In addition, we find differences of opinion among Bible students as to where the prophecies regarding Antiochus IV end, and those relating to the final Antichrist begin. In spite of these questions, it is clear that this personage is the clearest type of the coming man of sin that we find in the Old Testament.

Indeed, there are many things which Antiochus IV had in common with the predicted Antichrist. From what the Bible has to say about Antiochus and his rampages, we can make the following observations.

1. ANTIOCHUS, LIKE ANTICHRIST, STARTS OUT AS A "LITTLE HORN"

The first thing that Antiochus and the final Antichrist have in common is that they are each called a "little horn." In fact, each of these evil individuals becomes a person of great power after starting from a small beginning. We are told the following about Antiochus.

> From one of them came a small horn. But it grew to be very big, toward the south and the east and toward the beautiful land. It grew so big it reached the army of heaven, and it brought about the fall of some of the army and some of the stars to the ground, where it trampled them (Daniel 8:9 ESV).

This part of the Daniel's vision anticipated the rise of a ruler from the Greek Empire. Antiochus fulfilled this prediction.

This is true of the final Antichrist as well. His power will continue to grow from an obscure beginning. In fact, the final Antichrist will seemingly begin as an insignificant political figure. However, by the middle of the great tribulation period his power will be extended over the entire world. The Bible then says the following of him.

> The beast was permitted to go to war against the saints and conquer them. He was given ruling authority over every tribe, people, language, and nation (Revelation 13:7 NET).

2. ANTIOCHUS WAS THOUGHT TO BE A MAN OF PEACE

Antiochus deceived the people of Judea by appearing as a man of peace. The following prediction was made about him in the Book of Daniel.

> By his treachery he will succeed through deceit. He will have an arrogant attitude, and he will destroy many who are unaware of his schemes (Daniel 8:25 NET).

The Book of First Maccabees records the fulfillment of this prediction as it describe the treachery of Antiochus to Israel.

> Deceitfully he spoke peaceable words to them, and they believed him; but he suddenly fell upon the city, dealt

it a severe blow, and destroyed many people of Israel
(1 Maccabees 1:30 NRSV).

The same will be true of the final Antichrist. He will arrive on the
world scene as a man of peace.

3. ANTIOCHUS PERSECUTED THE JEWS

Probably the most obvious of all the parallels is that Antiochus IV
was a persecutor of the Jewish people. The apocryphal book of First
Maccabees describes him in this manner.

> After subduing Egypt, Antiochus returned in the one hun-
> dred forty- third year. He went up against Israel and came
> to Jerusalem with a strong force. He arrogantly entered the
> sanctuary and took the golden altar, the lampstand for the
> light, and all its utensils. He took also the table for the bread
> of the Presence, the cups for drink offerings, the bowls, the
> golden censers, the curtain, the crowns, and the gold deco-
> ration on the front of the temple; he stripped it all off. He
> took the silver and the gold, and the costly vessels; he took
> also the hidden treasures that he found. Taking them all, he
> went into his own land. He shed much blood, and spoke
> with great arrogance (1 Maccabees 1:20-24 NRSV).

Antiochus brought terrible agony upon the Jewish nation. As we are
told here in 1 Maccabees, he was an arrogant murderer.

In the last days of this present age, the man of sin, the final Antichrist
will also specifically separate the Jews for his own special persecution.
Scripture speaks of the dragon persecuting the woman.

> And when the dragon saw that he had been thrown down
> to the earth, he pursued the woman who had given birth to
> the male child (Revelation 12:13 ESV).

In this context, the woman represents the nation of Israel and her male child is Jesus. The dragon represents the devil. He is the one who empowers the Antichrist to destroy the Jewish people.

4. ANTIOCHUS WAS ON THE SCENE FOR ABOUT SEVEN YEARS

Interestingly, the time Antiochus would be on the scene is specifically given to us in the Book of Daniel. Scripture says.

> He said to me, "It will take 2,300 evenings and mornings; then the sanctuary will be reconsecrated" (Daniel 8:14 NIV).

The time 2,300 evening is just about seven years. This is the same amount of time the final Antichrist will be a public figure.

This coming Caesar will become prominent on the world's stage when he makes, or confirms, a seven-year covenant with the Jews. The Bible says.

> He will confirm a covenant with many for one 'seven.' In the middle of the 'seven' he will put an end to sacrifice and offering. And at the temple he will set up an abomination that causes desolation, until the end that is decreed is poured out on him (Daniel 9:27 NIV).

In this context, the word translated "seven" refers to seven "years." Therefore, the amount of time Antichrist will be on the world's stage will be about seven years, similar to the amount of time of Antiochus.

5. ANTIOCHUS PLACED IMAGES OF PAGAN GODS IN THE TEMPLE

Antiochus committed the ultimate sacrilege by desecrating the Holy Temple in Jerusalem. We read about his horrible deeds in the book of First Maccabees.

> And the king sent letters by messengers to Jerusalem and the towns of Judah; he directed them to follow customs

strange to the land, to forbid burnt offerings and sacrifices and drink offerings in the sanctuary, to profane sabbaths and festivals, to defile the sanctuary and the priests, to build altars and sacred precincts and shrines for idols, to sacrifice swine and other unclean animals, and to leave their sons uncircumcised. They were to make themselves abominable by everything unclean and profane, so that they would forget the law and change all the ordinances. He added, "And whoever does not obey the command of the king shall die" (First Maccabees 1:44-50 NRSV).

Among other things, Antiochus defiled the temple, ordered pigs to be sacrificed on altars, as well as building shrines for idols. He also changed the Laws that the Lord had set down. Those who did not obey the commands of Antiochus were put to death.

This prefigures what the final Antichrist will do. Like Antiochus, he will desecrate the temple in Jerusalem. In fact, when asked for a "specific sign" of the end of the age, we read the following words of Jesus.

So when you see standing in the holy place 'the abomination that causes desolation,' spoken of through the prophet Daniel—let the reader understand—(Matthew 24:15 NIV).

Jesus called this coming incident, the desecration of the temple, "the abomination which causes desolation.

The Apostle Paul also wrote about this coming event. He said.

He will oppose and will exalt himself over everything that is called God or is worshiped, so that he sets himself up in God's temple, proclaiming himself to be God (2 Thessalonians 2:4 NIV).

The comparisons here are obvious. Antiochus defiled the temple and claimed to be a god. The Antichrist will do likewise. In fact, he will claim to be "God himself." It is no wonder Jesus called this act an "abomination!"

6. ANTIOCHUS WAS HELPED BY A RELIGIOUS LEADER

Antiochus was primarily a political leader. He had a religious leader who promoted him named Menelaus. The coming Antichrist will also have a religious leader who will help his cause. He is called the second beast, the false prophet.

The false prophet, the second beast, will cause everyone to worship the first beast, the Antichrist. The Book of Revelation explains it as follows.

> Then I saw another beast, coming out of the earth. It had two horns like a lamb, but it spoke like a dragon. It exercised all the authority of the first beast on its behalf, and made the earth and its inhabitants worship the first beast, whose fatal wound had been healed. And it performed great signs, even causing fire to come down from heaven to the earth in full view of everyone. Because of the signs it was given power to perform on behalf of the first beast, it deceived the inhabitants of the earth. It ordered them to set up an image in honor of the beast who was wounded by the sword and yet lived (Revelation 13:11-14 NIV).

The world will be forced to worship Antichrist. The religious leader, the false prophet, will see to that.

7. ANTIOCHUS WAS REPORTED AS DEAD BUT APPEARED ALIVE AGAIN

Interestingly, there was a premature report circulating that Antiochus had died. The report turned out to be untrue.

The Book of Revelation tells us about the beast receiving a mortal head wound and then coming back to life.

> One of the heads of the beast seemed to have had a fatal
> wound, but the fatal wound had been healed. The whole
> world was filled with wonder and followed the beast
> (Revelation 13:3 NIV).

Therefore, each of these personages was once thought to be dead, but in actuality was not. In the case of Antichrist, there is the possibility that he actually will be dead but is somehow brought back to life.

8. ANTIOCHUS DEMANDED THAT EVERYONE WORSHIP HIM

Antiochus, in his arrogance, demanded that everyone worship him.

In the same manner, the false prophet, the second beast, will cause everyone to worship Antichrist and his image.

> All who dwell on the earth will worship him, whose names
> have not been written in the Book of Life of the Lamb slain
> from the foundation of the world (Revelation 13:8 NIV).

The entire world will be forced to worship the beast. In doing so, they will also be worshipping the devil himself.

9. A GROUP OF FAITHFUL JEWS OPPOSED ANTIOCHUS

There were a group of faithful Jews who opposed the deeds of Antiochus. They would not obey his commands. We read the following in First Maccabees.

> But many in Israel stood firm and were resolved in their
> hearts not to eat unclean food. They chose to die rather
> than to be defiled by food or to profane the holy cove-
> nant; and they did die. Very great wrath came upon Israel
> (First Maccabees 1:62-64 NRSV).

In the same way, there will be a remnant of the Jews which will oppose the coming man of sin. This includes the 144,000. Scripture says of them.

Then I saw another angel ascending from the rising of the sun, with the seal of the living God, and he called with a loud voice to the four angels who had been given power to harm earth and sea, saying, "Do not harm the earth or the sea or the trees, until we have sealed the servants of our God on their foreheads." And I heard the number of the sealed, 144,000, sealed from every tribe of the sons of Israel (Revelation 7:2-4 ESV).

These men, like the Jews who opposed Antiochus, would not bow to the demands of this evil ruler Antichrist.

10. ANTIOCHUS WAS DEFEATED BY A JEWISH DELIVERER

In the end, it was a deliverer from the chosen people, the Jews, who overthrew Antiochus. We read about the organized rebellion against Antiochus which was started by a man named Mattathias. The Book of First Maccabees records the following.

They organized an army, and struck down sinners in their anger and renegades in their wrath; the survivors fled to the Gentiles for safety. And Mattathias and his friends went around and tore down the altars; they forcibly circumcised all the uncircumcised boys that they found within the borders of Israel (First Maccabees 2:44-46 NRSV).

Of course, someday a Deliverer will overthrow Antichrist and then set up His eternal kingdom. This Deliver will also come from the chosen people, the Jews, according to His human nature. Jesus Christ will return and defeat the beast, the final Antichrist. The Bible says.

And the beast was captured, and with it the false prophet who in its presence had done the signs by which he deceived those who had received the mark of the beast and those who worshiped its image. These two were thrown alive into the lake of fire that burns with sulfur (Revelation 19:20 ESV).

This sums up some of the many ways in which the evil Seleucid ruler Antiochus IV pre-figured the coming beast, the Antichrist.

SUMMARY TO QUESTION 16
WHO WAS ANTIOCHUS IV? (EPIPHANES) WHY IS HE CONSIDERED TO BE THE CLEAREST PERSON WHO FORESHADOWS THE COMING ANTICHRIST?

The clearest type of the final Antichrist, the coming Caesar, was the Seleucid king Antiochus IV (168 B.C.) His coming is predicted in detail in the Book of Daniel. We find that Antiochus prefigures Antichrist in a number of specific ways.

To begin with, Antiochus, like the coming Antichrist, was a persecutor of the Jews. In particular, the Jews were set apart for horrific persecution by this evil ruler. Scripture says Antichrist will try to eliminate the entire Jewish race. However, like Antiochus, he will fail.

The Bible also gives us a specific limit as to the time Antiochus would be on the scene, 2,300 days. This is about seven years. In the same way, the coming Antichrist will be a public person for seven years.

Antiochus was also involved in the defiling of the Holy Temple in Jerusalem. He placed idols in the Holy of Holies and slaughtered a pig on the altar of sacrifice. A similar thing will happen in the future. An image of Antichrist himself will be set up in a future temple in Jerusalem. Jesus called this incident "the abomination of desolation."

Antiochus, a political leader, worked with a religious leader. Antichrist will also have a religious leader promoting him. He is the second beast, the false prophet. This personage will force the people of the world to follow this man of sin.

Antiochus demanded worship. Like Antiochus of old, Antichrist will demand that everyone worship him, as well as worship the devil. Those who do not will be put to death.

Antiochus was thought to be dead but appeared alive again. Antichrist will seemingly die or perhaps actually will die and then come back to life. His resurrection will cause everyone in the world to marvel after him. It is at this time he demands the worship of the people.

There was a remnant of godly Jews who resisted Antiochus. In the same way, there will be a remnant of Jews who will refuse to worship the beast. These Jews will be persecuted.

Finally, Antiochus was overthrown by a Jewish deliverer. The final Antichrist will be also be overthrown by a physical descendent of Abraham, the God/Man Jesus Christ.

Consequently, we find that Antiochus IV is the clearest pre-figurement, or type, that we have of the final Antichrist which is to come.

Why Do Most Bible Commentators Believe The Final Antichrist Will Come From Western Europe? Could He Come From The USA?

If the Bible teaches that a personal Antichrist will arise in the future, is there any indication as to where he comes from? Could this man come from the United States of America, the USA? What does the Bible have to say about the national origin of the final Antichrist?

THE FINAL EMPIRE: THE FEET OF IRON MIXED WITH CLAY

The answer to this question is found in the Book of Daniel. Daniel wrote of four major empires which will rule the world. The last empire is a revival of the fourth, the Roman Empire. It will be revived in the days before the coming of Jesus Christ. The Book of Daniel describes the fourth kingdom in this manner.

> And there shall be a fourth kingdom, strong as iron, because iron breaks to pieces and shatters all things. And like iron that crushes, it shall break and crush all these. And as you saw the feet and toes, partly of potter's clay and partly of iron, it shall be a divided kingdom, but some of the firmness of iron shall be in it, just as you saw iron mixed with the soft clay. And as the toes of the feet were partly iron and partly clay, so the kingdom shall be partly strong and partly brittle. As you saw the iron mixed with soft clay, so they will

mix with one another in marriage, but they will not hold together, just as iron does not mix with clay. And in the days of those kings the God of heaven will set up a kingdom that shall never be destroyed, nor shall the kingdom be left to another people. It shall break in pieces all these king-doms and bring them to an end, and it shall stand forever (Daniel 2:40-44 ESV).

The fourth kingdom was Rome. It is the leader of that revived Roman Empire who is the biblical Antichrist. This indicates that whoever this personage may be, he will come out of this geographical area.

Daniel saw this empire as a terrible beast, the leader was a little horn. He wrote.

After this I saw in the night visions, and behold, a fourth beast, terrifying and dreadful and exceedingly strong. It had great iron teeth; it devoured and broke in pieces and stamped what was left with its feet. It was different from all the beasts that were before it, and it had ten horns. I con-sidered the horns, and behold, there came up among them another horn, a little one, before which three of the first horns were plucked up by the roots. And behold, in this horn were eyes like the eyes of a man, and a mouth speaking great things (Daniel 7:7-8 ESV).

The little horn is a man who arises from the beast with "ten horns."

THE PRINCE THAT SHALL COME

There is a further prediction in the Book of Daniel which narrows the ethnicity of the man of sin even further. Daniel wrote of a coming prince.

And after the sixty-two weeks, an anointed one shall be cut off and shall have nothing. And the people of the prince who is to come shall destroy the city and the sanctuary. Its end shall come with a flood, and to the end there shall be war. Desolations are decreed (Daniel 9:26 ESV).

Daniel said that the people of this "coming prince" will destroy the city and the sanctuary. In A.D. 70 it was the Roman army, led by Titus who destroyed the temple and city. Therefore, the people of the coming prince were the Romans. This indicates that the future prince, the Antichrist, will himself be a Roman. This also fits with the idea that the man of sin will come from the revived Roman Empire.

Therefore, when we examine the totality of Scripture, it seems to indicate that the final Antichrist will arise out of the revived Roman Empire.

CAN THE ANTICHRIST COME FROM THE USA?

It is often asked if the coming Antichrist will arise out of the United States of America. Since the USA is the only superpower in the world at the present time, it would seem reasonable that the man of sin would come forth from such a powerful nation. Indeed, if he is going to be the world ruler, then the USA seems like the logical country from which he would arise.

One could even argue that since the United States was founded by people that came from Europe, the nations of the old Roman Empire, the present United States could be seen as somehow related to it. In this way a United States President could be viewed as someone who comes from a part of the old Roman Empire even though the USA, as a nation, did not exist when the Roman Empire was flourishing.

Although we do not know the answer for certain, Scripture seems to say that the final Antichrist will arise out of what was the geographical Roman Empire in the first century A.D. Indeed, the major events which are still to take place, as far as Scripture is concerned, will center on Europe and the Middle East.

For whatever reason, the other nations of the world will not be major participants in the final events leading up until the Second Coming of Jesus Christ. This includes the United States of America.

SUMMARY TO QUESTION 17
WHY DO MOST BIBLE COMMENTATORS BELIEVE THE FINAL ANTICHRIST WILL COME FROM WESTERN EUROPE? COULD HE COME FROM THE USA?

Many people ask about the origin of the Antichrist. Do we know what country he will come from? Could he be from the USA?

The reason as to why most people believe Antichrist will arise out of Western Europe has to do with a number of prophecies found in the Book of Daniel.

Daniel wrote of four great empires which would consecutively rule the world. They are Babylon, Media/Persia, Greece, and Rome. The last empire, Rome, will be revived before Jesus Christ comes back. It is the leader of this revived Roman Empire who will be the biblical Antichrist. He is called the "little horn" in the Book of Daniel.

Furthermore, in the Book of Daniel we find that it is predicted that "the people of the prince who shall come" will destroy Jerusalem. This coming prince is believed to be the final Antichrist. Since Jerusalem was destroyed by the Romans, it is assumed that the coming prince has to be a Roman. This, it is argued, is another indication that Antichrist comes from Western Europe.

There is the question of Antichrist arising out of the only superpower in the world, the United States of America. Since those who founded America were Europeans, countries that formerly belonged to the old Roman Empire, it could be argued that the United States is somehow connected with ancient Rome and its empire.

Yet Scripture does seem not allow for this possibility. The Antichrist will apparently arise from another part of the world; the geographical areas of the old Roman Empire. If this is the case, it means that a world leader will arise who will have more power and influence than the President of the United States.

What this says about the strength and authority of the United States at this time in history has been a matter of much speculation.

For whatever reason or reasons, the United States will not be the major player at the end times according to the biblical scenario. The old Roman Empire, as well as the Middle East, will be the scene where the major events take place.

What does seem to be clear is that Antichrist will arise from somewhere out of the old Roman Empire to become ruler of the world. The good news from Scripture is that his rule will be stopped by the Second Coming of Christ to the earth.

QUESTION 18

How Does The Bible Describe
The Final Antichrist?

We find a number of different terms, in both testaments, which seem to describe the final Antichrist of Scripture. Indeed, he has many aliases. There is, however, no consensus of opinion among interpreters as to whether all of these terms are describing the coming "man of sin," or possibly referring to some other personage.

This having been said, the following are the various designations which are *usually* ascribed to this future lawless one.

ANTICHRIST IN THE OLD TESTAMENT

The Antichrist is spoken of often in the Old Testament. Indeed, from looking at the Hebrew Scriptures we find that the following terms seem to describe the coming Antichrist.

GENESIS: THE SEED OR OFFSPRING OF THE SERPENT

In the Book of Genesis, the Lord predicts a struggle between the offspring of the woman and the offspring of the serpent. We read the Lord saying.

> And I will put enmity between you and the woman, and between your offspring and hers; he will crush your head, and you will strike his heel (Genesis 3:15 NIV).

There are those who say that the offspring, or seed, of the serpent has its ultimate fulfillment in the final Antichrist. As Jesus was the ultimate fulfillment of the offspring of the woman, it seems that the ultimate fulfillment of the offspring of the serpent will be the coming man of sin, the Antichrist.

DANIEL

The Book of Daniel contains a number of references to this coming man of sin. They are as follows.

1. HE IS THE LITTLE HORN

In the Book of Daniel, this terrible person is first introduced to us. Daniel describes an individual known as the "little horn." He wrote the following.

> While I was thinking about the horns, there before me was another horn, a little one, which came up among them; and three of the first horns were uprooted before it. This horn had eyes like the eyes of a human being and a mouth that spoke boastfully (Daniel 7:8 NIV).

This little horn is described a human being whose mouth speaks boastfully. Arrogance seems to characterize this personage.

2. THE STERN-FACE KING

Daniel also calls this particular individual a "stern-face king," or a "king of bold face." He wrote.

> And at the latter end of their kingdom, when the transgressors have reached their limit, a king of bold face, one who understands riddles, shall arise (Daniel 8:23 ESV).

This is another description of this evil personage.

3. THE PRINCE OR RULER OF THE PEOPLE THAT SHALL COME

In the Book of Daniel, we read of a person called "the prince that shall come" or the "ruler of the people who shall come." This is a description of the coming Antichrist. Scripture says.

> After the sixty-two 'sevens,' the Anointed One will be put to death and will have nothing. The people of the ruler who will come will destroy the city and the sanctuary. The end will come like a flood: War will continue until the end, and desolations have been decreed (Daniel 9:25 NIV).

However this is a controversial reference. Many people think this actually refers to Jesus Christ, not Antichrist. Jesus is the "coming prince."

Others think the coming prince refers to the man who was in charge of the destruction of the city of Jerusalem, Titus the Roman.

Yet the context seems to greatly favor the interpretation that the coming prince refers to the final Antichrist.

4. ONE WHO MAKES DESOLATE

He is also given the title "one who makes desolate." The Book of Daniel says the following.

> And he shall make a strong covenant with many for one week, and for half of the week he shall put an end to sacrifice and offering. And on the wing of abominations shall come one who makes desolate, until the decreed end is poured out on the desolator (Daniel 9:27 ESV).

The Antichrist is a "desolator."

5. THE WILLFUL KING OF THE KING WHO DOES AS HE PLEASES

He is also called the "willful king" or the king who "does as he pleases" in the Book of Daniel. The Bible says.

The king will do as he pleases. He will exalt and magnify himself above every god and will say unheard-of things against the God of gods. He will be successful until the time of wrath is completed, for what has been determined must take place (Daniel 11:36 NIV).

This description certainly reveals the arrogance of this person. The fact that he has the audacity to magnify himself above God indicates his evil nature.

MICAH: THE ASSYRIAN

The prophet Micah describes the coming Antichrist as "the Assyrian." We read the following.

And he shall be their peace. When the Assyrian comes into our land and treads in our palaces, then we will raise against him seven shepherds and eight princes of men (Micah 5:5 ESV).

The fact that he is called an "Assyrian" has led some to believe that Antichrist will actually be a literal descendant of the ancient Assyrians.

ZECHARIAH: THE WORTHLESS SHEPHERD

In the Book of Zechariah, there is a description of one known as the "worthless shepherd." The Bible describes him as follows.

This illustrates how I will give this nation a shepherd who will not care for those who are dying, nor look after the young nor heal the injured, nor feed the healthy. Instead, this shepherd will eat the meat of the fattest sheep and tear off their hooves. "What sorrow awaits this worthless shepherd who abandons the flock! The sword will cut his arm and pierce his right eye. His arm will become useless, and his right eye completely blind" (Zechariah 11:16-17 NLT).

This worthless shepherd is the final Antichrist. There may have been earlier historical fulfillments in other pseudo or false Messiahs, such as Bar Kochba.

He led a rebellion in A.D. 132-135 against the Romans and was proclaimed by Rabbi Akiva to be the Messiah. Nevertheless the ultimate fulfillment of this will be found in this coming "man of sin."

WILL HIS ARM BE CUT OFF AND HIS RIGHT EYE PUT OUT?

When it says "the sword would cut his arm and pierce his right eye" we should not understand that to mean that someone cuts off his arm or puts out his eye. In fact, many translations understand this as a prayer for judgment. For example we read what the NIV says.

> Woe to the worthless shepherd, who deserts the flock! May the sword strike his arm and his right eye! May his arm be completely withered, his right eye totally blinded! (Zechariah 11:17 NIV).

The prayer calls for his power to be paralyzed. The arm speaks of his power, while the eye refers to his intelligence.

Therefore, this passage is praying for his lack of power to fight, or even to take aim, against his enemy. This paralyzing of his ability will be literally fulfilled at the Second Coming of Christ when this final Antichrist and his armies are destroyed at the return of the Lord.

This sums up the various descriptions of Antichrist in the Old Testament. As we see, he is mentioned quite often.

ANTICHRIST IN THE NEW TESTAMENT

There are a number of New Testament designations of this future adversary of the people of God. We can note them as follows.

ANTICHRIST IN THE GOSPELS

The Antichrist is briefly alluded to in the four gospels. We can cite the following references.

1. THE ONE DESOLATING THE TEMPLE

Jesus spoke of a future profaning of the temple by this coming Antichrist. He called this event called the "abomination of desolation," or the "abomination that causes desolation." Matthew records Jesus saying the following.

> So when you see standing in the holy place 'the abomination that causes desolation,' spoken of through the prophet Daniel—let the reader understand—(Matthew 24:15 NIV).

This specifically refers to a defiling of the temple in Jerusalem. We discover from the writings of Paul (2 Thessalonians 2:1-4) that the final Antichrist is the one who performs this horrible deed.

2. A FALSE CHRIST

Jesus also spoke of false Christs, or false Messiahs, who would come before His return to the earth. He gave the following warning.

> For false messiahs and false prophets will rise up and perform great signs and wonders so as to deceive, if possible, even God's chosen ones (Matthew 24:24 NLT).

While there will be many false Christs or Antichrists who will arise on the scene, there will come an ultimate false Christ, the final Antichrist.

3. ONE COMING IN HIS OWN NAME

Jesus spoke of one coming in his own name. John records Him saying.

> I have come in my Father's name, and you do not receive me. If another comes in his own name, you will receive him (John 5:43 ESV).

Notice those who reject Jesus Christ will receive this personage. The Antichrist will come in his name, or authority, and the people will receive him.

ANTICHRIST IN THE WRITINGS OF PAUL

We also find the Antichrist in the writings of Paul though he does not use that specific name to depict this personage. Paul describes him as follows.

1. THE MAN OF LAWLESSNESS AND THE SON OF DESTRUCTION

When Paul wrote to the Thessalonians he referred to this personage as the "man of sin" or the "man of lawlessness," as well as the "son of destruction." He said.

> Let no one deceive you in any way. For that day will not come, unless the rebellion comes first, and the man of lawlessness is revealed, the son of destruction (2 Thessalonians 2:3 NIV).

There are two different descriptions of this personage in this one verse. He is a man "characterized by sin" or "lawlessness" and "the son of destruction." This describes a truly horrible person.

2. THE LAWLESS ONE

Later in that same chapter, he called the final Antichrist the "lawless one." Paul wrote.

> And then the lawless one will be revealed, whom the Lord Jesus will kill with the breath of his mouth and bring to nothing by the appearance of his coming (2 Thessalonians 2:8 ESV).

This man opposes all the laws of God.

3. BELIAL

Paul also speaks of the contrast between Christ and Belial. He wrote the following.

> What accord has Christ with Belial? Or what portion does a believer share with an unbeliever? (2 Corinthians 6:15 ESV).

While Belial is usually thought to be another title or name for the devil, this may be a reference to the final Antichrist. This seems to be the case because we find a reference to the temple spoken of in the same context. Paul wrote.

> What agreement has the temple of God with idols? For we are the temple of the living God; as God said, "I will make my dwelling among them and walk among them, and I will be their God, and they shall be my people" (2 Corinthians 6:16 ESV).

Therefore, this seems to be another reference to Antichrist. However, this particular reference is certainly debatable.

ANTICHRIST IN THE LETTERS OF JOHN

John is the only New Testament writer which actually uses the term "Antichrist" to describe this personage. We find him using the term twice to describe this coming "man of sin." He wrote.

> Children, it is the last hour, and as you have heard that Antichrist is coming, so now many Antichrists have come. Therefore we know that it is the last hour (1 John 2:18 ESV).

Later he writes.

> By this you know the Spirit of God: every spirit that confesses that Jesus Christ has come in the flesh is from God, and every spirit that does not confess Jesus is not from God.

This is the spirit of the Antichrist, which you heard was coming and now is in the world already (1 John 4:2,3 ESV).

These are specific references to this coming world leader.

ANTICHRIST IN THE BOOK OF REVELATION

John, who also wrote the Book of Revelation, provides further titles for this final Antichrist. He stated it this way.

THE FIRST BEAST

Apart from the title Antichrist, John calls this man "the beast" or the "first beast." We read of this description in the Book of Revelation.

> And when they have finished their testimony, the beast that rises from the bottomless pit will make war on them and conquer them and kill them (Revelation 11:7 ESV).

Here this personage is the "beast" which rises from the bottomless pit, the abyss.

John also gives a further description this personage. He wrote as follows.

> And the beast that I saw was like a leopard; its feet were like a bear's, and its mouth was like a lion's mouth. And to it the dragon gave his power and his throne and great authority (Revelation 13:2 NLT).

This evil individual is described as a horrible beast. There is no good in him whatsoever.

CONCLUSION: WE ARE DEALING WITH A PERSONAGE WHO IS COMPLETELY EVIL

These descriptions, from both testaments, give us further insight into the character of this final Antichrist. From these descriptions it is obvious that it is totally evil.

SUMMARY TO QUESTION 18
HOW DOES THE BIBLE DESCRIBE THE FINAL ANTICHRIST?

The Bible describes the final Antichrist with a number of different titles or aliases. Each of these gives us some insight into his dreaded character. We find these titles in both testaments. They can be listed as follows.

In the Old Testament he is known by numerous titles. There are some who see him in the Book of Genesis as the "seed of the serpent."

Daniel gives us the most titles of this coming individual. He is known as the "little horn" "the "desolator," the "stern-faced king" and "the king who does his own will."

Micah the prophet called this individual the "Assyrian." Some believe this indicates his actual nationality; he will be a descendant of the ancient Assyrians.

In the Book of Zechariah, this wicked being is called the "evil shepherd" or the "worthless shepherd."

This sums up the main designations of this character according to the Old Testament.

The New Testament also gives a variety of names to this personage.

In the gospels, the Lord Jesus predicted many false Christs would appear. Jesus called the final Antichrist "the one who will come in his own name."

This is in contrast to Jesus who came in the name, or authority, of God the Father. The Lord also spoke of an event in which this individual is the main character, the abomination of desolation. This speaks of the defiling of the Holy of Holies in the temple in Jerusalem.

An image of this final Antichrist will be placed in a rebuilt temple. He himself will come to the temple and claim to be God Himself. Little wonder, Jesus called this an abomination.

The writings of Paul also give us a number of titles of this evil man. When writing to the Thessalonians Paul referred to him as the lawless one, the man of sin, and the son of perdition, or the son doomed to destruction.

To the Corinthians, Paul called this person "Belial." This term could refer to the devil rather than the Antichrist but it is likely a term referring to this coming man of sin.

The letters of First and Second John are the only place where the title Antichrist is used of this coming man of sin. John spoke of many Antichrists already coming with one final person still to appear.

In the Book of Revelation this personage is described as the "beast," as well as the "first beast," to differentiate him and the second beast, the false prophet. He is described as having seven heads and ten horns and a "mouth speaking great things." He is inspired by the devil himself.

When we put these titles together we can get a composite idea of his character. Indeed, it is totally evil. In fact, there is no good in him whatsoever.

QUESTION 19

Is It Possible That The Final Antichrist Will Be A Homosexual In That He Has No Desire For Women? (Daniel 11:37)

The prophet Daniel made a statement regarding the character of the coming Antichrist that many understand as a reference to homosexuality. In the eleventh chapter, we read the following description of the future world leader.

> Neither shall he regard the God of his fathers, nor the desire of women, nor regard any god: for he shall magnify himself above all (Daniel 11:37 *King James Version*).

The New King James translation reads basically the same. This personage shall not regard "the desire of women." This particular phrase "the desire of women" has been variously interpreted.

IT IS A REFERENCE TO SEXUAL ORIENTATION?

Some believe it refers to his sexual orientation. In other words, this final Antichrist will either be celibate, or he will have an unnatural desire for men instead of women. Either seems to be possible with this translation. A number of Bible commentators believe this is the meaning here.

OTHER TRANSLATIONS HAVE A DIFFERENT UNDERSTANDING OF THE MEANING

Other translations, however, do not translate the verse in the same way. For example, the *English Standard Version* translates the phrase "the one beloved by women." It reads as follows.

> He shall pay no attention to the gods of his fathers, or to the one beloved by women. He shall not pay attention to any other god, for he shall magnify himself above all (Daniel 11:37 ESV).

The NIV has something similar. It says.

> He will show no regard for the gods of his ancestors or for the one desired by women, nor will he regard any god, but will exalt himself above them all (Daniel 11:37 NIV).

Some translations understand this to mean he has no desire for "the god loved by women." The New Living Translation says.

> He will have no respect for the gods of his ancestors, or for the god loved by women, or for any other god, for he will boast that he is greater than them all (Daniel 11:37 NLT).

With these translations, his sexual orientation is not an issue. Consequently, another meaning for this phrase has to be found.

WHAT DOES IT MEAN?

If it is not referring to his sexual orientation, then what does this phrase mean? There have been a number of suggestions offered.

OPTION 1: HE HAS NO DESIRE FOR THE GOD OF ISRAEL

Some take it to mean that Antichrist has no interest in the God of Israel. The phrase "desire of women" is translated to mean "the one desired by women." This is viewed as a reference to the longing desire of Jewish women to be the mother of the Messiah.

Thus, the phrase "the desire of women" is referring to a Person, the promised Messiah. Antichrist has contempt for the genuine Messiah.

OPTION 2: HE HAS DESIRE FOR ANY HUMAN LOVE

There are others who see this as a reference to human love. For whatever reason, Antichrist has no desire for human love from anyone, whether it be male or female.

OPTION 3: HE HAS NO DESIRE FOR FEMININE TRAITS SUCH AS MERCY AND KINDNESS

Some interpreters see this as a general description of his character. In other words, this final antichrist will have no regard for the feminine traits of grace, mercy, and kindness

Whatever the exact meaning of the phrase which Daniel uses to describe this coming man of sin, we do not have to assume that he indicates Antichrist will be a homosexual.

While this is a possible understanding of the phrase, it is certainly not the only way to interpret it.

SUMMARY TO QUESTION 19
IS IT POSSIBLE THAT THE FINAL ANTICHRIST WILL BE A HOMOSEXUAL IN THAT HE HAS NO DESIRE FOR WOMEN? (DANIEL 11:37)

The Book of Daniel has a statement regarding the final Antichrist which has puzzled many people. It has been translated to indicate that Antichrist will not regard the "desire of women." At issue is the meaning of this phrase.

Some have understood it to refer to the sexual orientation of the future man of sin. In other words, he will have no desire for females. This could mean he is celibate, or that his attraction is to other men. A number of Bible commentators have held this view.

However, this is not the only way the passage can be understood. Other translations render it in such a way that it has nothing to do with sexual orientation.

Certain translations render the phrase in such a way that he does not respect "the god loved by women." This is a possible way to understand the text.

There is also the possibility that the phrase "the desire of women" refers to a person, the long-awaited Messiah. It was the hope of every young Jewish girl to be the mother of the Messiah. Antichrist has no respect for this hope. Therefore, the phrase "the desire of women" would be referring to a Person, the Messiah.

There is also the possibility that Antichrist desires no love from any human being. Human love is not something he wants or needs.

In addition, some Bible students think this merely a general description of his character. In other words, he shows no interest whatsoever in the feminine traits of mercy and kindness.

Whatever the case may be, we should not assume, as some have, that this must refer to his sexual orientation.

QUESTION 20

Will A Personal Antichrist Be Jewish?

There is the question concerning the national origin of a personal Antichrist. Is he Jewish or non-Jewish? Commentators are divided over this issue. A popular idea is that Antichrist will be a Jew rather than a Gentile.

THE CASE FOR ANTICHRIST BEING A JEW

There are many reasons why the final Antichrist is thought to be a Jew, possibly from the tribe of Dan. They can be listed as follows.

1. THE MISSING TRIBE OF DAN GIVES A CLUE TO HIS IDENTITY

In the seventh chapter of the Book of Revelation we find that 144,000 Jews, or twelve thousand from each tribe, are said to be sealed by the Lord. Scripture says.

> And I heard the number of the sealed, 144,000, sealed from every tribe of the sons of Israel (Revelation 7:4 ESV).

However, the tribe of Dan is missing from the list. For some reason, nobody from this particular tribe is included in those which are sealed, protected by the Lord.

This has caused some to believe that the final Antichrist comes from the tribe of Dan, and that Dan is judged for the fact that one of theirs becomes the "man of sin." This particular interpretation goes all the way back to the second century church father Irenaeus.

We do know that Dan is not judged because this tribe has become extinct at that time. In fact, we find that Dan inherits a portion of the Promised Land in the Millennium. This is a period of time *after* the great tribulation and the Second Coming of Jesus Christ. We read about this in Ezekiel.

> Here is the list of the tribes of Israel and the territory each is to receive. The territory of Dan is in the extreme north. Its boundary line follows the Hethlon road to Lebo-hamath and then runs on to Hazar-enan on the border of Damascus, with Hamath to the north. Dan's territory extends all the way across the land of Israel from east to west (Ezekiel 48:1 NLT).

Therefore, there must be some reason for Dan being judged during this time of the great tribulation. It is possible that the first beast, the Antichrist, comes from Dan.

Possibly there is other biblical support that the final Antichrist comes from Dan. In the Book of Genesis, the patriarch Jacob predicted the following about his son Dan.

> Dan will provide justice for his people as one of the tribes of Israel. Dan will be a snake by the roadside, a viper along the path, that bites the horse's heels so that its rider tumbles backward (Genesis 49:16-17 NIV).

Here we are specifically told that Dan will be a snake. The snake is a biblical symbol of the devil.

There is perhaps further evidence in Scripture that Antichrist will come from Dan. Consider what the prophet Jeremiah recorded the Lord as saying.

The snorting of the enemy's horses is heard from Dan; at the neighing of their stallions the whole land trembles. They have come to devour the land and everything in it, the city and all who live there (Jeremiah 8:16 NIV).

Therefore, Scripture may give evidence of the origin of the coming Antichrist from one of the tribes of Israel, the tribe of Dan.

2. THE CONTRAST TO JESUS HIMSELF

When Jesus spoke to the religious leaders of His day, He said the following.

I have come in my Father's name, and you do not receive me. If another comes in his own name, you will receive him (John 5:43 ESV).

Jesus was rejected by His people. However, He said that someday they will receive another person. This person will be a different Messiah. To many, this seems to imply a person from their own nationality, a Jew.

Inasmuch as this one will enter into negotiations with the nation of Israel, it suggests that they can confidently trust this individual. If the coming man of sin were a Gentile, then it would be difficult to see how they could have complete faith in his promises. However, if he were one of their own, a Jew, then this would be different.

3. HE REJECTS THE GOD OF HIS FATHERS

One powerful argument seems to be the way he is described by the prophet Daniel. He is a man who disregards the "God of his fathers." We read.

Neither shall he regard the God of his fathers, nor the desire of women, nor regard any god: for he shall magnify himself above all (Daniel 11:37 *King James Version*).

This is a rather common phrase in the Old Testament. The words, "God of our fathers," or "God of their fathers," is used hundreds of times in the Old Testament. It always refers to the God of Abraham, Isaac, and Jacob. It *never* refers to a pagan god.

4. HE IS CALLED THE PRINCE OF ISRAEL

There is a passage in the Book of Ezekiel which has been applied to the final Antichrist. In it, he is called the "wicked one, prince of Israel."

> And you, O profane wicked one, prince of Israel, whose day has come, the time of your final punishment, thus says the Lord GOD: Remove the turban and take off the crown. Things shall not remain as they are. Exalt that which is low, and bring low that which is exalted. A ruin, ruin, ruin I will make it. This also shall not be, until he comes, the one to whom judgment belongs, and I will give it to him (Ezekiel 21:25-27 ESV).

This passage speaks of the end of the present age. The wicked prince, the final Antichrist, comes from Israel.

5. THE NAME ANTICHRIST SUGGESTS HE IS JEWISH

The fact that he is called the anti "Christ" seems to clearly mark his identity. Since the promised Christ must be Jewish, and that the Messiah is first and foremost the Savior of Israel, the logical conclusion is that the Antichrist must be a Jew.

6. THE JEWS WOULD NEVER ACCEPT A GENTILE MESSIAH

Probably the strongest reason in favor of the Antichrist being Jewish is that he is accepted by the Jews as their promised Messiah. The Jewish people will *never* accept a Gentile messiah.

It is for these reasons that many people anticipate the coming Antichrist will be Jewish.

SUMMARY TO QUESTION 20
WILL A PERSONAL ANTICHRIST BE JEWISH?

There is some question as to whether the final Antichrist will be a Jew or a Gentile. Many people assume that he will be, or must be, Jewish. There are a number of reasons as to why this position is held.

One reason has to do with the missing tribe of Dan. We are told that during the great tribulation period the Lord seals, or supernaturally protects, 144,000 from each of the twelve tribes of Israel. Noticeably missing is the tribe of Dan. For some unknown reason, Dan is absent during this time.

Since people from the tribe of Dan exist in the Millennium, their exclusion in this list in Revelation is not due to their non-existence. Seemingly, they are being judged, but we are not told why. It has been suggested that Dan is omitted because the final Antichrist comes from that tribe.

There are a couple of passages in the Old Testament which may allude to this. The patriarch Jacob, in predicting the future for the descendants of his son Dan, uses the word "snake" to describe them.

The prophet Jeremiah records the Lord's warning of a sinister threat coming from the area of Dan. These passages may indicate the origin of Antichrist is from the tribe of Dan.

There is also a statement by Jesus which has led many to conclude that the final Antichrist must be Jewish. He said that while the nation rejected Him, One who came in the name of God the Father, they would accept another one who will come in his own name. This also suggests they can trust the final Antichrist because he is one of their own, a Jew.

We also find a statement in the Book of Daniel which seems to indicate that Antichrist must be a Jew. It says he will not regard the "God" of his fathers. This phrase, or something similar, is used often in the Old Testament. It always refers to the God of the Bible. There are no exceptions to this.

In the Book of Ezekiel there is the prediction of a coming personage called the "prince of Israel." In context, it seems to be speaking of the future Antichrist. The fact that this profane one is Jewish is another indication that Antichrist comes from the chosen people.

There is also the name of this personage; Antichrist. The word "anti" can mean "in place of" or "instead of." He comes "in place of" the true Christ. The man of sin is therefore received by the Jews in place of the genuine Messiah. To do this, he must be Jewish.

Finally, there is the fact that the Jews could not possibly accept a Messiah other than someone from their own race. To many people, this settles the issue. The Messiah, or Christ, must be a Jew for the Jewish people to accept him.

Therefore, the false Christ, the Antichrist, must come from the physical line of Abraham.

These reasons have caused many people to anticipate a Jewish Antichrist.

Will A Personal Antichrist Be A Gentile?

There is the question concerning the national origin of the coming world ruler, the Antichrist. While many people think he will be Jewish, there are others who make the case that he will be a Gentile. The following reasons are put forth for believing the final Antichrist, the coming Caesar, must be non-Jewish.

1. HE COMES OUT OF THE ROMAN EMPIRE

The Antichrist will come out of the revived Roman Empire. In fact, it seems that he will be a Roman. Daniel wrote.

> And after the sixty-two weeks, an anointed one shall be cut off and shall have nothing. And the people of the prince who is to come shall destroy the city and the sanctuary. Its end shall come with a flood, and to the end there shall be war. Desolations are decreed (Daniel 9:26 ESV).

The people who destroyed the city of Jerusalem were Romans. Therefore, the people of the prince who is to come are Romans, Gentiles. If the people of the prince are Romans, or Gentiles, then the prince himself, the final Antichrist, must also be a Gentile.

In another passage, Antichrist is also seen as arising out of the Roman Empire in the dream of the prophet Daniel. Daniel saw four beasts arising in his dream. These four beasts represented four world kingdoms. It is out of the fourth kingdom, the revived Roman Empire, where the Antichrist will arise. Daniel describes him as a "little horn." He wrote.

> After that, in my vision at night I looked, and there before me was a fourth beast—terrifying and frightening and very powerful. It had large iron teeth; it crushed and devoured its victims and trampled underfoot whatever was left. It was different from all the former beasts, and it had ten horns. "While I was thinking about the horns, there before me was another horn, a little one, which came up among them; and three of the first horns were uprooted before it. This horn had eyes like the eyes of a human being and a mouth that spoke boastfully" (Daniel 7:7-8 NIV).

This gives further indication that Antichrist must be a Gentile.

2. HE COMES FROM THE SEA: A REFERENCE TO THE NATIONS

We are told that this first beast arises from "the sea." The Book of Revelation has the following to say about his origin.

> And I saw a beast rising out of the sea, with ten horns and seven heads, with ten diadems on its horns and blasphemous names on its heads. And the beast that I saw was like a leopard; its feet were like a bear's, and its mouth was like a lion's mouth. And to it the dragon gave his power and his throne and great authority (Revelation 13:1-2 ESV).

This seems to be a reference to the nations of the world, in contrast to the nation of Israel. The Gentile nations are often compared to the sea while the nation of Israel is compared to the "earth," or the "land." Therefore, coming out of the sea could mean coming from the Gentiles nations.

3. ALL THE MAJOR TYPES OF ANTICHRIST WERE GENTILES

There are a number of individuals in Scripture, and in history, who have been seen as a "type of Antichrist." This includes three main characters: Nimrod, the initial builder of the city of Babylon, Nebuchadnezzar, the King of Babylon, and the Seleucid King, Antiochus IV. They were all Gentiles. This seems to further indicate that the final Antichrist himself will be a Gentile.

In fact, the only non-Gentile type of Antichrist was Saul. While he was not a Gentile, neither was he from the promised line. He was from the tribe of Benjamin, not Judah.

4. HE IGNORES THE GOD, OR GODS, OF HIS ANCESTORS

The Book of Daniel says this personage will not respect "the God or the gods of his fathers." Either translation is possible. If "gods" is the correct reading, then he could not be Jewish. Some translations understand this to be the meaning. For example, the English Standard Version reads.

> He shall pay no attention to the gods of his fathers, or to the one beloved by women. He shall not pay attention to any other god, for he shall magnify himself above all (Daniel 11:37-38 ESV).

However, even if "the God of his fathers," is the correct reading it does not necessarily mean he is Jewish. Rather we find this verse simply stating that the final Antichrist will reject whatever religion is practiced by his ancestors. If he arises from the peoples of ancient Rome, as what the evidence seems to show, then his family religion probably would be some form of Christian faith.

> This passage emphasizes that he will not follow any god. In other words, he will be an atheist. In fact, he will exalt himself above any god or object of worship (2 Thessalonians 2:4).

5. ANTIOCHUS, THE ONLY PERSON SPECIFIED AS A TYPE OF ANTICHRIST WAS A GENTILE

There is also the fact that Antiochus IV, the only individual in Scripture who is specifically identified as a type of the Antichrist, was a Gentile. Both Antiochus, and the final Antichrist, are called "the little horn" in the Book of Daniel.

As we examine the Scripture, we find that Antiochus is the clearest pre-figurement of the coming man of sin. It stands to reason that if the pre-figurement of the final Antichrist is a Gentile, then the Antichrist himself must also be a Gentile.

6. ANTICHRIST SEPARATES THE JEWS FOR SPECIAL PERSECUTION

Finally, we discover from Scripture that the final Antichrist separates the Jews for special persecution. He breaks his agreement with the Jews, defiles the rebuilt Jewish temple, and then begins an attempt to wipe out the entire race of Jews.

Since the Jews are the ones who are specially persecuted by this man of sin, it does not seem likely that the Antichrist would himself be a Jew. Seemingly, he would not persecute his own people.

It is for these many reasons that a number of Bible students conclude that the final Antichrist will be a Gentile, rather than a Jew.

SUMMARY TO QUESTION 21
WILL A PERSONAL ANTICHRIST BE A GENTILE?

Bible believers have differences of opinion with respect to whether a personal Antichrist would be Jewish or Gentile. Some argue that the final Antichrist will not be Jewish but rather will be a Gentile leader. There are a number of reasons as to why this is held.

To begin with, he is called "the prince who is to come." Furthermore, we are told by Daniel that "the people of prince who is to come" would destroy the city of Jerusalem. This happened in A.D. 70 when the Roman legions destroyed both the city and the temple. His people were the Romans. Therefore, he himself must be from the Roman Empire, possibly even a Roman.

Scripture elsewhere teaches that Antichrist will arise from a revived version of the ancient Roman Empire. He will head up a last-days confederation of ten Gentile nations. This is another indication that he is a Gentile.

In the Book of Revelation, we are told that his origin is from "the sea." Often the sea depicts the Gentile nations in contrast to Israel. This provides further evidence of his Gentile nationality.

In addition, all major types of Antichrist in Scripture, Nimrod, Nebuchadnezzar, and Antiochus IV, were Gentiles. This seems to further indicate that Antichrist himself will be a Gentile rather than a Jew.

Daniel also says that he will not respect the "gods" of his fathers. This is not the God of Israel but rather false gods. Therefore, he cannot be Jewish. The Jews only worshipped one God.

There is also the fact that the clearest type of the final Antichrist, Antiochus IV, was a Gentile. Both he and the coming man of sin are called "the little horn."

Indeed, his life mirrored that of the Antichrist in many ways. If this type of Antichrist was a Gentile, then it seems to follow that the fulfillment of the type will also be a Gentile.

Finally, there is the fact that Jews are separated out for special persecution by this coming man of sin. The Bible says that the final Antichrist breaks his agreement with the Jews, defiles their rebuilt temple by going into its holiest area, openly defies their God by claiming that he is God, and then turns his attention to eradicate the nation. It seems difficult to imagine that a Jew would do this to his own people. Consequently, it seems more likely that the final Antichrist will be a Gentile.

These factors have caused many Bible students to assume the coming Antichrist will be a Gentile.

QUESTION 22

Will The Coming Antichrist Claim To Be The Long-Awaited Messiah?

One of the mostly commonly accepted beliefs with respect to the final Antichrist is that when he comes upon the scene of history he will claim to be the long-awaited Messiah of the Jews, and the nation will accept him as such. He will be the fulfillment of what the nation has longed for since the promises were first made to them so long ago. Their dream will finally be realized.

WHY IT IS ASSUMED ANTICHRIST PRETENDS TO BE THE REAL MESSIAH

There are a number of reasons as to why it is believed the coming Antichrist will pretend to be the genuine Christ, the Messiah.

1. HE IS CALLED THE ANTICHRIST

First, he is called the "anti-Christ;" the one who appears instead of Christ. This seems to assume that he attempts to take the place of Christ and claim for himself what rightfully belongs to Jesus, God the Son. Therefore, the very name which is used of him, "Antichrist," shows that this personage tries to usurp something that is not rightfully his.

2. HE COMES TO THE TEMPLE

Second, he will come to the temple of God in Jerusalem and demand worship from the Jews. Paul wrote.

> He will oppose and will exalt himself over everything
> that is called God or is worshiped, so that he sets him-
> self up in God's temple, proclaiming himself to be God
> (2 Thessalonians 2:4 NIV).

This seems to indicate that Antichrist will claim that the temple
and everything connected with it refers to him. He is the legitimate
Messiah.

3. JESUS' STATEMENT ABOUT ANTICHRIST

Third, there is the statement of Jesus with respect to the coming of the
Antichrist. He said.

> I have come in my Father's name, and you do not accept
> me; but if someone else comes in his own name, you will
> accept him (John 5:43 NIV).

These words of Jesus contrast Himself, whom the people did not
receive, with the coming Antichrist, whom they will receive. They will
accept a *false* Messiah. This is one of the main reasons as to why many
people assume the coming Antichrist has to be Jewish.

Indeed, for the Jews to embrace him as the Christ, the Messiah, he
must meet all the qualifications. Primary among those is that he will be
Jewish. It is argued that the Jews would never receive a Gentile Messiah.

Do these facts make it clear that Antichrist must be Jewish and that
the nation will receive him as their Messiah when he makes such
claims? Not everyone thinks so.

THERE ARE SOME WHO DO NOT THINK ANTICHRIST WILL CLAIM TO BE MESSIAH

There is one assumption in all of this which needs to be established;
that the Antichrist will actually *claim* to be the promised Messiah, and
that the Jews will accept him as such.

However, it is contended by some people that the final Antichrist will not claim to be the Messiah of the Jews. Though Antichrist makes an agreement with the nation which allows them to once again offer sacrifices in their temple, this does not mean that he will claim to be the Messiah, or that they will embrace him as their "Anointed one."

In point of fact, instead of accepting the Antichrist as their Messiah, it is contended that the Jews will actually long for the Messiah when this man of sin turns on them and demands their worship.

THE TERM ANTICHRIST CAN BE UNDERSTOOD IN ANOTHER WAY

In fact, one does not have to understand the term Antichrist in the sense that this man of sin will actually claim to be the Messiah. To the contrary, it says that he rejects everything that has to do with the religion of the Jews. In other words, he takes the rightful place of Christ, not by claiming to be the Messiah, but rather by substituting himself as a false god. In this way, he is an "anti Christ."

HE IS NOT RECEIVED AS MESSIAH BUT RATHER AS GOD

The words of Jesus, as to the reception of the man of sin, do not have to be understood in the sense that the Jews receive him as the Christ. Indeed, it is argued that the Antichrist will not be received as the Messiah, but rather he will be worshipped as God.

Therefore, the idea of receiving this man of sin is not so much receiving him as the long-awaited Christ, but actually receiving him as God visiting his creation!

Recall that Antichrist comes on the scene as a political leader who helps the Jewish people regain the practice of their ancient institutions such as animal sacrifices. He then stops their sacrifices, defiles their Holy Temple, and orders them to worship him.

If this is the correct understanding of what the Antichrist will claim to be, then it explains why most of the types of Antichrist in Scripture are *Gentiles* and not Jews. He is a Gentile ruler who introduces a different god to the people of Israel, and a different system of worship. He replaces the genuine worship, with worship of a false god. In this sense he is the Antichrist.

SUMMARY TO QUESTION 22
WILL THE COMING ANTICHRIST CLAIM TO BE THE LONG-AWAITED MESSIAH?

While many accept the idea, without questioning it, that the Jews will receive the final Antichrist as their promised Messiah not everyone assumes that this is what will happen. Indeed, there is some question as to whether Antichrist will even claim to be the coming Messiah.

Generally speaking, it is assumed that Antichrist will claim to be the genuine Messiah for a number of reasons. For one thing, the fact that he is called the "anti-Christ" seems to indicate that he attempts to assume the rightful role of Christ. "Anti" can mean "instead of" or "in place of." Hence, it seems to follow that he will attempt to usurp the role of the Jesus as the legitimate Messiah.

We are told that Antichrist will come to the Holy Temple in Jerusalem and defile the Holy of Holies. The fact that he enters the temple is seen as further evidence that he will claim to be the long-awaited Messiah of the Jews.

This seems to be further confirmed by Jesus' own statement. Christ said that while He came in the name of His Father, He was rejected by His people. However, another person will come in his own name and that person will be accepted. This is the Antichrist. The fact that Jesus said the Jewish people will receive this imposter indicates that he is welcomed as the genuine Messiah.

Consequently, this had led many to the conclusion that the final Antichrist must be Jewish, since the Jews would never accept a Gentile as their long-awaited Messiah.

Yet there is another way of looking at this. It is possible that Antichrist takes the place of the Messiah in the sense of claiming to be an alternative god to the God of Abraham, Isaac, and Jacob.

Therefore, the man of sin does not claim to be the Messiah, or is accepted as the Messiah, but rather claims to be a different god than the One which the Jews worship. In this way, he tries to take the place of Christ, who is God Himself.

This understanding would explain why all the prefigurements or types of the Messiah are, for the most part, Gentiles and not Jews. It would fit with how Scripture uses the pagan king Antiochus IV as the clearest type of Antichrist. He was a Gentile ruler who imposed himself on the Jews while claiming to be a god. He never claimed to be their Messiah, yet he is a clearest type of Antichrist in all of Scripture.

While there are many things about the coming Antichrist we do know about, there are still many matters which are uncertain. The question as to whether he will claim to be the Messiah may be one of these.

Is The Possible The Antichrist Is Caesar Nero Resurrected? (Nero Redivivus)

There have been many past identifications of the Antichrist. One of the favorite ones has been Caesar Nero. Not only do some people think the description of the Antichrist was a description of the historical Roman Emperor Nero, there was a theory that Antichrist was actually going to be Nero resurrected. This is also known as *Nero Redivivus*. Is there any reason we should believe this theory?

THE THEORY EXPLAINED

We are told that the beast, the Antichrist, dies and then comes back to life. Scripture explains it as follows.

> The dragon stood on the shore of the sea. And I saw a beast coming out of the sea. It had ten horns and seven heads, with ten crowns on its horns, and on each head a blasphemous name. The beast I saw resembled a leopard, but had feet like those of a bear and a mouth like that of a lion. The dragon gave the beast his power and his throne and great authority. One of the heads of the beast seemed to have had a fatal wound, but the fatal wound had been healed. The whole world was filled with wonder and followed the beast. People worshiped the dragon because he had given authority to the beast, and they also worshiped the beast and asked,

"Who is like the beast? Who can make war against it?" (Revelation 13:1-4 NIV).

This passage has been thought by some to explain certain events surrounding the life of Caesar Nero. Nero died in A.D. 68 by his own hand. However, a rumor arose that Nero was not really dead. Instead, it was thought that he had fled across the Euphrates River to the enemy of Rome, Parthia.

Furthermore, it was rumored that Nero would return as the new leader of Parthian armies in an attempt to destroy Rome. This became the basis of the *Nero Redivivus* myth.

PEOPLE APPEARED CLAIMING TO BE NERO

Interestingly, during the decades following Nero's death, three pretenders did come forth claiming to be Caesar Nero. This is recorded by the Roman historians Tacitus and Suetonius.

THE THEORY TAKES ON A NEW TWIST

At the end of the first century A.D. the story of Nero took a further twist. It was then said Caesar Nero had been dead after all but that he would actually rise from the dead, return to the city of Rome, and seize the Roman Empire back for himself.

This idea of the return of Nero to Rome captured the popular fancy. It found its way into certain Jewish and Christian writings of the time. This triumphant Nero was sometimes even pictured as the Antichrist. This is found in an apocryphal work called the "Ascension of Isaiah." We also find this in another written work, the "Sibylline Oracles."

Eventually, the idea that Nero would come back to the world as the long-predicted Antichrist was abandoned by the masses. However, this certainly did not happen immediately. Indeed, in the days of Augustine, the fifth century theologian, he notes that some people still expected to see the return of Nero. This was some three hundred and fifty years after Nero's death.

This basically explains the *Nero Redivivus* myth. However, there is no evidence whatsoever that the final Antichrist will be Caesar Nero resurrected. None.

SUMMARY TO QUESTION 23
IS IT POSSIBLE THE ANTICHRIST IS CAESAR NERO RESURRECTED? (NERO REDIVIVUS)

One ancient theory has Nero being the long-predicted Antichrist that dies and then comes back to life. This is also known as *Nero Redivivus* myth.

In Revelation 13, there is the account of the wounded beast, the Antichrist. He has a mortal wound but recovers from it. This story could be understood as an actual man who had been dead and then miraculously comes back to life. This account in the Book of Revelation became the basis of this story about Nero.

After Nero's death in A.D. 68, it was reported that he had not actually died but rather had escaped to join the enemies of Rome, Parthia. It was thought that he would return leading the Parthian armies in a triumph over Rome. Certain individuals did appear in the next few years claiming to be Nero.

At the end of the first century, the story circulated that Nero had actually died but that he had also risen from the dead. These stories circulated in the writings of both Jews and Christians. Certain Christians then taught that Nero was the beast of Revelation, the one who received the mortal head wound and then came back to life.

As time went by, this *Nero Redivivus* myth eventually fell out of favor. However, it lingered for several hundred years. We find from the fifth century theologian, Augustine of Hippo, that some people in his day were still expecting the return of Nero. However, the New Testament does not teach that this is what is going to occur.

In sum, there is no evidence that the final Antichrist will be a resurrected Nero.

What Is The Theory That Antichrist Will Be Judas Iscariot Reincarnated?

One theory as to the true identity of the coming Antichrist has him being the reincarnation of the man who betrayed Jesus, Judas Iscariot. Some people go even further and state that that Judas was either a demon or the devil himself incarnate! The following arguments are usually given to support this idea.

1. THE COMING ANTICHRIST IS RELATED TO THE NATION OF ISRAEL

First, it is claimed that the coming Antichrist has some relationship with the nation of Israel. Psalm 55 is cited in support of this idea. It says.

> My companion attacks his friends; he violates his covenant.
> His talk is smooth as butter, yet war is in his heart; his
> words are more soothing than oil, yet they are drawn swords
> (Psalm 55:20,21 NIV).

These verses are viewed as a specific reference to the covenant which Antichrist makes, or confirms, with the Jews and then ultimately breaks. Daniel wrote about this. He said.

> He will confirm a covenant with many for one 'seven.' In
> the middle of the 'seven' he will put an end to sacrifice and
> offering. And at the temple he will set up an abomination

that causes desolation, until the end that is decreed is poured out on him (Daniel 9:27 NIV).

Consequently, it is argued that the entire Psalm should be read in this context. It portrays the sufferings of the nation Israel and its godly remnant during the time of the great tribulation.

However, in the midst of this passage describing the great tribulation, we read about the betrayal of a trusted friend.

For it is not an enemy who taunts me—then I could bear it;

> it is not an adversary who deals insolently with me—then I could hide from him. But it is you, a man, my equal, my companion, my familiar friend. We used to take sweet counsel together; within God's house we walked in the throng (Psalm 55:12-14 ESV).

These verses not only describe the treachery of Judas toward Jesus the Messiah, they also give us the hint of something else. Judas shall be reincarnated in the person of Antichrist. In the future, he will betray and desert the nation of Israel.

In fact, what we discover is that the relationship of future Antichrist to Israel will be exactly the same as that of Judas to Jesus. While he will initially pose as the friend of the Jews, three and one half years later his true character will emerge, he will betray them. This is what happened with Judas Iscariot. He was Jesus' disciple for three and one half years before he betrayed the Lord.

As Jesus endured the bitterness and betrayal of one who was supposedly His trusted friend, the nation of Israel shall suffer the same fate. Hence, from the picture given to us in Psalm 55, we have the first clue that the Antichrist will be Judas Iscariot reincarnated.

2. A COVENANT IS MADE WITH DEATH

The next clue can be found in the writings of the prophet Isaiah. We read about the covenant which will be made with death. Isaiah the prophet wrote.

> Your covenant with death will be annulled; your agreement with the realm of the dead will not stand. When the overwhelming scourge sweeps by, you will be beaten down by it (Isaiah 28:18 NIV).

This is also viewed as a reference to the seven-year agreement which is mentioned in Daniel 9:27. The coming man of sin, the final Antichrist, makes, or confirms, a covenant, a contract, with the nation of Israel.

But here the person with whom this covenant is made is termed "Death and Hades" or "death and the realm of the dead." This is a title of the coming Antichrist, just as the title "the Resurrection and the Life" is one which belongs to the true Christ.

The idea that Antichrist is equated with Death and Hades in found in the sixth chapter of the Book of Revelation. In this chapter we have the unveiling of the four horsemen of the apocalypse.

It is a four-fold picture of Antichrist just as the gospels give a four-fold portrayal of the Lord Jesus. Antichrist is seen as the rider on four differently colored horses, which bring about four stages in his awful career. Finally, we are told this about him.

> I looked, and there before me was a pale horse! Its rider was named Death, and Hades was following close behind him. They were given power over a fourth of the earth to kill by sword, famine and plague, and by the wild beasts of the earth (Revelation 6:8 NIV).

"Hades" is the name of the place which receives the souls of the unbelieving dead. The fact that this name is here applied to Antichrist hints that he has come from there, the evil underworld. As we will discover, Hades is the place where Judas went after his suicide.

3. JUDAS IS CALLED THE SON OF DESTRUCTION (OR PERDITION)

Next we look at the New Testament. In John's gospel, we have further evidence that the Antichrist will be Judas Iscariot reincarnated. On the night of His betrayal, Jesus prayed the following to God the Father.

> While I was with them, I kept them in your name, which you have given me. I have guarded them, and not one of them has been lost except the son of destruction, that the Scripture might be fulfilled (John 17:12 ESV).

Judas is termed by Christ as, "the son of destruction" or the "son of perdition."

The Apostle Paul also gave the final Antichrist the same designation. He wrote.

> Let no one deceive you in any way. For that day will not come, unless the rebellion comes first, and the man of lawlessness is revealed, the son of destruction (2 Thessalonians 2:3 ESV).

These are the only two places in the entire Scripture where this name occurs. The fact that Judas was termed by Christ "the son of destruction" and the fact that the same designation is given by the Apostle Paul to the coming man of sin, the final Antichrist, shows that they are one-and-the-same person.

4. JUDAS WAS A MAN BUT MORE THAN A MAN

We find this further supported by what Jesus said about Judas. We know that Judas was a genuine human being. Jesus said.

The Son of Man will go just as it is written about him. But woe to that man who betrays the Son of Man! It would be better for him if he had not been born (Matthew 26:24 NIV).

Though Judas was a man, some believe he was more than a mere man. In fact, Jesus also said of him.

Jesus replied, "Didn't I choose you, the twelve, and yet one of you is the devil" (John 6:70 NIV).

While there are many demons, there is only one devil. Indeed, in no other passage in Scripture is the word "devil" applied to any one but to Satan himself. This has caused some to believe that Judas was the devil incarnate, just as the Lord Jesus was God incarnate.

Others do not go that far. They believe either a demon entered a human being, Judas Iscariot, or that the person of Judas was actually a demonic spirit who took on a human body. However, Judas was not the devil himself.

5. THE BEAST COMES FROM THE BOTTOMLESS PIT

There is further evidence of the demonic origin of Judas. In the eleventh chapter of the Book of Revelation "the beast" is first revealed to us. It says.

Now when they have finished their testimony, the beast that comes up from the Abyss will attack them, and overpower and kill them (Revelation 11:7 NIV).

The beast, the Antichrist, is seen coming forth from the Abyss, the bottomless pit. Scripture teaches that this pit is the place where the jailed spirits of lost souls reside in torment. It is their prison.

If this is the case, then how did the spirit of the beast, the Antichrist, get there in the first place? When did this spirit arrive in the Abyss?

Some say that this occurred when Judas Iscariot died. The Antichrist will be thus be the traitor Judas Iscariot reincarnated.

This is further supported in the New Testament. When Simon Peter spoke to his fellow disciples about the need to replace Judas he characterized this personage as follows.

> And they prayed and said, "You, Lord, who know the hearts of all, show which one of these two you have chosen to take the place in this ministry and apostleship from which Judas turned aside to go to his own place" (Acts 1:24,25 ESV).

It is said of no other character in the Bible that at his death he went "to his own place." When these two passages of Scripture are placed together we find that Judas went "to his own place," the Abyss, and that the beast ascends out of the Abyss. Thus, these two characters are the same person.

6. THE BEAST WAS NOT, IS, BUT WILL BE

We have a further description of the nature of this beast later in the Book of Revelation. The following explanation is given.

> The beast, which you saw, once was, now is not, and will come up out of the Abyss and go to its destruction. The inhabitants of the earth whose names have not been written in the book of life from the creation of the world will be astonished when they see the beast, because it once was, now is not, and yet will come (Revelation 17:8 NIV).

The Word of God says that the beast shall come up out of the Abyss and that he shall go into perdition or destruction. Then we are told

> The beast who once was, and now is not, is an eighth king. He belongs to the seven and is going to his destruction (Revelation 17:11 NIV).

We learn four things about the beast, or the final Antichrist, from comparing these verses. They can be summed up as follows.

First, he "was." This seems to mean that he once was living on the earth.

Second, he "is not." This description seems to mean that he was not on the earth at that time but that he formerly had been. In other words, he left the earth through his death. His spirit, after death went to the Abyss.

Third, he shall "come out of the Abyss." His spirit now comes up from the Abyss, the prison house of dead spirits, and returns to the earth.

Finally, he shall "go into perdition or destruction." In other words, he will eventually go away to eternal destruction.

These truths fit well with Judas being the coming Antichrist. He was alive, then died and his spirit went to Hades, the place of the dead. At some future time, his spirit will come up from Hades and will go back to the earth to live in another human being. Finally, he shall be sent away to eternal punishment.

7. THE END OF THE BEAST

The final fate for the beast is recorded in the Book of Revelation. It says.

> And the beast was captured, and with it the false prophet who in its presence had done the signs by which he deceived those who had received the mark of the beast and those who worshiped its image. These two were thrown alive into the lake of fire that burns with sulfur (Revelation 19:20 ESV).

Antichrist, along with the false prophet, will be thrown alive into the Lake of Fire. Instead of returning to the Abyss where he came from, he is sent away to his final fate.

The fact that the beast, the Antichrist, is distinct from Satan is clear. The devil is sent to the Abyss for this specific period of time only to be released at the end of the one thousand year Millennium.

This basically sums up the biblical case for the coming Antichrist to be a reincarnation of the disciple of Jesus, Judas Iscariot.

RESPONSE: JUDAS IS A TYPE OF ANTICHRIST

While there are Bible-believers who believe that Judas and Antichrist are one-in-the-same person, a better answer is that Judas is a type of Antichrist. Indeed, while there are resemblances between the two of them, there are a number of reasons as to why the idea of Antichrist being Judas reincarnated is ruled out.

For one thing, as we have explained in a previous book, *What Happens One Second After We Die?*, reincarnation, the belief that someone who dies can return in a later life as another person, is something that the Bible says cannot happen. Once a person is dead, they do not come back to life again as another human being. Therefore, Antichrist could not be Judas Iscariot reincarnated!

Second, the passages used to indicate that Antichrist is the reincarnation of Judas certainly do not have to be interpreted in that way. Indeed, there are other ways to understand what these passages are saying without resorting to the idea of reincarnation.

Third, as noted in previous questions, there is the timing factor. The devil does not know when the Antichrist will come upon the scene of history. Indeed, the return of Jesus Christ is something that God, and He alone, knows and controls. Jesus made that clear when He said the following about His return to the earth.

> But as for that day and hour no one knows it-not even the angels in heaven-except the Father alone (Matthew 24:36 NET).

Note that no created being, whether human or supernatural, knows when the Lord will return. Therefore, it is not possible that Antichrist could be Judas reincarnated because this coming Caesar suddenly appears on the scene during the last seven-year period before the Lord returns; a time which is unknown to Satan.

Consequently, these three reasons rule out any physical connection between the Antichrist and Judas.

However, there is perhaps some type of demonic link between the two. In fact, one could argue that the same demonic spirit who possessed Judas will also possess this final Antichrist. This is certainly possible. Yet there does not seem to be enough information to make the connection certain.

What we can conclude is this: when all is said and done, Judas Iscariot, and the final Antichrist will be two of the most despised individuals who have ever lived.

SUMMARY TO QUESTION 24
WHAT IS THE THEORY THAT ANTICHRIST WILL BE JUDAS ISCARIOT REINCARNATED?

It has been held by some Bible-believers that the final Antichrist is actually the reincarnation of the disciple of Jesus who betrayed Him, Judas Iscariot. The support for this view is as follows.

To begin with, the coming Antichrist is linked with the nation of Israel. At first, he will be their friend but he will eventually turn on them. This will occur after three and one half years. In the same manner, Judas was a friend of Jesus for three and one half years before he betrayed him.

We are also told that Israel will make an agreement with Death and Hades. The coming Antichrist, the rider on the pale horse in the Book of Revelation, is called Death and Hades. Hades is the place where the spirits of the unbelieving dead are housed. This is same place from where the final Antichrist originates. Hades is also where Judas went upon his death. This fact links Judas with the origin of Antichrist.

Judas is called "the son of perdition" by Jesus, while Paul calls the future Antichrist by the same name. This, it is claimed, indicates that they are the same personage.

While Judas was a genuine human being, he seems to be more than that, a demonic spirit inhabiting a human body. Indeed, Jesus called him both "a man" and "the devil." He was a human being who was possessed by some devilish spirit which took over his body.

When Judas died, Scripture says that he went to "his own place." This place is the Abyss, the bottomless pit. This is significant because the Book of Revelation tells us the beast, the Antichrist, will arise from the bottomless pit.

Revelation also tells us the beast, the Antichrist, did exist on the earth at one time, left the earth through death, and then returned to the earth from the bottomless pit. This precisely describes Judas Iscariot.

The final end of the beast will be the lake of fire. The fact that he is distinct from the devil is made clear. When the beast, Antichrist, is thrown into the lake of fire, the devil is sent to the Abyss. This shows that while the beast may be a human who is indwelt by a demonic spirit, that spirit is not the devil himself.

It is for these reasons that some Bible students have thought that the coming Antichrist will be the reincarnation of Judas Iscariot.

Yet a better answer is that Judas is a type of Antichrist rather than being the same human being reincarnated. Indeed, according to Scripture, reincarnation is not something that can occur. Therefore, the possibility of Antichrist being Judas is ruled out. Furthermore, the passages used to support the idea do not have to be interpreted in this manner.

Finally, the timing will not work. Antichrist appears at the end of this age, a few short years before the return of Christ. The timing of this is completely in the control of the Lord. While the Lord certainly knows who this final Antichrist will be, there is nothing in Scripture that indicates that the devil knows this ahead of time. To the contrary, the Bible is clear that this is something only the Lord knows. Therefore, Satan could not arrange ahead of time for Judas to reappear in the future as the "man of sin."

As we indicated, Judas is a type of Antichrist; possibly possessed by the same demonic spirit that will eventually possess this coming Caesar. However, to say they are the same personage is going way beyond what the Bible allows.

How Does The Final Antichrist Fit With The Period Known As, "The Times Of The Gentiles?

To correctly appreciate the place of the final Antichrist in biblical history, it is necessary to understand what Scripture says about a period known as "the times of the Gentiles." Once we understand how the times of the Gentiles fits into the overall plan of God, then the appearance and rule of the coming Antichrist will become much clearer.

THE TIMES OF THE GENTILES ACCORDING TO JESUS

Jesus alone spoke of a period known as the "times of the Gentiles." Luke records Him saying the following.

> They will fall by the edge of the sword and be led captive among all nations, and Jerusalem will be trampled underfoot by the Gentiles, until the times of the Gentiles are fulfilled (Luke 21:24 ESV).

Jesus' use of this phrase is the first and only time we find it in the Scripture. Basically it predicts that Gentiles will dominate the city of Jerusalem until this period of time, the times of the Gentiles, is fulfilled.

What does this phrase mean? Are we still in the "times of the Gentiles" since Jerusalem is no longer in Gentile control? Or, has the times of the Gentiles ended?

THE TIMES OF THE GENTILES DEFINED: GENTILE RULE OVER JERUSALEM

We can define the 'the times of the Gentiles" as follows: it refers to the period of time when Gentiles rule over the city of Jerusalem. This began about 606 B.C. with King Nebuchadnezzar's deportation of the people from Jerusalem to Babylon. The times of the Gentiles will conclude at the Second Coming of Jesus Christ when Jerusalem will no longer be subject to Gentile rule.

While Jerusalem has had periodic times in the last two thousand six hundred years when Gentiles did not dominate the city, as they are presently, there is another component of the "times of the Gentiles" which is essential to understand. Jerusalem must again be ruled by a King from the line of David for the times of the Gentiles to end. This has not occurred for over 2,600 years!

NO DESCENDANT OF DAVID HAS RULED SINCE 587 B.C.

We need to explain the historical situation. Around 587 B.C., King Zedekiah of Judah was blinded by the Babylonians and then taken captive to the city of Babylon. He was the last King of Judah who was a physical descendent of the royal line of David who ruled in Jerusalem. Nobody from David's line has ruled since that time.

After the Jews returned from Babylonian captivity they were placed under the rule of a number of different nations. This includes the Persians, the Greeks led by Alexander the Great, the Ptolemies of Egypt, and the Seleucid's of Syria.

166 B.C. ISRAEL AGAIN HAD KINGS BUT THEY WERE NOT FROM DAVID'S LINE

However, there was about a one hundred year period when the Jews were again ruled by their own kings. Between the time of the Maccabean revolt, 166 B.C. and the time the Romans began to rule Jerusalem, 64 B.C., there were Jewish kings who ruled over the people of Jerusalem.

However, these installed kings were from the Hasmonean dynasty, which was a priestly family. They were not from the tribe of Judah, or the line of David, as the Scriptures demands of the legitimate kings.

The Romans ruled Jerusalem from about 64 B.C. until they destroyed the city and temple in A.D. 70. At that time the Jews were sent into exile. In A.D. 135 the Jews again ruled Jerusalem for a few short years but this revolt was soon crushed. The people then became scattered throughout the earth.

Yet one of the greatest miracles of history occurred on May 14, 1948, when the modern state of Israel was reborn. However, the city of Jerusalem was still under Gentile rule. It was not until 1967 that the Old City of Jerusalem was captured by the Israelis and that the entire city was unified under Jewish control. This is how it remains until the present. Although the Jews again control the city of Jerusalem there is no king ruling in Israel from the line of David.

In other words, the rule from David's family ceased at the time of the Babylonian captivity and it has not ever returned. It will return again when the greater Son of David, the Lord Jesus, begins His rule in Jerusalem. This will only happen when He returns to the earth. Until this occurs, we are in the times of the Gentiles.

THERE WILL BE GENTILE RULE OVER JERUSALEM IN THE FUTURE BY ANTICHRIST

As we mentioned, while there have been periodic episodes of Jewish rule over the city of Jerusalem in the last two thousand six hundred years, Jerusalem has been characterized by Gentile domination.

Though presently there is Jewish control over the city, according to the prophetic Scripture, this control will again be lost to the Gentiles. This is where the predicted Antichrist enters the scene.

ANTICHRIST WILL BE THE LAST GENTILE KING

He will be the last Gentile king who rules over Jerusalem. After making a pact or agreement with the Jewish people to reinstitute their sacrifices and their worship, he will break that agreement. Antichrist will become a worldwide ruler with the seat of His power near the city of Jerusalem. Like Nebuchadnezzar of old, a Gentile king will again dominate the city of Jerusalem.

However, this will be the last time that this occurs. The Second Coming of Jesus Christ will end Gentile rule over Jerusalem once and for all. Yet before this happens, Jerusalem will again be subject to the rule of the Gentiles.

SUMMARY TO QUESTION 25
HOW DOES THE FINAL ANTICHRIST FIT WITH IN WITH THE PERIOD KNOWN AS "THE TIMES OF THE GENTILES?

It is important that we know where the coming Antichrist fits into the plan of biblical history. To be able to understand this, we must appreciate what the Scripture has to say about a period of time Jesus spoke of. It is known as "the times of the Gentiles."

Simply stated, the "times of the Gentiles" consists of the period when the city of Jerusalem has been without a king from the line of David. This began about 587 B.C. at the time of the destruction of the city and the temple, as well as the deportation of the people to Babylon. This time period continues until the present. For the greater part of the last twenty six hundred years, Jerusalem has been under Gentile domination.

While Jerusalem had a few kings which ruled for about a one hundred year period before the time of Christ, 166 B.C. to 64 B.C., none of them were from the royal line of David.

Israel became a modern state in 1948. The city of Jerusalem came under complete Jewish control in 1967 and it is now in the hands of

Jews, not Gentiles. While there is presently Jewish, not Gentile, rule over the city, there is no king ruling from David's line. We are still in the times of the Gentiles.

This is where the predicted Antichrist enters the scene. Once again, there will be Gentile domination over the city when the coming man of sin makes a treaty with the Jewish nation, and then breaks his treaty. At that time he exerts his authoritarian rule over them.

His oppressive domination over Jerusalem will come to an end when Jesus Christ returns to the earth. Until this wonderful event occurs, we are still in the times of the Gentiles. When Christ comes back to the earth the times of the Gentiles will be once-and-for-all over. Jerusalem will again be ruled by a rightful King, the King of Kings!

QUESTION 26

What Qualities Will
Antichrist Possess?

If there is a final Antichrist, who is an actual human being, then what are the qualities which he possesses? What attributes does this man have which makes him distinct from all others? Scripture has the following to say about the characteristics the coming Antichrist will have.

1. HE WILL BE DIFFERENT FROM OTHER MEN

The first thing that we note is that Antichrist will be different from all other men, so different that all the people of the world will be saying, "Who is like him?" John described the response in this manner.

> One of its heads seemed to have a mortal wound, but its mortal wound was healed, and the whole earth marveled as they followed the beast. And they worshiped the dragon, for he had given his authority to the beast, and they worshiped the beast, saying, "Who is like the beast, and who can fight against it?" (Revelation 13:3–4 ESV).

He is one-of-a-kind. With this sort of leader at the control, his kingdom will differ from all other kingdoms, past and present.

2. HE WILL HAVE GREAT INTELLECT

We also find that he will be a person of great intellect. Daniel called him an "insolent king skilled in intrigue." We read.

> And at the latter end of their kingdom, when the transgressors have reached their limit, a king of bold face, one who understands riddles, shall arise (Daniel 8:23 ESV).

The New Testament also emphasizes that this man of sin, the beast, will possess an amazingly high degree of intelligence. For one thing, he rises up out of the sea of nations. The Bible says.

> And I saw a beast rising out of the sea, with ten horns and seven heads, with ten diadems on its horns and blasphemous names on its heads (Revelation 13:1 ESV).

He demonstrates his unique abilities among these ten kings, so that they decide to give their power into his hands. The Bible says.

> These are of one mind, and they hand over their power and authority to the beast (Revelation 17:13 ESV).

Satan himself recognizes his qualifications for leadership and gives to the beast "his power, his throne, and his authority." The Bible says.

> And the beast that I saw was like a leopard; its feet were like a bear's, and its mouth was like a lion's mouth. And to it the dragon gave his power and his throne and great authority (Revelation 13:2 ESV).

This brilliant personage is in the complete control of Satan.

3. HE WILL BE AN OUTSTANDING SPEAKER

Another trait of the beast is his public speaking ability. It seems that he will be able to communicate to the masses. In fact, both testaments emphasize the fact that this future man of sin will be a great speaker; perhaps the greatest orator ever.

The Book of Revelation describes him as having a "mouth like that of a lion." The Scripture reads.

The beast I saw resembled a leopard, but had feet like those of a bear and a mouth like that of a lion. The dragon gave the beast his power and his throne and great authority (Revelation 13:2 NIV).

This passage suggests he has regal or kingly authority with which he speaks.

The content of his speaking is "great blasphemies against God." John wrote.

Then the beast was allowed to speak great blasphemies against God. And he was given authority to do what he wanted for forty-two months. And he spoke terrible words of blasphemy against God, slandering his name and all who live in heaven, who are his temple (Revelation 13:5,6 NLT).

Indeed, he is introduced as a person of blasphemy. Again, we read in the Book of Revelation.

The dragon stood on the shore of the sea. And I saw a beast coming out of the sea. It had ten horns and seven heads, with ten crowns on its horns, and on each head a blasphemous name (Revelation 13:1 NIV).

In the Gospel of John, Jesus described the coming Antichrist as one who comes in his own name. He put it this way.

I have come in my Father's name, and you do not receive me. If another comes in his own name, you will receive him (John 5:43 ESV).

The favorite subject of Antichrist will be himself.

We also read in the book of Daniel that his speech will consist of horrific things against the true God.

> And the king shall do as he wills. He shall exalt himself and magnify himself above every god, and shall speak astonishing things against the God of gods. He shall prosper till the indignation is accomplished; for what is decreed shall be done (Daniel 11:36 ESV).

Therefore, we can conclude that he will be an outstanding orator who will continuously speak evil things against the living and true God.

4. HE WILL BE A GREAT POLITICAL LEADER

The Bible emphasizes the ability of the beast as a political leader. He is described as follows.

> As for the beast that was and is not, it is an eighth but it belongs to the seven, and it goes to destruction. And the ten horns that you saw are ten kings who have not yet received royal power, but they are to receive authority as kings for one hour, together with the beast (Revelation 17:11,12 ESV).

The Antichrist will be the supreme ruler at the head of an organization which will seemingly be controlling the whole earth. The Bible says.

> And they worshiped the dragon, for he had given his authority to the beast, and they worshiped the beast, saying, "Who is like the beast, and who can fight against it?" And the beast was given a mouth uttering haughty and blasphemous words, and it was allowed to exercise authority for forty-two months (Revelation 13:4-5 ESV).

The world will be his for forty-two months.

5. ANTICHRIST WILL BE A GREAT MILITARY LEADER

He also has the qualities of a great military leader. The initial description of him is as follows.

> And I looked, and behold, a white horse! And its rider had a bow, and a crown was given to him, and he came out conquering, and to conquer (Revelation 6:2 ESV).

He will be a great military leader. Indeed, he will be able to conquer nations.

In fact, we are told that he honors "the god of fortresses."

> What he will honor is a god of fortresses-a god his fathers did not acknowledge (Daniel 11:37 NET).

The only "god" he will honor is the god of military power. In other words, his "god," his religion, is to build up his military might so that he might conquer others. Indeed, with this overwhelming military power as his god he will destroy all those who challenge him.

On the other hand, those who give their allegiance to this "coming Caesar" will be rewarded by him.

> To those who recognize him he will grant considerable honor. He will place them in authority over many people, and he will parcel out land for a price (Daniel 11:39 NET).

6. HE WILL BE AN ECONOMIC GENIUS: HE WILL CONTROL THE COMMERCE OF THE WORLD

This man of sin will also control the economics of the world. Indeed, no commerce will be able to take place without recognizing him. The Bible says his promoter, the false prophet, causes everyone in the world to take the mark of this beast.

> He also caused everyone (small and great, rich and poor, free and slave) to obtain a mark on their right hand or on their forehead. Thus no one was allowed to buy or sell things unless he bore the mark of the beast- that is, his name or his number. This calls for wisdom: Let the one who has insight

calculate the beast's number, for it is man's number, and his number is 666 (Revelation 13:16-18 ESV).

He will be in control of everything.

7. HE WILL BE THE OBJECT OF WORSHIP

Since this coming "man of sin" has all of these abilities, he will also be an object of worship. The Word of God informs us of the following.

And all those who live on the earth will worship the beast, everyone whose name has not been written since the foundation of the world in the book of life belonging to the Lamb who was killed (Revelation 13:8 NET).

These things characterize the coming Antichrist according to Scripture. As can readily be seen, he will be a unique individual with outstanding abilities. Tragically, these abilities will be used for evil, not for good.

SUMMARY TO QUESTION 26
WHAT QUALITIES WILL A FINAL ANTICHRIST POSSESS?

The Bible speaks of a final Antichrist which will come on the world scene some seven years before the return of Jesus Christ. This man of sin, the beast, will have some amazing qualities.

Scripture says that he will be unlike all other men. This final Antichrist will be a one-of-a-kind human being. He has no peers, nobody has ever appeared who is like him.

Among his unique abilities is that of public speaking. Antichrist will speak like a king. He will have an uncanny ability to sway the masses in his speech. Seemingly, it will be almost hypnotic. The content of his speech will be words of blasphemy against the God of Scripture.

Coupled with his public speaking capacity is the great intellect he will possess. This lawless one will seemingly have all the answers to the problems of the world. People will flock to him because of his problem-solving ability, and his magnetic way of explaining how they can be solved. Everyone will want to hear him.

Because of these abilities he possesses, the final Antichrist will be the greatest political leader the world has ever known. He will be able to accomplish things which other politicians have not been able to accomplish. Antichrist will make the impossible possible.

His abilities will not be limited to political realities. He will also be a military genius who defeats enemy armies with ease. Nothing seems beyond his abilities.

The man of sin will eventually be a world ruler who will control the economy of the entire world. He will seemingly own everything.

This will lead to the final quality or characteristic he will possess, the need to be worshipped. He will, in fact, demand worship from those who live upon the earth.

The worship of this individual will be facilitated by the religious leader who is his promoter, the false prophet. Those who do not worship this Antichrist will be put to death. The entire world will be his for a short period of time.

This briefly sums up the unique attributes that the coming Antichrist will possess.

What Will Be The Career Of Antichrist?

Scripture tells us a number of things about the events in the life of the coming man of sin, the final Antichrist. Though we cannot be absolutely certain about the exact chronology of these events, we are able to list the highlights. They can be summed up as follows.

1. HE WILL APPEAR AT THE TIME OF THE END

Scripture is clear that the final Antichrist will not appear on the stage of history until the time of the end. The Lord said the following to the prophet Daniel.

> As Gabriel approached the place where I was standing, I became so terrified that I fell with my face to the ground. "Son of man," he said, "you must understand that the events you have seen in your vision relate to the time of the end" (Daniel 8:17 NLT).

Indeed, his coming signals the time of the end. He cannot appear before these last days, since his coming sets the stage for the soon return of Jesus Christ. Therefore, it is clear that the final Antichrist has not yet arrived on the scene.

2. HIS ARRIVAL WILL SIGNAL THE BEGINNING OF THE PROPHETIC PERIOD, THE DAY OF THE LORD

The Bible says that Antichrist's coming will commence a prophetic period known as the "Day of the Lord." Paul wrote about this time to the church at Thessalonica. He said.

> And now, brothers and sisters, let us tell you about the coming again of our Lord Jesus Christ and how we will be gathered together to meet him. Please don't be so easily shaken and troubled by those who say that the day of the Lord has already begun. Even if they claim to have had a vision, a revelation, or a letter supposedly from us, don't believe them. Don't be fooled by what they say. For that day will not come until there is a great rebellion against God and the man of lawlessness is revealed—the one who brings destruction (2 Thessalonians 2:1-3 NLT).

This period cannot begin until Antichrist arrives on the scene.

3. HE IS PRESENTLY BEING RESTRAINED BY SOMEONE OR SOMETHING

We know that someone or something is presently restraining the appearance of Antichrist. Paul wrote the following to the Thessalonians.

> And you know what is holding him back, for he can be revealed only when his time comes (2 Thessalonians 2:6 NLT).

The pre-tribulation rapture view holds that the Lord will take the true believers out of the world before the great tribulation period. According to this view, immediately following the rapture of the church, the final Antichrist will be revealed. Until that time, his identity will remain unknown to the world.

The reason he cannot be revealed before this time is because the Holy Spirit of God, through the believers living upon the earth, is presently restraining the coming man of sin. Once the believers are removed through the rapture, this evil personage can then be revealed.

Other views of the rapture of the church, the mid-tribulation, the pre-wrath, and post-tribulation view, believe the restrainer of Antichrist consists of something else. However, all agree on this point: the final Antichrist is presently being restrained.

4. HE WILL APPEAR AS AN INCONSPICUOUS FIGURE

Antichrist appears on the scene of world history as an inconspicuous figure. This is explained for us in the Book of Daniel. We read of his rise from obscurity.

> After that, in my vision at night I looked, and there before me was a fourth beast—terrifying and frightening and very powerful. It had large iron teeth; it crushed and devoured its victims and trampled underfoot whatever was left. It was different from all the former beasts, and it had ten horns. "While I was thinking about the horns, there before me was another horn, a little one, which came up among them; and three of the first horns were uprooted before it. This horn had eyes like the eyes of a human being and a mouth that spoke boastfully" (Daniel 7:7-8 NIV).

He is called a little horn. This indicates his rise is from relative obscurity. Therefore, he will not be someone who has an immediate high profile.

5. HE WILL APPEAR AS A MAN OF PEACE

He starts out upon a career of conquest by peaceful means. In the Book of Revelation, we are introduced to the four horsemen of the apocalypse. Scripture says.

> I watched as the Lamb opened the first of the seven seals. Then I heard one of the four living creatures say in a voice

like thunder, "Come!" I looked, and there before me was a white horse! Its rider held a bow, and he was given a crown, and he rode out as a conqueror bent on conquest (Revelation 6:1–2 NIV).

While the rider on the white horse may not be a direct reference to Antichrist but rather to many antichrists, we do know that his career will begin by peaceful means.

6. HE WILL MAKE A PEACE TREATY WITH ISRAEL

The final Antichrist makes, or confirms, a peace treaty with the Jews, a covenant of peace. Daniel wrote about this agreement.

He will make a treaty with the people for a period of one set of seven (Daniel 9:27 NLT).

The phrase "one set of seven" refers to a period of seven years. It is a seven year agreement that involves the nation of Israel.

This man of sin will do all of this in his own name, or authority. Jesus said of him.

I have come in my Father's name, and you do not receive me. If another comes in his own name, you will receive him (John 5:43 ESV).

He will be welcomed by the Jews because of this treaty. The nation which rejected Jesus as their Messiah will receive this man.

The particular peace treaty will begin the seventieth week of Daniel, the last seven years in this age in which we live before Jesus Christ returns. Therefore, this is a very significant event.

5. THIS TREATY WILL INVOLVE JERUSALEM AND THE TEMPLE MOUNT

This treaty will seemingly allow the Jews to take possession of the area of the Temple Mount, the place where the First and Second Temple stood. We read about the measuring of the temple in the Book of Revelation. It says.

> Then I was given a measuring rod like a staff, and I was told, "Rise and measure the temple of God and the altar and those who worship there, but do not measure the court outside the temple; leave that out, for it is given over to the nations, and they will trample the holy city for forty-two months. And I will grant authority to my two witnesses, and they will prophesy for 1,260 days, clothed in sackcloth" (Revelation 11:1–3 ESV).

The fact that the temple is measured assumes that it exists at that time. We are not told what Antichrist receives in return for making this deal with the nation.

6. HE WILL HEAD UP A TEN NATION POLITICAL CONFEDERACY

It seems that at the same time he negotiates this peace treaty with the Jews, he becomes the head of a ten-nation confederacy. Scripture speaks of this confederacy in the following manner.

> The dragon stood on the shore of the sea. And I saw a beast coming out of the sea. It had ten horns and seven heads, with ten crowns on its horns, and on each head a blasphemous name (Revelation 13:1 NIV).

We read the explanation of the ten horns in the Book of Revelation. It says.

> The ten horns you saw are ten kings who have not yet received a kingdom, but who for one hour will receive authority as kings along with the beast. They have one purpose and will give their power and authority to the beast (Revelation 17:12–13 NIV).

The ten horns are ten kings. They give their complete authority to this beast.

9. THE CONFEDERACY WILL BECOME A WORLD POWER

By the middle of the final seven-year great tribulation period, this ten-nation confederacy will be a world power. The Book of Revelation says.

> It was given power to make war against God's people and to conquer them. And it was given authority over every tribe, people, language and nation (Revelation 13:7 NIV).

He has complete authority over everything and everyone.

10. HE WILL BREAK THE AGREEMENTS HE MADE

Since this final Antichrist is the ultimate liar, he will break the agreements and various the alliances which he had previously made.

First, the Babylonian system of this time, which is described as a woman riding a beast, is no longer needed. Antichrist only used it to gain world power. Once he has the power, this institution can be done away with. The ten nation confederation, which is under his control, destroys this system called the harlot or prostitute. The Bible says.

> The beast and the ten horns you saw will hate the prostitute. They will bring her to ruin and leave her naked; they will eat her flesh and burn her with fire. For God has put it into their hearts to accomplish his purpose by agreeing to give the beast their power to rule, until God's words are fulfilled (Revelation 17:16–17 NIV).

This reveals that it was foolish to place any trust in this man.

11. HE WILL BREAK THE COVENANT WITH THE JEWS

The agreement with the Jews will also be broken in the midst of the seven year period. The Bible explains it this way.

He will confirm a covenant with many for one 'seven.' In the middle of the 'seven' he will put an end to sacrifice and offering. And at the temple he will set up an abomination that causes desolation, until the end that is decreed is poured out on him (Daniel 9:27 NIV).

Antichrist will put an end to the sacrifices which were being offered in the temple. He will then turn upon the nation which embraced him.

Paul wrote about what will occur when the people think they are at peace.

Now, brothers and sisters, about times and dates we do not need to write to you, for you know very well that the day of the Lord will come like a thief in the night. While people are saying, "Peace and safety," destruction will come on them suddenly, as labor pains on a pregnant woman, and they will not escape (1 Thessalonians 5:1-3 NIV).

There will be no safety for them. In fact, when they think they have peace then destruction will suddenly come upon them.

12. HE WILL RECEIVE A FATAL HEAD WOUND

This seems to be *the* significant event in the life of the coming Antichrist. Scripture tells us that his personality changes after he receives this wound to the head. The Bible says.

One of its heads seemed to have a mortal wound, but its mortal wound was healed, and the whole earth marveled as they followed the beast (Revelation 13:3 ESV).

Whether or not he actually dies, it certainly appears that way to everyone on the earth.

13. HE WILL DESCEND INTO THE ABYSS

After this head wound occurs, this personage descends into the abyss, the bottomless pit. The Book of Revelation says.

> And when they [the two witnesses] have finished their testimony, the beast that rises from the bottomless pit will make war on them and conquer them and kill them (Revelation 11:7 ESV).

The abyss is the bottomless pit, the prison house of evil spirits. The beast becomes a different person after he goes down into the abyss and then returns.

14. HE IS RAISED BACK TO LIFE: THE WORLD IS AMAZED

Something happens to this political leader at this point, he is raised back to life. This event is described as follows.

> One of the beast's heads appeared to have been killed, but the lethal wound had been healed. And the whole world followed the beast in amazement. . . He exercised all the ruling authority of the first beast on his behalf, and made the earth and those who inhabit it worship the first beast, the one whose lethal wound had been healed. . . . and, by the signs he was permitted to perform on behalf of the beast, he deceived those who live on the earth. He told those who live on the earth to make an image to the beast who had been wounded by the sword, but still lived (Revelation 13:3,12,14 NET).

This causes the people of the world to be astonished. The Word of God puts it this way.

> The beast that you saw was, and is not, and is about to rise from the bottomless pit and go to destruction. And the dwellers on earth whose names have not been written in the

book of life from the foundation of the world will marvel to see the beast, because it was and is not and is to come (Revelation 17:8 ESV).

This beast seemingly rises from the dead.

15. HE BECOMES THE BEAST, A MAN CONTROLLED BY SATAN

This man goes from a world leader in politics to a worldwide dictator. He is now the beast, a satanically controlled individual. The Bible says.

> Now the beast that I saw was like a leopard, but its feet were like a bear's, and its mouth was like a lion's mouth. The dragon gave the beast his power, his throne, and great authority to rule. One of the beast's heads appeared to have been killed, but the lethal wound had been healed. And the whole world followed the beast in amazement; they worshiped the dragon because he had given ruling authority to the beast, and they worshiped the beast too, saying: "Who is like the beast?" and "Who is able to make war against him?" The beast was given a mouth speaking proud words and blasphemies, and he was permitted to exercise ruling authority for forty-two months (Revelation 13:2-5 NET).

There is an entire change of character of this personage.

16. HE SUBDUES THREE OF THE TEN KINGS

Three of the ten kings of the ten nation confederation are uprooted by this beast. The Book of Daniel says.

> As for the ten horns, out of this kingdom ten kings shall arise, and another shall arise after them; he shall be different from the former ones, and shall put down three kings (Daniel 7:24 NIV).

This leader now is in complete control of these nations. As to exactly when this happens during the final seven year period is a matter of debate.

17. HE DESECRATES THE TEMPLE IN JERUSALEM

The holiest spot on earth for the Jews is the Temple Mount in Jerusalem. It was the site of the First and Second Temple and will also be the site of the Third Temple.

This Third Temple now becomes a place of desecration. The man of sin, who is the unholiest of all the people on the earth, comes to the most Holy Place. Indeed, in five different places in Scripture we are told of the horrific event (Daniel 9:27; Daniel 12:11; Matthew 24:15; 2 Thessalonians 2:1-4; Revelation 11:2).

This beast will claim Deity for himself. Paul wrote.

> He will exalt himself and defy every god there is and tear down every object of adoration and worship. He will position himself in the temple of God, claiming that he himself is God (2 Thessalonians 2:4 NLT).

He defies the living God and makes outrageous claims. Included is the claim to Deity. This beast offers himself to the world as a god in the place of Jesus Christ, the true and living God. He is truly an "anti" Christ.

18. THE BEAST PERSECUTES THE JEWS

Persecution of the Jews now begins. The Book of Daniel says.

> As I looked, this horn made war with the saints and prevailed over them (Daniel 7:21 ESV).

We also read of this in the Book of Revelation. It says the following.

Its tail swept a third of the stars out of the sky and flung them to the earth. The dragon stood in front of the woman who was about to give birth, so that it might devour her child the moment he was born. She gave birth to a son, a male child, who "will rule all the nations with an iron scepter." And her child was snatched up to God and to his throne. The woman fled into the wilderness to a place prepared for her by God, where she might be taken care of for 1,260 days (Revelation 12:4-6 NIV).

In this context, the woman refers to the nation of Israel. The Jews are his special target. This is not surprising since the devil has targeted the chosen people, from the very beginning.

19. HE RULES POLITICALLY AND CURSES THE LIVING GOD

The political rule of the entire world begins. The Bible says the following will happen.

They worshiped the dragon for giving the beast such power, and they also worshiped the beast. "Who is as great as the beast?" they exclaimed. "Who is able to fight against him?" Then the beast was allowed to speak great blasphemies against God. And he was given authority to do whatever he wanted for forty-two months. And he spoke terrible words of blasphemy against God, slandering his name and his dwelling—that is, those who dwell in heaven. And the beast was allowed to wage war against God's holy people and to conquer them. And he was given authority to rule over every tribe and people and language and nation. And all the people who belong to this world worshiped the beast. They are the ones whose names were not written in the Book of Life before the world was made—the Book that belongs to the Lamb who was slaughtered (Revelation 13:4-8 NLT).

As a worldwide ruler, the beast feels free to curse the God of Scripture.

The Book of Daniel talks about this personage speaking boastfully. We read.

> While I was thinking about the horns, there before me was another horn, a little one, which came up among them; and three of the first horns were uprooted before it. This horn had eyes like the eyes of a human being and a mouth that spoke boastfully (Daniel 7:8 NIV).

Thus, his ability to speak boastfully is emphasized in both testaments.

HE WILL ATTEMPT TO MAKE CHANGES IN THE CALENDAR

He will also attempt to make changes in the calendar that have been established by the law.

> He will speak words against the Most High. He will harass the holy ones of the Most High continually. His intention will be to change times established by law (Daniel 7:25 NET).

This could refer to the calendar itself or it may be a specific reference to changing "holy days." In other words, he may change the calendar from A.D. and B.C., refuse to recognize Easter and Christmas, etc. In sum, there will be no acknowledgement of Jesus Christ as long as he is ruling.

Interestingly, there was an unsuccessful attempt during the French Revolution to replace the Christian (Gregorian) calendar with a Revolutionary calendar. It seems the Antichrist will do something similar.

20. HE IS PROMOTED BY A SECOND BEAST: THE FALSE PROPHET

Another beast comes on the scene to promote Antichrist. He is known as the "false prophet." The Bible explains him as follows.

Then I saw another beast come up out of the earth. He had two horns like those of a lamb, but he spoke with the voice of a dragon. He exercised all the authority of the first beast. And he required all the earth and its people to worship the first beast, whose fatal wound had been healed. He did astounding miracles, even making fire flash down to earth from the sky while everyone was watching (Revelation 13:11-13 NLT).

This second beast looks like a lamb but is, in point of fact, a dragon. The dragon is one of many symbols of the devil.

21. PEOPLE ARE FORCED TO WORSHIP A LIKENESS OF HIM

There is a tangible image made of the beast which the people of the earth are forced to worship. The Book of Revelation says.

He performed momentous signs, even making fire come down from heaven in front of people and, by the signs he was permitted to perform on behalf of the beast, he deceived those who live on the earth. He told those who live on the earth to make an image to the beast who had been wounded by the sword, but still lived. The second beast was empowered to give life to the image of the first beast so that it could speak, and could cause all those who did not worship the image of the beast to be killed (Revelation 13:13-15 NET).

While there are those who willingly worship the beast, others have no choice. Indeed, they must worship or die!

22. EVERYONE MUST RECEIVE THE MARK OF THE BEAST

Scripture says that the false prophet, the second beast, then forces everyone to take a particular "mark of the beast." Nobody is exempt. The Bible says.

He required everyone—great and small, rich and poor, slave and free—to be given a mark on the right hand or on the forehead. And no one could buy or sell anything without that mark, which was either the name of the beast or the number representing his name. Wisdom is needed to understand this. Let the one who has understanding solve the number of the beast, for it is the number of a man. His number is 666 (Revelation 13:16-18 NLT).

The false prophet will attempt to make everyone on the face of the earth receive the "mark of the beast." Nobody will be able to buy or sell without this mark.

23. HE KILLS THE TWO WITNESSES

There are two witnesses who testify to the Lord for three and one half years. Eventually the Lord will allow the first beast, the man of sin, to murder them. The Bible says.

And when they have finished their testimony, the beast that rises from the bottomless pit will make war on them and conquer them and kill them (Revelation 11:7 ESV).

The Lord allows this beast to prevail for a short period of time.

24. HE WAGES WAR ON GOD'S PEOPLE

The man of sin, the first beast, then wages an all-out war on the people of God. The Bible describes it as follows.

This means that God's holy people must endure persecution patiently, obeying his commands and maintaining their faith in Jesus. And I heard a voice from heaven saying, "Write this down: Blessed are those who die in the Lord from now on. Yes, says the Spirit, they are blessed indeed, for they will rest from their hard work; for their good deeds follow them!" (Revelation 14:12,13 NLT).

He will persecute those who come to faith in Jesus during the period. They are known as the "tribulation saints." In other words, he attempts to destroy all those who belong to the Lord.

25. THE TEN KINGS WILL DESTROY BABYLON

The ten kings, who are under the control of the beast, will destroy Babylon. We read the following.

> 'Woe! Woe to you, great city, dressed in fine linen, purple and scarlet, and glittering with gold, precious stones and pearls! In one hour such great wealth has been brought to ruin! "Every sea captain, and all who travel by ship, the sailors, and all who earn their living from the sea, will stand far off" (Revelation 18:16-17 NIV).

Babylon the Great is destroyed.

26. HE GATHERS ALL NATIONS AGAINST JERUSALEM

The preparation is now made for a final war. All nations are gathered against Jerusalem in the final conflict, the War, or Campaign, of Armageddon. In the Old Testament, we read.

> A prophecy: The word of the LORD concerning Israel. The LORD, who stretches out the heavens, who lays the foundation of the earth, and who forms the spirit in human beings, declares: I am going to make Jerusalem a cup that sends all the surrounding peoples reeling. Judah will be besieged as well as Jerusalem (Zechariah 12:1-2 NIV).

Later in the Book of Zechariah we read about this conflict. It says.

> A day of the LORD is coming, Jerusalem, when your possessions will be plundered and divided up within your very walls. I will gather all the nations to Jerusalem to fight against it; the city will be captured, the houses ransacked,

and the women ravished. Half of the city will go into exile, but the rest of the people will not be taken from the city. Then the LORD will go out and fight against those nations, as he fights on a day of battle (Zechariah 14:1-3 NIV).

We also read about this awesome conflict in the Book of Revelation.

So they assembled them at the place called in Hebrew, Armagedon (Revelation 16:16 HCSB).

The beast then attempts to make war with the Living God. Scripture speaks of this feeble attempt.

Then I saw the beast and the kings of the earth and their armies gathered together to make war against the rider on the horse and his army (Revelation 19:19 NIV).

All of this is in preparation for the final battle.

The carnage of this battle is unimaginable. Scripture explains it this way.

So the angel swung his sickle on the earth and loaded the grapes into the great winepress of God's wrath. And the grapes were trodden in the winepress outside the city, and blood flowed from the winepress in a stream about 180 miles long and as high as a horse's bridle (Revelation 14:19-20 NLT).

Such is the punishment for those who do not turn to the Lord.

27. HE ATTEMPTS TO FIGHT THE LORD HIMSELF

This beast foolishly attempts to fight the Lord Jesus, the rider on the horse, as He returns to the earth with His saints. The Book of Revelation explains it this way.

And I saw the beast and the kings of the earth with their armies gathered to make war against him who was sitting on the horse and against his army (Revelation 19:19 ESV).

As can be imagined, this will be a one-sided battle.

28. HE IS CAPTURED AND THEN CAST ALIVE INTO THE LAKE OF FIRE

The end to the beast was predicted long ago. We first read about it in Daniel. It says.

I looked then because of the sound of the great words that the horn was speaking. And as I looked, the beast was killed, and its body destroyed and given over to be burned with fire (Daniel 7:11 ESV).

His end is also recorded in the book of Revelation. The Bible says the following about his demise.

Now the beast was seized, and along with him the false prophet who had performed the signs on his behalf signs by which he deceived those who had received the mark of the beast and those who worshiped his image. Both of them were thrown alive into the lake of fire burning with sulfur (Revelation 19:20 NET).

This gives us the main highlights of the personage who is to come, the final Antichrist. His career consists of one evil deed after another.

Fortunately, his time on the earth is limited. However, it will be the worst period in the history of the world.

SUMMARY TO QUESTION 27
WHAT WILL BE THE CAREER OF ANTICHRIST?

The coming man of sin, the beast, the Antichrist, is a prominent figure in Scripture. Indeed, he is the outstanding figure on the earth at the end times. We find that the Bible tells us a number of things about this personage. We can sum up the highlights as follows.

First, he cannot come on the scene until the time of the end. It occurs when the restrainer is taken out of the way. Once this occurs, then the final Antichrist can then be revealed. This will begin a period of time called the "Day of the Lord."

His career will begin in relative obscurity but he will quickly rise to leadership. Antichrist will rule over a ten-nation confederation which makes up part of the old Roman Empire. He will seem to be a man of peace. This man of sin will make a treaty involving the nation of Israel. It appears that this treaty will allow the Jews to rebuild their temple and restore their system of sacrifices.

After three and one half years, everything changes. A significant event takes place around this time. Antichrist will receive a fatal head wound by means of a sword. He will recover from this death blow. However, after his recovery this loving man of peace now becomes an evil beast. It is at this time he begins to terrorize the world and all its inhabitants. This wicked personage will break the treaty with Israel. He will stop the sacrifices in the temple in Jerusalem.

There are two witnesses which the Lord raises up to counter the beast. The Lord allows the beast to kill them after their three and one half year ministry.

The beast will then begin an unrelenting persecution of the chosen people, the Jews. Providentially, the Lord will supernaturally protect His chosen people from ultimate annihilation.

The people of the world will be forced to worship a likeness of the beast. This will be instituted by a religious leader who is his promoter, the false prophet. Each individual must personally receive the mark, or branding, of the beast. Those who do not will be put to death.

Eventually this beast gathers all the nations against the city of Jerusalem as the campaign of Armageddon is waged. His attempt to destroy the chosen people is again thwarted by the Lord. In this case, it occurs at the Second Coming of Jesus Christ to the earth. This beast will foolishly attempt to do battle with the Lord Jesus when He returns to the earth with His saints. Clearly, this battle will be one-sided.

This beast, along with the false Prophet, is thrown alive into the Lake of Fire where they will be tormented day and night forever and ever.

This is a brief summation of what Scripture says will happen to the final Antichrist.

QUESTION 28

How Long Will The Antichrist Rule?

We know that the Bible says that the final Antichrist will rule for a limited period of time. Scripture specifically tells us the exact amount of time he will govern. It is for three and one half years. The evidence is as follows.

WE MUST UNDERSTAND DANIEL'S PROPHECY OF THE SEVENTY SEVENS (SEVENTY WEEKS)

To understand why it is only three and one half years that this man of sin rules the world, we must first look at the prophecy of Daniel's seventy sevens. It is also known as the seventy "weeks" for the Hebrew term translated as week means seven. Daniel the prophet was told that seventy weeks, or seventy sevens, are determined upon the nation of Israel. He wrote.

> "Seventy 'sevens' are decreed for your people and your holy city to finish transgression, to put an end to sin, to atone for wickedness, to bring in everlasting righteousness, to seal up vision and prophecy and to anoint the Most Holy Place (Daniel 9:24 NIV).

In this context, the "sevens" are years. Therefore, the seventy sevens consist of a total of four hundred and ninety years. Hence there are four hundred and ninety years which are determined upon the people of Israel until everlasting righteousness is brought about.

Four hundred and eighty three of these years, sixty-nine of the seventy sevens, have already been fulfilled. One seven year period remains. This is known, among other things, as "the seventieth week of Daniel." In other words, it is the last of the seventy sevens.

We are told that this man of sin will make, or confirm, a covenant, or agreement, with the nation Israel. This covenant is supposed to last seven years. The Bible says.

> And he shall make a strong covenant with many for one week, and for half of the week he shall put an end to sacrifice and offering. And on the wing of abominations shall come one who makes desolate, until the decreed end is poured out on the desolator (Daniel 9:27 ESV).

Therefore, one more period of seven years remains to be fulfilled.

HIS RULE WILL BE THREE AND ONE HALF YEARS LONG

There are a number of different passages in the Bible which make it clear that Antichrist will reign for only three and one half years of these seven years. The first three and one half years of the seventieth week of Daniel constitutes the rise of this final Antichrist. His real power will only take place in the final three and one half years. Scripture has the following to say.

HE WILL RULE FORTY-TWO MONTHS

In the Book of Revelation it says his rule will be for forty-two months. Scripture says the following.

> And the beast was given a mouth uttering haughty and blasphemous words, and it was allowed to exercise authority for forty-two months (Revelation 13:5 ESV).

The time of forty-two months equals three and one half years.

IT WILL BE FOR A TIME, TIMES, AND HALF A TIME

In the Book of Daniel we are told that his rule will be a time, times, and half a time. It reads in this manner.

> And I heard the man clothed in linen, who was above the waters of the stream; he raised his right hand and his left hand toward heaven and swore by him who lives forever that it would be for a time, times, and half a time, and that when the shattering of the power of the holy people comes to an end all these things would be finished (Daniel 7:25 ESV).

This expression is repeated later in Daniel. We read.

> The man clothed in linen, who was above the waters of the river, lifted his right hand and his left hand toward heaven, and I heard him swear by him who lives forever, saying, "It will be for a time, times and half a time. When the power of the holy people has been finally broken, all these things will be completed" (Daniel 12:7 NIV).

The Book of Revelation also describes it this way. The Bible says.

> The woman was given the two wings of a great eagle, so that she might fly to the place prepared for her in the wilderness, where she would be taken care of for a time, times and half a time, out of the serpent's reach (Revelation 12:14 NIV).

This is another way of describing three and one half years. A time equals one year, times or two times equals two years, and half a time is six months. When we add these numbers together the total amount becomes three and one half years.

THE LENGTH WILL BE 1,260 DAYS

Finally we have his rule calculated at 1,260 days. The Book of Revelation says.

> And I will appoint my two witnesses, and they will prophesy for 1,260 days, clothed in sackcloth (Revelation 11:3 NIV).

This number is later repeated. It constitutes the time the woman, most likely Israel, is taken care of by God.

> The woman fled into the wilderness to a place prepared for her by God, where she might be taken care of for 1,260 days (Revelation 12:6 NIV).

Therefore, the same period of time, three and one half years, is described for us in Scripture in three different ways. This is the amount of time which the beast, this coming Caesar, will rule upon the earth. While his worldwide rule will be horrific, the good news is that it will come to an end after a relatively short period of time.

SUMMARY TO QUESTION 28
HOW LONG WILL THE ANTICHRIST RULE?

The Bible does not let us speculate as to the exact time Antichrist will be on the stage of history. Rather it tells us. For seven years he will be a public figure but it is the last three and one half years in which he will terrorize the world. His great power and authority will, therefore, be limited to the final three and one half year period.

There are a number of passages in Scripture which help us determine this. To begin with, the prophecy of the seventy weeks, the seventy sevens, which the prophet Daniel received, divided the history of the nation Israel into three distinct periods. This adds up to four hundred and ninety years.

The first two periods have been fulfilled. They encompassed four hundred and eighty three years. There is one future seven-year period which needs to take place. This is known as the seventieth week of Daniel, the time of Jacob's trouble, or the great tribulation.

This period begins when the man of sin, the beast, the Antichrist, signs a peace treaty with the nation of Israel. From a relatively lowly position, he will become a world leader some three and one half years later. It is in these three and one half years which the great judgments of the Lord will come upon the earth.

The fact that his reign is limited to three and one half years is made clear in a number of different places in Scripture through three different expressions: forty-two months, one thousand two hundred and sixty days, and a time, two times, and one half a time. Each of these expressions adds up to three and one half years.

Consequently there is no room for doubt about the time this evil personage will be on center-stage.

The fact that the rule of Antichrist is limited to this time period is indeed good news; he will not be around for very long. The bad news is that he is indeed coming.

QUESTION 29

Is There An Exact Time
When Antichrist Is Coming?

One of the interesting questions regarding the coming Antichrist concerns the exact timing of his arrival on the scene of history. The Bible says that Jesus came in the "fullness of time."

> But when the fullness of time had come, God sent forth his Son, born of woman, born under the law (Galatians 4:4 ESV).

Is there such a thing as the "fullness of time" for the Antichrist? Is there a time when he must arrive on the earth? What does the Bible say?

IT IS GOD'S PLAN, NOT HIS

The timing of the return of the Lord is entirely up to God Himself. Nobody else is consulted, and nothing can slow it down or speed it up. We read the following dialogue of the Lord Jesus with His disciples after Jesus had come back from the dead.

> When the apostles were with Jesus, they kept asking him, "Lord, are you going to free Israel now and restore our kingdom?" "The Father sets those dates," he replied, "and they are not for you to know. But when the Holy Spirit has come upon you, you will receive power and will tell people

261

about me everywhere—in Jerusalem, throughout Judea, in
Samaria, and to the ends of the earth" (Acts 1:6-8 NLT).

Jesus said that God the Father sets the times of His kingdom. Therefore,
there is no specific time the Lord has committed Himself to return.
This being the case, then the question becomes this: how can Satan
know when the Lord will return? The simple answer is, "he cannot."

In fact, Christ made this clear earlier when He explained who knows
about the timing of His return.

> But about that day or hour no one knows, not even the
> angels in heaven, nor the Son, but only the Father (Matthew
> 24:36 NIV).

It is only the Father who knows. Therefore, the timing of the Lord's
return is unknown to the devil.

Consequently, Satan must always have someone available in each generation to fulfill the predictions of the final Antichrist.

HE IS PRESENTLY BEING RESTRAINED

We are told that the Lord is presently restraining the final Antichrist.
Paul emphasized this when he wrote to the Thessalonians. He said.

> And you know what is restraining him now so that he may
> be revealed in his time (2 Thessalonians 2:6 ESV).

There is a time when the man of sin will come, but this timing is not
in his hands. It is completely in the hands of the Lord.

THERE ARE MANY ANTICHRISTS

Antichrists have always existed. John made it clear that there had been
many Antichrists who had already come on the scene at his time.
He wrote.

Children, it is the last hour, and as you have heard that antichrist is coming, so now many antichrists have come. Therefore we know that it is the last hour (1 John 2:18 ESV).

Therefore, the final Antichrist will be one in the long list of many antichrists who have already appeared. Each and every generation has their own "Antichrist." Consequently, there is always a candidate for the "man of sin." It will all depend upon when the Lord wants to institute His end-time program.

While this predicted "man of sin," will be the final Antichrist, he certainly will not be the only "antichrist" the world has seen.

HE WILL BE A NORMAL HUMAN BEING

Therefore, we assume that this coming world leader is born like any other human being. He only becomes the "final Antichrist" when it is time for the Lord's kingdom to be established.

Consequently, there is nothing supernatural about his birth, or his upbringing. Indeed, he will not even know that he is this final Antichrist until the Lord removes His church, the true believers, from the earth, the rapture.

We can make the comparison between this final Antichrist and Jesus. At His temptation, the devil offered Jesus all the kingdoms of this world. Christ merely had to worship the devil and the kingdoms would be His. He refused. It seems that the final Antichrist will receive the same temptation from Satan.

However, instead of refusing, he will bow to the devil. Satan will then empower him and, therefore, the kingdoms of this world will belong to this "man of sin" for a short period of time. Yet his reign will end with the Second Coming of Jesus Christ to the earth.

SUMMARY TO QUESTION 29
IS THERE AN EXACT TIME WHEN ANTICHRIST IS COMING?

One of the many fascinating questions with respect to the coming Antichrist concerns the time of his appearing on the world scene. Is there a set time in which he will appear? If so, does the devil know when this time will occur?

While there is indeed a set time in which the Antichrist is coming, this is something which is known to God, and to Him alone. Nobody, not even the angels in heaven, knows when the Lord Jesus is coming back to the earth. This being the case, there has to be an available Antichrist living at every time period in history. Unless the Lord reveals the timing of His coming to the devil, the devil must always be prepared to have someone available to fill the role of Antichrist.

Scripture also tells us that the Antichrist is presently being restrained by the Lord. Until the time the restrainer is taken out of the way, the Antichrist cannot be revealed. This restraining is something the Lord continues to do and will continue to do. Only when He gives the word can the restrainer be removed.

Furthermore, John said that many Antichrists had already come in his day (late first century). The coming Antichrist will be the final one in a long line of those who have opposed the Lord. Every generation has its own Antichrist.

Therefore, the time of the revelation of the predicted man of sin is something which God alone knows. Consequently, it will occur when the Lord desires it to occur, not before.

QUESTION 30

Will The Antichrist Actually Be Raised From The Dead?

The resurrection of Jesus Christ is the cornerstone of the Christian faith. Without the resurrection, there is no Christianity. Paul wrote to the Corinthians.

> For I delivered to you as of first importance what I also received: that Christ died for our sins in accordance with the Scriptures, that he was buried, that he was raised on the third day in accordance with the Scriptures (1 Corinthians 15:3,4 ESV).

No resurrection of Jesus, no Christianity, it's that simple.

ANTICHRIST TRIES TO IMITATE JESUS CHRIST

We know that the Antichrist, by definition, attempts to parody or imitate Jesus Christ. Indeed, he is the "anti" Christ. Consequently, we should not be surprised if he attempts to imitate the greatest miracle which Jesus performed, the resurrection from the dead.

In the Book of Revelation, there are several passages which seem to indicate that the final Antichrist actually dies and is soon thereafter brought back to life. Does this mean Antichrist duplicates the greatest miracle of Jesus? Does he actually supernaturally return from the dead?

Christians are divided on this issue as to whether this recorded resurrection is counterfeit or genuine. We can present the case for each of these viewpoints as follows.

THE CASE FOR A GENUINE RESURRECTION OF ANTICHRIST

There are a number of reasons as to why the Bible speaks of an actual resurrection of the beast, this coming "man of sin." They can be listed as follows.

ANTICHRIST ACTUALLY DIES

Scripture makes it clear that the final Antichrist actually does die. The same expression that is used in the Book of Revelation of Jesus' violent death is also used for the violent death of this beast, this man of sin. We read of what happened to Jesus.

> And between the throne and the four living creatures and among the elders I saw a Lamb standing, as though it had been slain, with seven horns and with seven eyes, which are the seven spirits of God sent out into all the earth (Revelation 5:6 ESV).

Jesus is the Lamb that was slain. However, as we know, death could not hold Him.

In a similar manner, we are told that the final Antichrist experiences a violent death and is likewise raised from the dead. The Book of Revelation says.

> And I saw a beast rising out of the sea, with ten horns and seven heads, with ten diadems on its horns and blasphemous names on its heads. And the beast that I saw was like a leopard; its feet were like a bear's, and its mouth was like a lion's mouth. And to it the dragon gave his power and his throne and great authority. One of its heads seemed to have a mortal

wound, but its mortal wound was healed, and the whole earth marveled as they followed the beast. And they worshiped the dragon, for he had given his authority to the beast, and they worshiped the beast, saying, "Who is like the beast, and who can fight against it?" (Revelation 13:1-4 ESV).

In another place, we read of the same thing. It says.

> The beast, which you saw, once was, now is not, and will come up out of the Abyss and go to its destruction. The inhabitants of the earth whose names have not been written in the book of life from the creation of the world will be astonished when they see the beast, because it once was, now is not, and yet will come (Revelation 17:8 NIV).

In this passage it speaks of the beast which "is not." He is dead for a short period of time, goes to the Abyss, the bottomless pit, and is then brought back to life. This is further evidence that he does, in reality, die and then he actually comes back to life.

Indeed, in at least six different places in the Book of Revelation, the death and resurrection of this first beast, the final Antichrist, is alluded to. While we may not be able to explain how or why this happens, it seems that this is what Scripture teaches on this issue.

Therefore, most likely, the beast experiences an actual death and seemingly a genuine resurrection.

For some reason, the God of the Bible, the only One who has power over life and death, allows this evil personage to come back to life. Scripture does not explain why this is so.

THE CASE FOR A COUNTERFEIT RESURRECTION

Many people believe this beast will have a counterfeit resurrection rather than a genuine one. Consider the following reasons.

ONLY GOD CAN RAISE THE DEAD

For one thing, Scripture makes it clear that the resurrection of the dead is something which is in the power of the God of the Bible. We find the Apostle saying the following to a pagan king.

> Why should any of you consider it incredible that God raises the dead? (Acts 26:8 NIV).

God alone gives life, and God takes it away. Satan has no power whatsoever over life and death. Therefore, if Antichrist actually comes back to life, it must be something which God allows to happen. To many people, it seems inconsistent with God's character to do such a thing. Why would he allow Satan to duplicate the miracle of the resurrection?

ANTICHRIST IS THE GREAT DECEIVER

There is also the fact that Antichrist is the great imitator and deceiver. Paul said his time on the earth will consist of lying wonders.

> The arrival of the lawless one will be by Satan's working with all kinds of miracles and signs and false wonders, and with every kind of evil deception directed against those who are perishing, because they found no place in their hearts for the truth so as to be saved (2 Thessalonians 2:9-10 NET).

His miracles are called "false." This seems to indicate they are not genuine but rather are illusions, or tricks. This also includes his so-called resurrection from the dead. Whether or not Antichrist actually comes back from the dead, the people of that time will believe that he has.

Therefore, he will be in a position to challenge the true and living God by claiming he is able to do the same sort of miracles which Jesus did. This includes coming back from the dead. Fortunately, the Lord has warned us of this deception ahead of time.

IT WILL NOT BE A RESURRECTION LIKE THAT OF JESUS!

One thing which cannot be stressed enough is that even if Antichrist truly comes back to life after he is literally dead, it will not be the same as a biblical resurrection. Certainly it will not be the same thing as the resurrection of Jesus.

Jesus came back from the dead in a *new body*, a glorified one. Indeed, Jesus' body was immortal and indestructible. He came back in a body which is fit for eternity.

There is no indication whatsoever that the body of the final Antichrist is somehow changed after his return from the dead. He is certainly not indestructible. His experience would be more of a re-animation or resuscitation. Whatever the nature of his body, it is not one made for eternity to experience the blessings of the Lord. If anything, is it a body that will be able to be tormented while alive in the lake of fire.

Indeed, the Bible says the following destiny awaits this man of sin.

> But the beast was captured, and with him the false prophet who had performed the signs on his behalf. With these signs he had deluded those who had received the mark of the beast and worshiped his image. The two of them were thrown alive into the fiery lake of burning sulfur (Revelation 19:20 NIV).

We can safely say that this is not a body anyone would desire to possess!

Consequently, whatever will happen to the man of sin is not an example of what anyone else would like to imitate.

SUMMARY TO QUESTION 30
WILL THE ANTICHRIST ACTUALLY BE RAISED FROM THE DEAD?

We know from Scripture that the coming Antichrist will try to mimic or parody the true Christ in every conceivable way. Consequently, we are not surprised to learn that Scripture speaks of the final Antichrist dying and then coming back from the dead. This act of rising from the dead causes the entire world to worship this beast.

The question naturally arises as to whether this man of sin actually comes back from the dead, or merely fakes his resurrection. Christians are divided on this issue.

Those who believe that there is an actual resurrection from the dead state their case as follows.

To begin with, the fact that Antichrist suffers a horrifying death is made plain by Scripture. The fact that he comes back to life is also made clear. The Bible says that after his death he goes down to the Abyss, the bottomless pit, and then returns to the earth. While we may not be able to explain how he is able to do this, it seems that God allows this to happen to suit His own purposes.

Those who reject the idea of an actual resurrection of this beast point out the fact that only God has the power to raise the dead. Since Satan is the great counterfeiter, it is only fitting that he attempts to pull off the biggest counterfeit of all by offering the world a phony resurrection. Paul clearly states that the man of sin will produce "lying wonders." It seems that one of these lies is a counterfeit resurrection.

Whatever the case may actually be, the world will assume that a genuine resurrection has occurred. The fact that the world believes in an actual resurrection, whether it truly took place or not, has the same outcome; the people will worship this evil individual as well as the devil who inspires him.

Therefore, whether or not this wicked personage actually comes back from the dead, the influence this event will have upon the world will be astonishing.

One last thing which does need to be stressed is this. Whatever the nature of the death and return to life of the final Antichrist, he does not receive a resurrected body like that of Jesus. Jesus' resurrected body is eternal and immortal. It is not subject to decay and it certainly is not subject to suffering. The body of the final Antichrist will be able to experience suffering. Indeed, we are told that he is cast alive in the lake of fire where he is consciously tormented for all eternity.

Therefore, whatever body he may have, after his brush with death, will not be a body like that of Jesus. At best, it seems to be a re-animation or resuscitation. However, it is certainly not a resurrection in the biblical sense of the word.

QUESTION 31

What Is The Identity Of The Two Witnesses Which The Beast, Or Antichrist, Kills?

One of the most fascinating episodes recorded in the Book of Revelation concerns the two witnesses which come on the scene and testify to the truth of God's Word. As we have seen, Satan will have his two men, the beast and the false prophet, to do his bidding during the time of the great tribulation. In like manner the Lord will also have His two men to testify to the truth.

The Bible has the following to say about the ministry of these two personages, the two witnesses.

THE MINISTRY OF THE TWO WITNESSES

Scripture records the ministry of the two witnesses as follows.

> And I will appoint my two witnesses, and they will prophesy for 1,260 days, clothed in sackcloth. They are "the two olive trees" and the two lampstands, and "they stand before the Lord of the earth." If anyone tries to harm them, fire comes from their mouths and devours their enemies. This is how anyone who wants to harm them must die. They have power to shut up the sky so that it will not rain during the time they are prophesying; and they have power to turn the waters into blood and to strike the earth with every kind of plague as often as they want (Revelation 11:3-6 NIV).

They will stand up for God's truth for some three and one half years. In doing so, they will exhibit supernatural powers from the Lord.

THE MURDER OF THE TWO WITNESSES

After their earthly ministry is complete, we are told that the beast kills them. The Bible has the following to say.

> And when they have finished their testimony, the beast that rises from the bottomless pit will make war on them and conquer them and kill them, and their dead bodies will lie in the street of the great city that symbolically is called Sodom and Egypt, where their Lord was crucified. For three and a half days some from the peoples and tribes and languages and nations will gaze at their dead bodies and refuse to let them be placed in a tomb, and those who dwell on the earth will rejoice over them and make merry and exchange presents, because these two prophets had been a torment to those who dwell on the earth (Revelation 11:7-10 ESV).

The celebration goes on around the world.

THE RESURRECTION OF THE TWO WITNESSES

However, the Bible says that a miracle then happens. Scripture tells us that they will be brought back to life.

> But after the three and a half days a breath of life from God entered them, and they stood up on their feet, and great fear fell on those who saw them. Then they heard a loud voice from heaven saying to them, "Come up here!" And they went up to heaven in a cloud, and their enemies watched them. And at that hour there was a great earthquake, and a tenth of the city fell. Seven thousand people were killed in the earthquake, and the rest were terrified and gave glory to the God of heaven (Revelation 11:10-13 ESV).

We find that after their resurrection, they will be brought into heaven.

WHO ARE THE TWO WITNESSES?

We now come to the question of the identity of the two witnesses. Who are they? Are they real people, or are they symbolic of something? If they are real people, are they biblical characters from the past returning to the earth, or are they two contemporary people whom God inspires as His prophets? The various options can be listed as follows.

OPTION 1: THE TWO WITNESSES ARE BIBLICAL CHARACTERS FROM THE PAST

A popular view is to see the two witnesses as two biblical characters from the past. A number of suggestions have been given as to whom they might be.

MOSES

Moses is a likely candidate for one of the two witnesses which will face the beast and the false prophet. For one thing, Moses was a prophet. Therefore, he has the proper biblical credentials to speak out against these two evil beings.

In addition, he had the power to strike the earth with plagues. Using the power of the Lord, he turned the Nile River into blood. The two witnesses will have the power to do the same.

> They have power to shut up the sky so that it will not rain during the time they are prophesying; and they have power to turn the waters into blood and to strike the earth with every kind of plague as often as they want (Revelation 11:6 NIV).

Therefore, this miracle-working ability fits with what we know of the ability God gave to Moses.

Moreover, at Jesus' Transfiguration, Moses appeared. He spoke with Jesus of things concerning the coming kingdom, the Second Coming of Christ. This may be another indication that Moses will appear shortly before Christ returns.

Interestingly, though Moses did die, we are told that the Lord Himself buried him. This may indicate that He had further plans for this prophet of God.

These things make Moses an apt candidate to be one of the two witnesses.

ELIJAH

Elijah is another popular candidate to be one of the two witnesses. There are a number of reasons as to why this is so.

For one thing, like Moses, Elijah was a prophet of God. Hence, he has the proper credentials to prophesy and do miracles in the name of the Lord.

Next, Elijah never experienced physical death. While death is not a requirement for every human being, it is possible he was not allowed to die because the Lord had plans for him to be one of the two witnesses.

Third, what is even more significant is that the Scripture expressly says that Elijah will come back to the earth before the return of the Lord.

> See, I will send the prophet Elijah to you before that great and dreadful day of the LORD comes (Malachi 4:5 NIV).

Fourth, Scripture speaks of Elijah calling fire down from heaven and consuming a sacrifice in front of the false prophets of Baal. We read.

> And the water ran around the altar and even overflowed the trench. At the customary time for offering the evening sac-rifice, Elijah the prophet walked up to the altar and prayed, "O LORD, God of Abraham, Isaac, and Jacob, prove today that you are God in Israel and that I am your servant. Prove

that I have done all this at your command. O LORD, answer me! Answer me so these people will know that you, O LORD, are God and that you have brought them back to yourself." Immediately the fire of the LORD flashed down from heaven and burned up the young bull, the wood, the stones, and the dust. It even licked up all the water in the ditch! (1 Kings 18:35-38 NLT).

As we have observed, one of the specific miracles attributed to the two witnesses is the calling down of fire from heaven.

Fifth, Elijah was given the ability to cause the land to be without rain for a number of years. Again, this is one of the specific miracles attributed to the two witnesses.

Finally, at the Transfiguration of Jesus, Elijah appeared with Moses.

Many Bible students believe that the fact that Elijah and Moses appeared together at the Transfiguration shows that they are the two witnesses which will appear to combat Antichrist and the false Prophet. However, Moses and Elijah are not the only possible candidates among the characters which we find on the pages of Scripture.

ENOCH

Another possibility is Enoch. The reason Enoch is preferred above Moses is that Enoch, like Elijah, did not die a physical death. The Bible says he left earth in the following way.

> Altogether, Enoch lived a total of 365 years. Enoch walked faithfully with God; then he was no more, because God took him away (Genesis 5:23-24 NIV).

Enoch did not die. Again, we emphasize that it is not necessary that every human being must die. Indeed, an entire generation of believers will not experience physical death but rather will be caught away into heaven at the rapture of the church.

Consequently, the fact that Enoch did not die does not necessarily make him one of the two witnesses. However, it does make him a prime candidate.

In addition, Enoch is also mentioned in the context of the return of the Lord. The Book of Jude notes that Enoch preached God's judgment before the flood.

> Enoch, the seventh from Adam, prophesied about them: "See, the Lord is coming with thousands upon thousands of his holy ones to judge everyone, and to convict all the ungodly of all the ungodly acts they have done in an ungodly way, and of all the defiant words ungodly sinners have spoken against him" (Jude 14-15 NIV).

He was a prophet of judgment before the Lord sent the Great Flood to the world. Interestingly, Jesus compared the conditions at the time of His Second Coming to the conditions in Noah's day.

> For as were the days of Noah, so will be the coming of the Son of Man. For as in those days before the flood they were eating and drinking, marrying and giving in marriage, until the day when Noah entered the ark, and they were unaware until the flood came and swept them all away, so will be the coming of the Son of Man (Matthew 24:37-39 ESV).

Since Enoch pronounced judgment to come upon the world, the first time the entire world was judged, he may appear again to announce a "second" coming judgment of the world. Therefore, Enoch remains a viable candidate for one of the two witnesses.

JOHN THE BAPTIST

There has also been the suggestion that John the Baptist is one of the two witnesses. For one thing, Jesus said that John the Baptist was Elijah.

If Elijah has to come to the earth before the day of the Lord, then it is argued that he will return in the person of John the Baptist.

While there are some who hold out for John the Baptist as one of the two witnesses, it is not likely that this is the case. The evidence is scant.

OPTION 2: THE TWO WITNESSES ARE TWO MEN LIVING AT THE TIME OF THE EVENTS

It is possible, even likely, that if the two witnesses are literal human beings, they are two people from the great tribulation period who have qualities which were similar to Moses and Elijah. In other words, they are godly people who will be living on the earth at the time these events take place. God chooses them to be His special witnesses to the earth.

Since the two witnesses are unnamed, and we would expect the return of Moses, Elijah or Enoch to be noted in Scripture if they were the two witnesses, the idea that they are two people living at that time has much going for it.

OPTION 3: THE TWO WITNESSES ARE NOT LITERAL PEOPLE

Among those who do not interpret the Book of Revelation in a literal manner interpret the two witnesses as something symbolic, not literal.

THE WORD OF GOD: THE OLD AND NEW TESTAMENT

There are some who see the two witnesses as the Bible, the Old Testament and the New Testament. Yet this breaks down when we try to interpret Revelation 11 with this in mind. The context calls for two human beings, not two testaments.

THE TWO PEOPLE OF GOD: ISRAEL AND THE CHURCH

Some see the two witnesses as representing the two people of God, the nation of Israel and the New Testament church. However, the same problems arise as with the previous possibility. The passage reads as though two human beings are in view.

CONCLUSION: NOBODY KNOWS THEIR IDENTITY FOR CERTAIN

The specific identity of the two witnesses is not revealed to us. Any attempt to identify them is only speculation. It does, however, seem best to view the two witnesses as two actual people who perform this special ministry.

It would not be inconsistent with the rest of Scripture to believe that the Lord actually brings Moses and Elijah back to earth for this ministry. However, it would also be in line with Scripture if we assume the two witnesses will be two godly people whom the Lord raises up at that time. Since we do not know the answer for certain, it is best that we hold our view with humility.

SUMMARY TO QUESTION 31
WHAT IS THE IDENTITY OF THE TWO WITNESSES WHICH THE BEAST, OR ANTICHRIST, KILLS?

One of the major events in the career of Antichrist is the murder of the "two witnesses." According to the Book of Revelation these two witnesses testify to the Lord for some three and one half years. During this time they are given the ability to perform miraculous deeds. After their three and one half year ministry, these two witnesses are murdered by the beast, the final Antichrist.

However, three and one half days later, the two witnesses are raised back to life. Then, in full view of everyone, they ascend into heaven. Therefore, while the Book of Revelation highlights the deeds of these two evil witnesses of the devil, the beast and the false prophet, we find victorious things happening with two godly witnesses whom the Lord sends to the earth.

The identity of these two witnesses continues to be debated among Bible-believers. There are those who believe they are actual people while others think they are symbolic of something or some particular people.

Some think they are biblical characters from the past who return to the earth. Suggestions include Moses, Elijah, Enoch and John the Baptist. Moses and Elijah are popular candidates because the ministry of these two individual mirrors that of these two prophets of God.

There is also the possibility that these two witnesses are two contemporary individuals whom the Lord raises up to be His prophets. This is a very real possibility.

A number of interpreters of Revelation see the two witnesses as symbolic figures, not literal people. Yet there is no consensus of opinion, among those who view these witnesses symbolically, as to what they may refer to.

Ultimately we cannot be certain as to their identity. However, it does seem that Scripture is speaking of two specific individuals who will personally perform this important ministry during this critical time in the history of the earth. Yet, nobody can be certain of their exact identity.

QUESTION 32

What Will Be The Doom Of Antichrist?

For three and one half years the man of sin, the final Antichrist, will rule the world. However, the inglorious career of the beast will come to a quick and violent end. Scripture says it will happen in this manner.

GOD WILL POUR OUT HIS WRATH

As the rebellion against the Lord continues during the period of the great tribulation, the Book of Revelation says that the fifth angel will pour out his bowl of wrath upon the throne of the beast and his kingdom. We read.

> Then the fifth angel poured out his bowl on the throne of the beast, and his kingdom was plunged into darkness. His subjects ground their teeth in anguish, and they cursed the God of heaven for their pains and sores. But they did not repent of their evil deeds and turn to God (Revelation 16:10–11 NLT).

The moral and spiritual darkness of the entire world is obvious at this point in time. Though these people are plagued with indescribable pain, they continue to blaspheme the God of heaven. They do not stop their evil deeds.

THE ARMIES GATHER FOR ARMAGEDDON

Antichrist then organizes a campaign against the Jews and against the city of Jerusalem. This is known as the Battle, or War, of Armageddon. We read about this gathering of the armies.

> Then the sixth angel poured out his bowl on the great Euphrates River, and it dried up so that the kings from the east could march their armies toward the west without hindrance. And I saw three evil spirits that looked like frogs leap from the mouths of the dragon, the beast, and the false prophet. They are demonic spirits who work miracles and go out to all the rulers of the world to gather them for battle against the Lord on that great judgment day of God the Almighty. "Look, I will come as unexpectedly as a thief! Blessed are all who are watching for me, who keep their clothing ready so they will not have to walk around naked and ashamed." And the demonic spirits gathered all the rulers and their armies to a place with the Hebrew name Armageddon (Revelation 16:12–16 NLT).

At this time, the War of Armageddon is about to transpire.

HE WILL CAMPAIGN AGAINST THE LAMB

The beast will gather his armies to fight against the Lord. Of course, the Antichrist and his armies do not have any chance whatsoever of prevailing against the God of Heaven. We further read.

> Then I saw the beast and the kings of the earth and their armies gathered together to make war against the rider on the horse and his army (Revelation 19:19 NIV).

John also wrote.

> They will make war against the Lamb, but the Lamb will triumph over them because he is Lord of lords and King of

kings—and with him will be his called, chosen and faithful followers (Revelation 17:14 NIV).

This is the height of absurdity. These puny human armies are gathered together to fight the One, True God, the only God who exists!

THE BEAST WILL BE DESTROYED AT THE SECOND COMING OF CHRIST

In one sense, the final War, or Battle, of Armageddon is not much of a battle. The Lord destroys His enemies at His return. John wrote.

Coming out of his mouth is a sharp sword with which to strike down the nations. "He will rule them with an iron scepter." He treads the winepress of the fury of the wrath of God Almighty. (Revelation 19:15 NIV).

Paul describes it this way.

Then the man of lawlessness will be revealed, whom the Lord Jesus will consume with the breath of his mouth and destroy by the splendor of his coming (2 Thessalonians 2:8 NLT).

This last battle is over. The result is clear.

Their entire army was killed by the sharp sword that came out of the mouth of the one riding the white horse. And all the vultures of the sky gorged themselves on the dead bodies (Revelation 19:21 NLT).

The rebellion comes to an end. The birds of prey feast upon the bodies of these enemies of Christ. Judgment has come to the earth.

THE BEAST WILL BE CAST INTO THE LAKE OF FIRE

Both the beast and the false Prophet are then taken alive and cast into the lake of fire forever. The Book of Revelation says the following.

But the beast was captured, and with him the false prophet who had performed the signs on his behalf. With these signs he had deluded those who had received the mark of the beast and worshiped his image. The two of them were thrown alive into the fiery lake of burning sulfur (Revelation 19:20 NIV).

This brings his inglorious career to its end. The man of sin had his time, it is now over. Jesus Christ will be the Ruler of the universe for the remainder of eternity.

In contrast to the evil rule of the beast, we are told that the rule of Christ will be a rule of righteousness. The writer to the Hebrews put it this way.

But about the Son he says, "Your throne, O God, will last for ever and ever; a scepter of justice will be the scepter of your kingdom. You have loved righteousness and hated wickedness; therefore God, your God, has set you above your companions by anointing you with the oil of joy" (Hebrews 1:8,9 NIV).

Righteousness will rule upon the earth in the Person of the righteous King!

THE DEVIL WILL EVENTUALLY JOIN THE BEAST AND FALSE PROPHET

The devil will be thrown into the bottomless pit, the abyss, at that time. Eventually he will join these other two beings in that horrible place, the lake of fire.

And the devil who had deceived them was thrown into the lake of fire and sulfur where the beast and the false prophet were, and they will be tormented day and night forever and ever (Revelation 20:10 ESV).

This sums up how the short career of the man of sin will end. It will be a horrific time for all those who dwell upon the earth. However, the good news is that after this terrible period in earth's history, the greatest period ever will be dawning, the kingdom of God will come to this earth!

SUMMARY TO QUESTION 32
WHAT WILL BE THE DOOM OF ANTICHRIST?

The Antichrist, though he will rule the world for some three and one half years, will eventually meet his doom. His evil reign will not last forever!

The beast will gather his armies in a final attempt to destroy the remnant of Jews which are still living upon the earth. This is the famous Battle, or War, of Armageddon. However, this attempt will be thwarted by the return of Christ to the earth.

When He returns with His saints the Lord Jesus destroys the armies of the beast. The beast and the false prophet will be thrown alive in the lake of fire where they will be tormented forever and ever. This ends the career of the man of sin.

With the return of Christ to the earth, the rule of righteousness and justice will begin. This righteous rule will never end!

The devil will be thrown in the bottomless pit, the abyss. He will eventually join these other two evil beings in the lake of fire. What a contrast to the future of those who belong to Christ!

Who Is The Second Beast, The False Prophet?

False prophets and false teachers have been around from the very beginning. These evil individuals always pervert the message of the God of the Bible. The Apostle John said there were many of these false prophets in his day. He wrote.

> Dear friends, do not believe every spirit, but test the spirits to see whether they are from God, because many false prophets have gone out into the world. This is how you can recognize the Spirit of God: Every spirit that acknowledges that Jesus Christ has come in the flesh is from God, but every spirit that does not acknowledge Jesus is not from God. This is the spirit of the antichrist, which you have heard is coming and even now is already in the world (1 John 4:1-3 NIV).

These particular false prophets denied Jesus was a genuine human being. In other words, they denied His true humanity. This is consistent with the false prophets, they are always denying some essential truth of the Christian faith.

FALSE PROPHETS WILL CONTINUE UNTIL THE END

The Bible stresses the fact that false prophets will continue to emerge until the time of the end. Jesus warned that many false prophets would appear.

> For false christs and false prophets will arise and perform great signs and wonders, so as to lead astray, if possible, even the elect (Matthew 24:24 ESV).

Therefore, we should always expect to have false prophets among us.

THE ULTIMATE FALSE PROPHET, THE SECOND BEAST

The Bible speaks of an ultimate or "final" false prophet. He will come on the scene of history at the end of time. He is called the "second beast," or "another beast." This makes it clear that the second beast is a different personage from the first beast, the man of sin, the Antichrist. This second beast is introduced as follows.

> Then I saw another beast rising out of the earth. It had two horns like a lamb and it spoke like a dragon (Revelation 13:11 ESV).

Two things are immediately apparent about this second beast. To begin with, he comes out of the earth. This could mean that his origin is from this world as opposed to heaven, or it could be emphasizing that he has no divine authority whatsoever.

There is also the possibility that this description is emphasizing that he is Jewish. The word "earth" could also be translated as "land." Consequently, the false prophet may actually come from the Promised Land and from the chosen people. Thus, he is Jewish. This would be in contrast with the first beast, who seemingly is a Gentile.

We are also told that this second beast looks like a harmless lamb but speaks as a dragon. His appearance and speech make him appear to be not dangerous. Yet, in actuality, his words originate from the pit of hell.

Who then is this second beast? What exactly is the role of this false prophet in the end times? Scripture has the following to say.

THE SECOND BEAST IS CALLED "THE" FALSE PROPHET

On three occasions, the second beast is called "the false prophet." In each of these instances, he is aligned with the first beast, the man of sin, the final Antichrist.

We first read of this title "the false prophet" in the sixteenth chapter of the Book of Revelation, where it says the following.

> Then I saw three evil spirits that looked like frogs; they came out of the mouth of the dragon, out of the mouth of the beast and out of the mouth of the false prophet (Revelation 16:13 NIV).

In this instance, evil spirits proceed from the dragon, the beast, as well as from the false prophet, the unholy trinity.

We are told the false prophet is captured along with the beast at the time of the Second Coming of Jesus Christ to the earth. Scripture says.

> But the beast was captured, and with him the false prophet who had performed the signs on his behalf. With these signs he had deluded those who had received the mark of the beast and worshiped his image. The two of them were thrown alive into the fiery lake of burning sulfur (Revelation 19:20 NIV).

The final reference to the false prophet is when he is thrown into the lake of fire. His demise is recorded in the following manner.

> And the devil, who deceived them, was thrown into the lake of burning sulfur, where the beast and the false prophet had been thrown. They will be tormented day and night for ever and ever (Revelation 20:10 NIV).

These are the only three passages which specifically describe the second beast as the false prophet.

WHO IS THE SECOND BEAST, THE FALSE PROPHET?

It is clear that the second beast is also called *the* false prophet. This brings up an obvious question. Who is this second beast, "the" false prophet? From Scripture we can make the following conclusions.

1. HE IS DISTINCT FROM THE FIRST BEAST AND THE DEVIL

The false prophet is distinct from the first beast. He is called the "second beast." This makes a clear distinction between this beast and the first beast. They are not the same personage.

Furthermore, as we have just noted, he is distinguished from the first beast and the devil in Revelation chapters nineteen and twenty. The beast and the false prophet are thrown into the lake of fire in chapter nineteen of the Book of Revelation while the devil is not. Later, in chapter twenty, we are told that the devil joins them in the lake of fire. Therefore, we can rightly conclude that the false prophet is a distinct personage from the first beast and the devil himself.

His character and mission are also distinct from the first beast. While the first beast is more of a political and military leader, the false prophet will be a religious leader.

2. HE IS A MIRACLE WORKER

We also find that the second beast, the false prophet, works miracles. Scripture says.

> He did astounding miracles, even making fire flash down to earth from the sky while everyone was watching (Revelation 13:13 NLT).

In fact, he is a greater miracle worker than the first beast.

There is something we must note about his miracles. We are told that the false prophet mimics the two witnesses of Revelation 11 in their miraculous deeds.

Indeed, the same miracles which the Bible says the two witnesses perform are also performed by this false prophet. This includes calling fire down from heaven.

Such mimicking of God's miracles reminds us of the battle of Moses and Aaron with the magicians of the Pharaoh of Egypt. We find them mimicking some of the miracles that the Lord performed through Moses and Aaron. This mimicking of the miracles is repeated by the deeds of the false prophet.

3. HE IS A SATANIC VERSION OF JOHN THE BAPTIST

The false prophet can be compared to John the Baptist. As John prepared the way for the genuine Messiah, the false prophet will point people to the false Messiah. In this sense, he is like a devilish version of John the Baptist. This second beast will be the chief promoter of the first beast.

4. HE WILL MAKE AN IMAGE OF THE FIRST BEAST

As the promoter of the first beast, he causes the people to make an image of this evil personage. The Bible says.

> And with all the miracles he was allowed to perform on behalf of the first beast, he deceived all the people who belong to this world. He ordered the people of the world to make a great statue of the first beast, who was fatally wounded and then came back to life (Revelation 13:14 NLT).

This image or statue is of the first beast who survived a seemingly fatal wound.

This act of sacrilege is called the "abomination of desolation" by Jesus.

> So when you see standing in the holy place 'the abomination that causes desolation,' spoken of through the prophet Daniel—let the reader understand (Matthew 24:15 NIV).

The image of the first beast will be placed in the Holy of Holies in the rebuilt temple in Jerusalem, the place where the Holy Ark of the Covenant stood. This act will be the ultimate blasphemy against the God of Scripture.

5. HE IS ABLE TO GIVE LIFE TO THE STATUE OF THE FIRST BEAST

The false prophet performs a great miracle. Somehow he is able to give life to the statue or image that he made of the first beast.

> He was permitted to give a spirit to the image of the beast, so that the image of the beast could both speak and cause whoever would not worship the image of the beast to be killed (Revelation 13:15 HCSB).

This seems to be an incredible miracle. We are not told how he is able to do it.

6. THE FALSE PROPHET CAUSES PEOPLE TO WORSHIP THE IMAGE OF THE BEAST

As the false prophet, he then causes people of the world to worship a false god, the first beast. The Bible says

> The second beast was empowered to give life to the image of the first beast so that it could speak, and could cause all those who did not worship the image of the beast to be killed (Revelation 13:15 NET).

The false prophet will order the death of all who refuse to worship this image of the first beast.

7. HE MAKES PEOPLE TAKE THE MARK OF THE FIRST BEAST

We also find that all who worship the first beast will receive his mark. The false prophet is the one who enforces this. The Book of Revelation says.

> And he requires everyone—small and great, rich and poor,
> free and slave—to be given a mark on his right hand or
> on his forehead, so that no one can buy or sell unless he
> has the mark: the beast's name or the number of his name
> (Revelation 13:16-17 HCSB).

Those who refuse to worship the first beast are denied the right to buy and sell. In other words, they cannot do anything without the mark of the first beast. All of this is facilitated by the false prophet. Consequently, he is the one who ultimately controls the commerce of the world.

8. HE MAY BE THE ONE WHO BRINGS THE FIRST BEAST BACK TO LIFE

There is another matter which we should consider about this second beast. Though it is not directly stated in Scripture, it is possible that the false prophet is the one who brings the first beast, the final Antichrist back to life after he receives a mortal head wound.

We are told that the first beast dies and then comes back to life. While not stated, it may be inferred that the second beast is the one who performs this miracle. Since the second beast, the false prophet, has the ability to give life to a statue of the first beast, it is not out of the question that he will be able to facilitate the resurrection of the first beast.

Of course, all this has to happen under the control of God. These personages have no power in and of themselves to give life to the dead.

9. THE FALSE PROPHET HAS THE SAME DESTINY AS SATAN AND THE FIRST BEAST

As the devil and the first beast will eventually be cast into the lake of fire, the false prophet, the second beast, will experience the same fate. The Bible says.

> Then the Devil, who betrayed them, was thrown into the
> lake of fire that burns with sulfur, joining the beast and the

false prophet. There they will be tormented day and night forever and ever (Revelation 20:10 NLT).

Each of these despicable humans will suffer the same punishment.

A LOOK AT THE DEEDS OF THE CHARACTER AND DEEDS OF THE SECOND BEAST, THE FALSE PROPHET

From a look at the Scripture we find the following things said about the deeds and character of this second beast.

1. HE WILL MIMIC HOLY SPIRIT

As the Antichrist, the first beast, attempts to usurp the rightful place of Jesus Christ, God the Son, while the second beast, the false prophet, will mimic the Third Person of the Trinity, the Holy Spirit.

As the Holy Spirit is a distinct Person from Jesus, God the Son, so the second beast, the false prophet, is a distinct person from the first beast, the Antichrist. In this unholy group of three personages, the devil is the parody of God the Father, the first beast of God the Son, and the false prophet, the second beast, is a mimic of God the Holy Spirit.

2. HE WILL PROMOTE OR GLORIFY THE FIRST BEAST

The job of the false prophet will be to glorify the first beast, he will not glorify himself. In this aspect, he will mimic the Holy Spirit.

Jesus said the ministry of the Holy Spirit is to testify to Him [Jesus], not of Himself. He said.

> When the Spirit of truth comes, he will guide you into all the truth, for he will not speak on his own authority, but whatever he hears he will speak, and he will declare to you the things that are to come. He will glorify me, for he will take what is mine and declare it to you (John 16:13-15 ESV).

The Holy Spirit teaches us about Jesus. In the same way, the false prophet will mimic the ministry of the Holy Spirit. However, the false prophet will lead people into error instead of the truth. He will encourage them to worship the false Christ.

3. HE WILL BUILD THE KINGDOM OF ANTICHRIST

As the Holy Spirit is the one who builds the church, the body of Christ, here upon the earth, it is the false prophet who builds the kingdom of Antichrist. This is another way in which this personage will mimic the work of God the Holy Spirit.

4. HE WILL BE THIRD PERSON OF THE UNHOLY GROUP OF THREE PERSONAGES

The false prophet is part of an unholy group of three personal beings. Each one of them is individually mentioned in Revelation chapter twenty. Scripture says.

> And the devil who had deceived them was thrown into the lake of fire and sulfur where the beast and the false prophet were, and they will be tormented day and night forever and ever (Revelation 20:10 ESV).

This emphasizes that he is distinct from the first beast, the Antichrist, and the devil.

5. THE FALSE PROPHET BRINGS DEATH INSTEAD OF LIFE

The false prophet, this second beast, brings death instead of life. This is in contrast to the Holy Spirit of God who gives life. Indeed, we are told that it was the Spirit of God who raised Jesus from the dead. Paul wrote about this to the Romans.

> And if the Spirit of him who raised Jesus from the dead is living in you, he who raised Christ from the dead will also give life to your mortal bodies because of his Spirit who lives in you (Romans 8:11 NIV).

The contrast between God the Holy Spirit and this false prophet in this particular instance is obvious; One brings life while the other brings death.

6. HE MARKS THOSE WHO BELONG TO ANTICHRIST

The false prophet marks those who worship the beast. In contrast to this, the Holy Spirit seals or marks those who believe in Jesus. Paul wrote.

> In him you also, when you heard the word of truth, the gospel of your salvation, and believed in him, were sealed with the promised Holy Spirit, who is the guarantee of our inheritance until we acquire possession of it, to the praise of his glory (Ephesians 1:13-14 ESV).

As the Lord marks or seals His people, the devil does the same.

These are some of the things which we learn about the second beast of the Book of Revelation, the false prophet. Like the first beast, this second beast is completely and thoroughly evil.

SUMMARY TO QUESTION 33
WHO IS THE SECOND BEAST, THE FALSE PROPHET?

While false prophets have always existed, and will always exist, Scripture speaks of a final false prophet who appears at the end of this present age. The Word of God tells us a number of things about him.

The Bible speaks of two beasts in the Book of Revelation. The first beast is a political and military leader, while the second beast is called "the" false prophet. He is more of a religious leader.

From the Bible, we learn the following things about things about this second beast, this ultimate false prophet.

We are told that he arises up from "the earth." This is in contrast to the first beast which comes from "the sea." "From the earth" could indicate that he has a non-heavenly origin. It is also possible that it could mean he is Jewish since the word translate "earth" could also be translated as "land," meaning the Holy Land.

Scripture says that he appears like a harmless lamb in his speech and appearance but is actually a dragon. This description aligns him with the devil who is also called a dragon.

We also discover that the second beast is not the same personage as the first beast. Neither is he the same personage as the devil. The Bible distinguishes between these three. Therefore, this second beast is a distinct personage from these other two beings.

We also find that this second beast is a worker of miracles. While the first beast also has miracles attributed to him, it seems that the false prophet performs more miracles as well as greater miracles. The miracles of the second beast are similar to the ones in which the two witnesses of Revelation 11 performed. It seems that he wants to prove that he can duplicate anything that the Lord's prophets can do.

This second beast, therefore, appears to be a satanic John the Baptist. As John prepared the way for Jesus the Christ, this false prophet will prepare the world for the false Christ, the Antichrist.

This second beast causes the people to make a physical image of the first beast. Somehow the false prophet is able to give life to this image or statue. This image will be placed in the Holy of Holies in a rebuilt temple in the city of Jerusalem. Jesus called this act of sacrilege the "abomination of desolation."

The false prophet then forces the people of the earth to worship this image. He also forces everyone upon the earth to be branded with the mark of this first beast. Without the mark, nobody will be able to buy or sell anything. Therefore, he is a facilitator of the program of the first beast.

It is also possible that the second beast is the instrument that brings the first beast back from the dead after the first beast suffers a violent death. Since the second beast has the ability to give life to a lifeless statue of the first beast, it does not seem out of the question that he could also be given the power to raise the dead man of sin, the Antichrist, back to life.

If this is what occurs then it is obvious these unique abilities must be granted by God; for He is the only One who has the power over life and death. For reasons, known to God alone, He allows this false prophet to deceive the people of the earth in this manner.

We also find that the second beast, the false prophet, will experience the same fate as the devil and the first beast. Each of them will be thrown into the lake of fire where they will be tormented forever and ever. Such is the fate of these evil beings.

There are a number of things which we learn about the character of the second beast, or the false prophet. They can be summed up as follows.

As the first beast mimics Christ, the second beast mimics the Holy Spirit. For example, as the Holy Spirit draws people to Jesus Christ, the false prophet draws people to the man of sin.

The second beast also glorifies the first beast in the same way the Holy Spirit glorifies God the Son, Jesus. The job of each of these personages is to glorify someone else rather than themselves.

In addition, the false prophet is the third person in the unholy trinity. In this way, Satan counterfeits the God of the Bible in His very nature. As God is made up of three distinct Persons, or centers of consciousness, God the Father, God the Son, and God the Holy Spirit, the devil counterfeits this with himself, the beast, and the false prophet.

The Holy Spirit of God brings life. Indeed, He is called the One who brought Jesus Christ back from the dead. He gives life. The false prophet, on the other hand, brings death.

Finally as the Holy Spirit marks those who believe in the God of the Bible, the false prophet marks those who belong to the Antichrist. Each group is branded, or marked, by their master.

This is a brief summation of actions of the second beast of the Book of Revelation, the false prophet. Truly, he is a hideous personage.

Is The Second Beast, The False Prophet, An Actual Person?

In the Book of Revelation we are introduced to a personage called the "second beast" or "false prophet." The Bible says the following of this personage.

> Then I saw another beast rising out of the earth. It had two horns like a lamb and it spoke like a dragon. It exercises all the authority of the first beast in its presence, and makes the earth and its inhabitants worship the first beast, whose mortal wound was healed (Revelation 13:11-12 ESV).

Who is this second beast? Is it a genuine person, an evil force, or perhaps some evil institution? The false prophet has been identified with either a person, or some type of false religious system.

What, therefore, is the best way to understand this reference? What is the author of the Book of Revelation attempting to communicate in his references to the second beast?

THE SYMBOLIC INTERPRETATION OF BIBLE PROPHECY

Usually those who hold that the second beast, the false prophet, is a mere symbol rather than an actual human being, think that Bible prophecy should be interpreted in a symbolic rather than a literal manner.

Consequently, we should not attempt to see these as literal people who actually exist but rather as symbols or metaphors of evil. They contend that literal interpretation of Bible prophecy was not what the original authors had in mind.

However, behind every symbol is some literal object. The problem we find with this viewpoint is that there is no consensus of opinion whatsoever as to what these symbols are symbolic of.

The fact that no agreement can be reached as to what exactly these symbols do mean shows the meaninglessness of such a view.

RESPONSE: HE IS AN ACTUAL PERSON

While some try to connect the passages concerning the false prophet with some type of evil system or false religion, there is much evidence to demonstrate that we are dealing with an actual human being. In other words, all the evidence seems to indicate that we must understand these references in a literal manner referring to a literal person. A number of points need to be made.

1. HE IS LINKED WITH SATAN AND THE FIRST BEAST THEY ARE ALWAYS TREATED AS REAL BEINGS

To begin with, we find that the false prophet is linked with Satan as well as with the first beast. Scripture says that they all receive the same final punishment. The Bible says.

> But the beast was captured, and with him the false prophet who had performed the signs on his behalf. With these signs he had deluded those who had received the mark of the beast and worshiped his image. The two of them were thrown alive into the fiery lake of burning sulfur (Revelation 19:20 NIV).

Later we find that the devil is thrown into the same place as the beast and false prophet.

> And the devil, who deceived them, was thrown into the lake of burning sulfur, where the beast and the false prophet had been thrown. They will be tormented day and night for ever and ever (Revelation 20:10 NIV).

Satan is always treated in Scripture as an actual personage; he is never viewed as a non-real character. Since the beast and false prophet are thrown into the same lake of fire as the devil, we should assume that they are all genuine beings, not symbols. Consequently, we should assume that the false prophet is an actual person.

2. EVERYTHING ABOUT HIM INDICATES A PERSON

As we look at the way the false prophet is described in the Bible, we find that he is always treated as an actual human being. For one thing, we find that personal pronouns are used of the false prophet. This is another indication that he is an actual person, rather than some type of evil institution.

Indeed, every description of him in the Book of Revelation indicates that we are dealing with an genuine individual. Nothing indicates we are dealing with some type of symbol.

Add to this the fact that there are no other examples in Scripture of a non-personage who is spoken of as a singular "false prophet." Every reference to a false prophet in Scripture concerns an actual person. We have no symbolic false prophets.

CONCLUSION: THE FALSE PROPHET IS AN ACTUAL PERSON

Therefore, it seems best to view this coming "false prophet" as an genuine human being who encourages the people of this world to follow the first beast, the man of sin.

In addition, this apostate religious leader leads the people of the earth to worship the devil himself. Consequently, the world should expect to see a literal person whom the Bible labels the "second beast," the "false prophet."

SUMMARY TO QUESTION 34
IS THE SECOND BEAST, THE FALSE PROPHET, AN ACTUAL PERSON?

The Book of Revelation speaks of two specific beasts. They are known as the first beast and the second beast. The second beast is also called the false prophet.

There have been those who believe the false prophet will not be an actual person but rather is representative or symbolic of something evil. Those who hold this view do not interpret all Bible prophecy in a literal manner.

Indeed, the ones who hold this perspective do not believe that the writers of Scripture intend for us to understand prophetic matters literally but rather symbolically.

The problem is that there is no consensus of opinion as to what the false prophet, the second beast, is symbolic of.

On the other hand, there is every reason to interpret Scripture, wherever possible, in a literal manner. This includes prophetic issues. For one thing, Satan, the devil, is always treated in the Bible as an actual personage.

Since he is mentioned alongside the first beast and the false prophet, and all three of them are eventually tossed into the lake of fire, it gives further evidence that the false prophet is an actual human being.

Consequently, it is consistent with the rest of Scripture to see the false prophet as a literal human being who appears on the scene of history shortly before the Second Coming of Jesus Christ.

QUESTION 35

Who Are The Two Beasts In The Book Of Revelation?

The Book of Revelation speaks of two coming beasts. They are called "the first beast" and "the second beast." It is important that we understand the differences between these two personages. We can make the following observations.

THE FIRST BEAST: THE POLITICAL LEADER, THE FINAL ANTICHRIST

The first beast we are introduced to is a political leader. He is the personage who heads up the final ten-nation confederation. He is described in this manner.

> And I saw a beast rising out of the sea, with ten horns and seven heads, with ten diadems on its horns and blasphemous names on its heads. And the beast that I saw was like a leopard; its feet were like a bear's, and its mouth was like a lion's mouth. And to it the dragon gave his power and his throne and great authority (Revelation 13:1-2 ESV).

The first beast is the final Antichrist.

THE SECOND BEAST: THE RELIGIOUS LEADER, THE FALSE PROPHET

The second beast is in contrast to the first beast. He is a religious leader. The Bible describes him in this manner.

> Then I saw another beast rising out of the earth. It had two horns like a lamb and it spoke like a dragon (Revelation 13:11 ESV).

The second beast calls attention to, and promotes, the first beast. He causes the people to follow the first beast.

THE SECOND BEAST HAS A DIFFERENT ORIGIN THAN THE FIRST BEAST

While the origin of the first beast is "from the sea," the origin of the second beast is "from the earth." This could mean several possible things.

"From the sea" could mean from the Gentile nations. In Scripture, the sea is often used to describe nations other than Israel.

On the other hand, the phrase "from the earth" may indicate the land of Israel. The word translated "earth" can also be translated as "land." It all depends upon the context.

THE BEASTS ARE DESCRIBED DIFFERENTLY

Each beast is described differently. The first beast is pictured as something ferocious. He is describes as a leopard with feet like a bear and a mouth like a lion.

On the other hand, the second beast has the appearance of something harmless, a lamb. However, this second beast speaks like a dragon. Interestingly, we find the dragon in the description of each of these beasts.

THEY HAVE DIFFERENT MISSIONS

The mission of each of these beasts is distinct. The second beast causes the people to worship the first beast. Scripture says the following of the "second beast."

It exercises all the authority of the first beast in its presence, and makes the earth and its inhabitants worship the first beast, whose mortal wound was healed (Revelation 13:12 ESV).

The first beast is the one to whom all the attention is given. He is the leader, while the second beast is his promoter.

Therefore, we find numerous differences in the description and mission of the two beasts. However, they are both united in their allegiance to the dragon, the devil himself.

SUMMARY TO QUESTION 35
WHO ARE THE TWO BEASTS IN THE BOOK OF REVELATION?

The Book of Revelation mentions two coming beasts. The first beast is a political leader who is the head of a ten nation confederation. He is the biblical Antichrist, the man of sin.

The second beast is a religious leader. He causes the people of the world to worship the first beast. Indeed, he does not demand worship for himself. He is known as the "false prophet."

The two beasts are different in a number of ways. For one thing they are distinguished from each other by their titles, the first beast and the second beast, as well as by their descriptions.

The first beast is described as something ferocious while the second beast is pictured as a lamb, something harmless. However, each of them is energized by the dragon, Satan.

Also they have different origins. The first beast originates from the sea. This may indicate the Gentile nations. The second beast originates from the earth, or the land. This could mean that he is Jewish; though this is not a necessary conclusion.

The mission of each of these beasts is different. The first beast is the world ruler while the second is the promoter of the first beast. This second beast makes an image of the first beast and causes the people of the world to worship the image.

While these two evil personages work together to deceive the world they are distinct from one another although they are one in purpose.

Is The False Prophet, Rather Than The First Beast, The Predicted Antichrist?

The Book of Revelation speaks of two "beasts." The first beast is the political leader who rules the world. The second beast comes on the scene and causes people to worship the first beast. The second beast seems to be more of a religious leader. It is almost universally assumed that the predicted Antichrist in Scripture is to be identified with the first beast.

However, there have been some commentators who believe the predicted Antichrist is actually the second beast of Revelation, not the first beast. The reasoning for this is as follows.

THE ANTICHRIST IS A RELIGIOUS FIGURE

One reason concerns the nature of the Antichrist. He is usually viewed as a religious figure. If this is the case, then it seems that the second beast, the false prophet, would be the long-awaited Antichrist. The first beast is a political leader, the second beast is a religious leader. Indeed, the second beast is called "the false prophet."

When John wrote about the final Antichrist, he linked this personage to "false prophets." He put it this way.

> Beloved, do not believe every spirit, but test the spirits to see whether they are from God, for many false prophets

have gone out into the world. By this you know the Spirit of God: every spirit that confesses that Jesus Christ has come in the flesh is from God, and every spirit that does not confess Jesus is not from God. This is the spirit of the antichrist, which you heard was coming and now is in the world already (1 John 4:1-3 ESV).

Here the final Antichrist is clearly linked to someone who is a false prophet. The spirit of Antichrist is what energizes false prophets. This would seem to indicate that the predicted Antichrist is a false prophet rather than a political leader.

THE FIRST BEAST IS A GENTILE, THE SECOND A JEW

Another reason as to why the Antichrist is more likely to be the false prophet rather than the first beast, the political leader, concerns their origin.

The first beast is described as coming out from the sea. Scripture says.

Then I saw a beast rising up out of the sea. It had seven heads and ten horns, with ten crowns on its horns. And written on each head were names that blasphemed God (Revelation 13:1 NLT).

The second beast, on the other hand, comes from the earth. The Bible puts it this way.

Then I saw another beast come up out of the earth. He had two horns like those of a lamb, and he spoke with the voice of a dragon (Revelation 13:11 NLT).

The sea is likely symbolic of the Gentile nations. This would make the first beast a Gentile. The second beast is from the earth, or the land. This may indicate that he is most likely Jewish.

Since the final Antichrist is the "anti" Messiah, many assume that he will be Jewish. If this is the case, then the second beast, the false prophet, is the predicted Antichrist.

It is for these reasons that a minority of Bible students believe the predicted Antichrist is actually the second beast of Revelation rather than the first beast.

EACH OF THESE INDIVIDUALS OPPOSE CHRIST

No matter which of these two personages turns out to be the final Antichrist, each of these individuals has the same purpose. Indeed, they willingly and maliciously turn people away from the true and living God of Scripture to serve and worship a false god. Consequently, they are both "antichrist."

SUMMARY TO QUESTION 36
IS THE FALSE PROPHET, RATHER THAN THE BEAST, THE PREDICTED ANTICHRIST?

The Book of Revelation mentions two "beasts" who are going to terrorize the world. These beasts are actually human beings. The first beast is a political leader while the second beast is a religious leader, the false prophet. Almost all commentators believe that the first beast is the predicted man of sin, or Antichrist.

Yet there is a minority of commentators who think this is not the case. They believe the final Antichrist is actually the second beast, the false prophet. Since this second beast is a religious leader, rather than a political leader, it seems to make more sense to see him as the predicted Antichrist.

Furthermore, there is evidence that the first beast is a Gentile and not a Jew. If this is the case, then he could not be received by the Jews as their Messiah. This would mean the Antichrist, or false Christ, is the second beast, the false prophet.

Actually each of these beasts act in the role of Antichrist. Indeed each of these is opposed to Christ and His kingdom and each of them intentionally attempts to pull people away from the true God. No matter which of these two personages is the final Antichrist of Scripture, each of them should be considered to be totally evil.

Will The False Prophet Actually Make People Worship The Antichrist And The Devil?

From the beginning of his existence, it seems that the devil has wanted to be worshipped. He now gets his chance during the period of the great tribulation which comes upon the earth. The Book of Revelation says the false prophet will cause the world to worship the first beast as well as the devil. Scripture says.

> People worshiped the dragon because he had given authority to the beast, and they also worshiped the beast and asked, "Who is like the beast? Who can make war against it?" (Revelation 13:4 NIV).

The beast is worshipped for his miraculous return to life after experiencing a mortal head wound. This event awes the world. However, the worship is not limited to this beast. The devil, who gives the authority to the beast, also receives worship.

DEVIL WORSHIP HAS ALWAYS BEEN IN THE MINORITY

While there have been examples of people worshipping the devil throughout history, it has only been a very small percentage which have publicly or privately done this. This will all change during the period known as the great tribulation. Devil worship will be the norm.

THE DEVIL HAS ALWAYS WANTED WORSHIP

From a study of Scripture, it seems that the created being who became the devil has always desired to be worshipped.

In fact, one of the temptations aimed at Jesus was the challenge to fall down and worship of the devil. We find the following exchange took place between Jesus and Satan.

> Again, the devil took him to a very high mountain and showed him all the kingdoms of the world and their splendor. "All this I will give you," he said, "if you will bow down and worship me." Jesus said to him, "Away from me, Satan! For it is written: 'Worship the Lord your God, and serve him only' (Matthew 4:8-10 NIV).

Jesus was told that He could bypass the cross if He would bow down and worship the devil. Jesus refused. This evil personage certainly does not deserve worship. Rather it is Jesus Christ, and Him alone, who deserves our worship.

HE WILL NOT DESERVE THE WORSHIP

Therefore, while the people of the earth will be forced to worship the first beast, the final Antichrist, as well as the devil, this worship will be completely undeserved. As we have stressed, worship belongs to the God of the Bible and to nobody else.

SUMMARY TO QUESTION 37
WILL THE FALSE PROPHET ACTUALLY MAKE PEOPLE WORSHIP THE ANTICHRIST AND THE DEVIL?

One of the predicted events in the Book of Revelation concerns the actual worship of the first beast, the man of sin. In addition to this, we also find that the people will worship the devil himself. The Bible says that the second beast, the false prophet, will cause the people of the earth to worship this first beast. Yet this is not all that he will do. We are also told that the people on the earth will also be forced to worship Satan, the devil. This seems to be a public acknowledgement of the devil. In other words, they will knowingly worship him.

In the past, devil worship has been limited to a minority of people. However, in the great tribulation period, everyone upon the earth will be forced to publicly acknowledge Satan as their object of worship. If they do not, they will die.

Consequently, whether it will be freely or unwillingly, the devil will be publicly worshipped by those who live upon the earth at that time. There will be those who refuse. Scripture says that many of them will pay for their refusal with their lives.

This public worship will fulfill what the devil has always wanted for himself, adoration. Indeed, one of the temptations that he addressed to Christ concerned worshipping him. Satan said that if Jesus would only fall down and worship him, then Christ would not have had to go through the necessary sufferings to secure our salvation and establish His kingdom.

Jesus refused to worship Satan. Instead He paid the price for our salvation by His death on the cross. This is why He alone deserves our worship.

QUESTION 38

What Is The Mark
Of The Beast?

In the thirteen chapter of the Book of Revelation we are told about one of the things which is forced upon the people who live in the world shortly before the Second Coming of Christ. To be able to buy or sell, each individual must take the "mark of the beast." John wrote.

> He [the false prophet] also caused everyone (small and great, rich and poor, free and slave) to obtain a mark on their right hand or on their forehead. Thus no one was allowed to buy or sell things unless he bore the mark of the beast-that is, his name or his number (Revelation 13:16-17 NET).

There are several things which we learn from Scripture about this coming mark. They include the following.

1. THE FALSE PROPHET IS THE ONE WHO INSTITUTES AND ENFORCES THIS

The promoter of the first beast, the second beast, the false prophet, is the one who enforces this mark. He is the one who makes everyone receive this mark. It is not done by the final Antichrist himself.

2. IT SEEMS TO BE A PHYSICAL MARK

The mark of the beast seems to be some type of physical image which is placed upon the forehead or right hand. Therefore, Scripture seems to say that this mark will be observable with the naked eye. It does not seem to be some type of computer chip which is implanted underneath the skin. Seemingly, everyone will be able to see the mark.

However, we certainly cannot be confident of this. It is possible that it will be invisible to the naked eye. We just do not know enough to be certain about this point.

3. IT IS PLACED UPON THE RIGHT HAND OR FOREHEAD

The next thing we learn about the mark is its placement of it. It will go on either the right hand or the forehead of the person. This will seemingly make it obvious to everyone whether or not someone has this particular mark. Apparently it will be in plain sight.

4. EVERYONE HAS TO RECEIVE THIS MARK TO BUY OR SELL

Scripture is also clear that everyone has to receive this mark, there are no exceptions. Rich or poor, young or old, everyone must have it. Without this mark, there would be no buying or selling, no commerce whatsoever.

5. IT CANNOT BE REMOVED FROM THE PERSON

Once the mark of the beast has been given to a person, it cannot be removed. It remains upon that person as long as they are alive. In other words, it is a permanent mark.

6. THE MARK IS A NUMBER

The mark constitutes a specific number. It is 666. No other mark or tattoo will be acceptable. It must be the 666.

7. IT IS THE NUMBER OF THE BEAST

We also find that this mark is the number of the name of the beast. In some way, this number is linked to the first beast.

8. IT IS A SIGN OF OWNERSHIP

Receiving the mark, the brand of the beast, indicates ownership. Scripture gives examples of God marking certain people.

For example, the Lord marked Cain. We read about this in the Book of Genesis.

> Then the LORD put a mark on Cain to warn anyone who might try to kill him (Genesis 4:15 NLT).

In this instance, it was a mark of protection.

In addition, during the great tribulation period, the Lord will mark 144,000 separate individuals who will be His witnesses.

> After this I saw four angels standing at the four corners of the earth, holding back the four winds of the earth to prevent any wind from blowing on the land or on the sea or on any tree. Then I saw another angel coming up from the east, having the seal of the living God. He called out in a loud voice to the four angels who had been given power to harm the land and the sea: "Do not harm the land or the sea or the trees until we put a seal on the foreheads of the servants of our God." Then I heard the number of those who were sealed: 144,000 from all the tribes of Israel (Revelation 7:1-4 NIV).

This will also be a mark of protection and ownership; they belong to Him.

As the Lord marks His people, the beast will mark his own. This is another way in which this man of sin mimics the Lord.

MANY PEOPLE WILL REFUSE TO ACCEPT THE MARK

We know from Scripture that there will be a number of people who will refuse to take this "mark of the beast." The Book of Revelation says.

> I saw thrones on which were seated those who had been given authority to judge. And I saw the souls of those who had been beheaded because of their testimony about Jesus and because of the word of God. They had not worshiped the beast or his image and had not received his mark on their foreheads or their hands. They came to life and reigned with Christ a thousand years (Revelation 20:4 NIV).

These people will pay with their lives. Yet this is a small price to pay to be able to spend eternity with the Lord.

This sums up what the Scripture has to say about the mark of the beast.

SUMMARY TO QUESTION 38
WHAT IS THE MARK OF THE BEAST?

The Book of Revelation speaks of something known as the "mark of the beast." This is some type of physical brand that the second beast, the false prophet, the promoter of Antichrist, will force upon all the people of the world. Each person will have to receive this mark. It is the mark of the first beast, the final Antichrist.

The Bible is clear that nobody at that time will be able to buy or sell without having the mark of the beast on their person. There will be no exceptions. This will be placed either upon their right hand, or upon their forehead.

The mark will consist of a specific number 666. This number is somehow related to the name of the first beast, the man of sin.

The mark is a sign of ownership. Indeed, Scripture give examples of the Lord marking certain people as His own. This includes the Old Testament character Cain. He was marked for his own protection.

During the great tribulation period, before the mark of the beast is instituted, the Lord will place His mark on 144,000 men, twelve thousand out of each of the twelve tribes of Israel. These "marked individuals will function as His witnesses during that horrific period of judgment which will come upon the people of the earth.

Therefore, just as the Lord marked His own people with His particular mark, the Antichrist will counterfeit God's ways by marking his own people. This mark signifies that the person is fully owned by this first beast, the Antichrist.

The mark seems to be permanent. Once the person receives this mark the beast seemingly owns them as long as they are alive. If this is the case, then all hope for them is gone. Therefore, it is a horrific thing for someone to receive the mark of the beast.

Scripture tells us that there will be many people who do not receive this mark of the beast. While many of them will pay for this refusal with their lives, this is much better than going into eternity separated from the Lord.

The good news is that people have been warned ahead of time about this mark. The bad news is that people will still receive this mark in defiance of the Lord.

Can Anyone Be Saved If They Receive The Mark Of The Beast?

The mark of the beast indicates his ownership. Those who willingly receive his mark are allowing him to literally "own" their souls. Does this mean that those who take the mark of the beast are forever owned by the man of sin and the devil that inspires him? What does the Scripture have to say about this?

WHAT IS THE MARK OF THE BEAST?

The mark is a brand which will be placed upon the right hand or the forehead of a person. This will only occur in the last three and one half years before the return of Jesus Christ to the earth. The Book of Revelation says the following about the reception of the mark.

> And he requires everyone—small and great, rich and poor, free and slave—to be given a mark on his right hand or on his forehead, so that no one can buy or sell unless he has the mark: the beast's name or the number of his name (Revelation 13:16,17 HCSB).

Without the mark of the beast, nobody will be able to buy anything or sell anything. In other words, without the mark, nobody will be able to survive.

WHAT HAPPENS WHEN THE MARK IS RECEIVED

When the mark of the beast is willingly received by a person, then their eternity is once and for all settled. In other words, their fate is sealed, they have no hope. The Bible explains it this way.

> And another angel, a third, followed them, saying with a loud voice, "If anyone worships the beast and its image and receives a mark on his forehead or on his hand, he also will drink the wine of God' wrath, poured full strength into the cup of his anger, and he will be tormented with fire and sulfur in the presence of the holy angels and in the presence of the Lamb. And the smoke of their torment goes up forever and ever, and they have no rest, day or night, these worshipers of the beast and its image, and whoever receives the mark of its name" (Revelation 14:9-11 ESV).

These words seem to make clear the terrible fate of those who willingly receive the mark of the beast. They will be eternally punished for their act of defiance against the Lord.

NOT EVERYONE AGREES THEY ARE WITHOUT HOPE

There are those commentators who believe that it will be possible for a person to turn to Jesus Christ even after they have received the mark of the beast. The reasoning is this: as long as a person is alive they have the choice whether to receive the forgiveness of Christ, or to reject it. This includes those who have received the mark of the beast.

THE HOLY SPIRIT MUST DRAW PEOPLE TO CHRIST

This is, however, a minority view among Bible students. Furthermore, it is questionable as to whether the Holy Spirit would even work with these individuals who have denied Jesus Christ by taking the mark of the beast. Scripture makes it clear that nobody is able to be saved from their sins apart from the work of the Holy Spirit. This being the case, we should not hold out hope for those who have willingly received this mark.

THE MARK OF THE BEAST HAS NOT HAPPENED YET!

We cannot emphasize this too much. Nobody has yet received the mark of the beast. Therefore, people should not be concerned at this time about taking the mark by accident. That cannot happen!

When the mark of the beast is eventually administered, it will be given to those who *willingly* take it, and who know exactly what it means. Indeed, they are dedicating themselves to the worship of the beast.

Consequently, we should not be worried that we may take the mark of the beast by mistake, or accident.

SUMMARY TO QUESTION 39
CAN ANYONE BE SAVED IF THEY RECEIVE THE MARK OF THE BEAST?

There is a legitimate concern by people about receiving the mark of the beast, the branding that the false prophet attempts to place upon every human being during the time of the great tribulation. The mark will be either the name of the beast, the Antichrist, or the number of his name, 666. It will be placed upon either the right hand or the forehead.

Scripture says that nobody will be able to buy or sell without having this mark. The Bible says that the punishment that God will mete out for those taking this mark is eternal damnation. Consequently, it is crucial that the people living at that time should refuse to take the mark of the beast.

The Bible seems to clearly say that once a person willingly receives that particular mark no hope remains for them. Indeed, they are forever lost in sin. Salvation from sin now becomes impossible.

Some, however, dispute this. They think that as long as a person remains alive there is still hope for them to turn to Christ and be saved. This includes those who have received the mark of the beast.

Yet, the Bible clearly says that nobody can come to Christ apart from the drawing of the Holy Spirit. It is questionable as to whether the Holy Spirit would attempt to convict a person of their need for Jesus Christ after they have willingly rejected him by receiving the mark of the beast.

Whatever the case may be, it is essential for those who are alive when the mark of the beast is administered to refuse to take the mark. While this will most likely result in their own death, the consequences of receiving the mark are so much worse.

How Can A Person Calculate The Number Of The Beast? Is The Number Of The Beast 666 Or 616?

One of the most well-known parts of the Bible, by believer and unbeliever alike, is the famous, or infamous, number of the coming beast of Revelation, the man of sin. His number is 666. Scripture says.

> This calls for wisdom: Let the one who has insight calculate the beast's number, for it is man's number, and his number is 666 (Revelation 13:18 NET).

The number of the beast will be 666. People living at the time of his appearance will be able to confirm his identity. The question is this: how will they be able to do this?

HOW THE IDENTITY OF THE BEAST IS CONFIRMED

To confirm the identity of the coming beast, the final Antichrist, it will be a matter of calculating the number of the name of that person, it will add up to 666. This is done by a process called Gematria. This refers to giving a numeric value to letters of the alphabet. Some languages, including Hebrew, Greek, and Latin, have numeric value for each letter.

HEBREW

In Hebrew, the first ten letters represent the numbers 1-10. The remainder of the letters represents the numbers 20, 30, etc., all the way up until 100, then 200, 300 and 400. Therefore, using these letters to represent numbers, the names in the Hebrew language can be given specific numeric values.

GREEK

In the same way, the Greek alphabet also has numbers which represent each letter. Latin also gives numeric value to the letters of the alphabet.

WHICH ALPHABET TO USE?

One of the issues which must be addressed concerns which of these three languages should be used to calculate the identity of the beast. Should Hebrew, Greek, or Latin be used? Among scholars there is no consensus of opinion; though most scholars would argue that Greek is the language which should be utilized.

A few, however, believe it is Hebrew which should be employed. Very few argue that we should use Latin to calculate the identity of this first beast of Revelation, the coming Antichrist.

666 OR 616?

However, another problem arises. A few manuscripts of the Book of Revelation, including the earliest existing one which dates to about A.D. 300, have the number 616 instead of 666! The number 665 is also found in some manuscripts.

What are we to make of this? What is the real number of the beast? How can his identity be confirmed if we do not know the exact number to calculate?

666 IS THE BEST READING FOR NOW

While it is true that a few biblical manuscripts read 616 instead of 666, most New Testament textual scholars still regard the 666 as the true reading. The early church Father Irenaeus, writing around A.D. 200, called attention to the manuscripts in his day which read 616. He gave a number of reasons as to why this particular number should be rejected.

However, from the statements of Irenaeus, we know that such a reading did exist at an early date. The Greek manuscript, called p115, which has been recently published, and dated about A.D. 300, only confirms what was already known; the 616 reading was around at an early date.

616 IS THE NUMBER OF NERO IN LATIN AND CALIGULA IN GREEK

It seems that one of the reasons why 616 may have showed up in certain manuscripts has to do with identifying the beast with two Roman Emperors, Caesar Nero and Caligula. Indeed, 616 is the number of Caesar Nero when written in Latin, and the number of Caligula in Greek.

Therefore, it seems that this particular reading of these few manuscripts was motivated in an attempt to link one of these two evil Roman Emperors to the first beast of the Book of Revelation.

666 SEEMS TO BE HIS NUMBER

When all is said and done, right now there is no reason to reject the evidence which gives the number of the beast at 666.

However, this does not mean that 616 can be completely ruled out. This is one of these issues where further evidence may change our opinion.

SUMMARY TO QUESTION 40
HOW CAN A PERSON CALCULATE THE NUMBER OF THE BEAST? IS THE NUMBER OF THE BEAST 666 OR 616?

The famous number 666 is the number of the name of the first beast, the final Antichrist in the Book of Revelation. This number is to be used by those living at the time of his appearance to confirm his identity. To do this, the letters of his name must be given a numeric value. The numbers of the letters of the name of this coming man of sin will add up to 666.

This being the case, it is important that 666 is the correct number. There are, however, some manuscripts of the Book of Revelation which have the number as 616 instead of 666. Which one of these numbers is correct?

We know that the number 616 was found in biblical manuscripts at an early date. Irenaeus, who died about A.D. 200, reported that a number of manuscripts in his day read 616. While he rejected 616 in favor of 666, the fact remains that some early manuscripts had this reading.

It seems that the number 616 may have been put in these manuscripts for a specific reason; it is the number of Caesar Nero when put into Latin. It is also argued that it is the number of the name of the Roman Emperor Caligula in Greek.

Since most textual scholars believe that 666 is the correct reading here, this is probably the best way to view the issue at the present. However, if further evidence is brought forward for the reading 616, then it must be considered. Yet as of now there is no real compelling reason to reject the traditional understanding that 666 is the number of the beast.

It must be emphasized that this number will only be important for those living at that time in history. If the true believers in Jesus Christ, the New Testament Church, are taken out of the world before the last seven year great tribulation period, then calculating the number of the coming beast will have no meaning for them whatsoever. Indeed, at that time they will have better things on their mind, the Lord Jesus Christ Himself!

QUESTION 41

How Will The Antichrist
Imitate Jesus?

The idea behind the term Antichrist is one who imitates Christ, or attempts to usurp the authority of the rightful Messiah. From a study of Scripture, we find that this final Antichrist will imitate or mimic Jesus Christ in a number of significant ways. These include the following

1. HE WILL MAKE A COVENANT, AN AGREEMENT, WITH ISRAEL

The final Antichrist starts his career by making an agreement with Israel. This is explained in the Book of Daniel. It says.

> And he shall make a strong covenant with many for one week, and for half of the week he shall put an end to sacrifice and offering. And on the wing of abominations shall come one who makes desolate, until the decreed end is poured out on the desolator (Daniel 9:27 ESV).

Jesus, the genuine Messiah, also makes a peace covenant with the nation. The prophet Ezekiel recorded the Lord saying.

> I will make a covenant of peace with them. It shall be an everlasting covenant with them. And I will set them in their land and multiply them, and will set my sanctuary in their midst forevermore (Ezekiel 37:26 ESV).

Each has their own covenant of peace. However, the covenant made with Antichrist is called a "covenant of death." The Lord said.

> Because you have said, "We have made a covenant with death, and with Sheol we have an agreement, when the overwhelming whip passes through it will not come to us, for we have made lies our refuge, and in falsehood we have taken shelter" (Isaiah 28:15 ESV).

The two covenants could not be more different. Indeed, one is from "heaven" and the other from "hell."

2. HE WILL RIDE A WHITE HORSE

As the judgments recorded in the Book of Revelation begin, we are introduced to a rider on a white horse. The Bible says.

> Now I watched when the Lamb opened one of the seven seals, and I heard one of the four living creatures say with a voice like thunder, "Come!" And I looked, and behold, a white horse! And its rider had a bow, and a crown was given to him, and he came out conquering, and to conquer (Revelation 6:1-2 ESV).

Many people believe this will be the Antichrist, or at the very least, individuals making the way for the final Antichrist.

When Jesus Christ returns to the earth, He will come back riding upon a white horse. The Book of Revelation records His return in this manner.

> Then I saw heaven opened, and behold, a white horse! The one sitting on it is called Faithful and True, and in righteousness he judges and makes war (Revelation 19:11 ESV).

This is another way in which Christ is imitated.

3. HE WILL PERFORM MIRACLES

Jesus performed miracles. They were part of the credentials of the pre-dicted Messiah. These miracles were performed to further the king-dom of God. The Gospel according to Matthew explains it as follows.

> Now when John heard in prison about the deeds of the Christ, he sent word by his disciples and said to him, "Are you the one who is to come, or shall we look for another?" And Jesus answered them, "Go and tell John what you hear and see: the blind receive their sight and the lame walk, lepers are cleansed and the deaf hear, and the dead are raised up, and the poor have good news preached to them" (Matthew 11:2-5 ESV).

The final Antichrist will also perform miraculous signs but his mira-cles will further the kingdom of Satan. Paul wrote the following to the Thessalonians.

> The coming of the lawless one is by the activity of Satan with all power and false signs and wonders, and with all wicked deception for those who are perishing, because they refused to love the truth and so be saved (2 Thessalonians 2:9,10 ESV).

Therefore, the man of sin mimics the Lord in miracle-working.

4. HE WILL CLAIM TO BE GOD

Jesus Christ was God in human flesh. Scripture says.

> In the beginning was the Word, and the Word was with God, and the Word was God (John 1:1 NIV).

Antichrist, a mere human, will claim to be God. The Bible says.

> Who opposes and exalts himself against every so-called god or object of worship, so that he takes his seat in

the temple of God, proclaiming himself to be God (2 Thessalonians 2:4 ESV).

His claim, of course, is false.

5. HE WILL CAUSE PEOPLE TO WORSHIP HIM

Jesus rightfully received the worship from His creation. Indeed, the writer to the Hebrews stated that even the angels were commanded to worship Jesus, God the Son. We read.

> For to which of the angels did God ever say, "You are my Son; today I have become your Father"? Or again, "I will be his Father, and he will be my Son"? And again, when God brings his firstborn into the world, he says, "Let all God's angels worship him" (Hebrews 1:5-6 NIV).

The final Antichrist, who does not deserve worship, desires to be adored by the people. Scripture says that he will be worshipped by the inhabitants of the world.

> People worshiped the dragon because he had given authority to the beast, and they also worshiped the beast and asked, "Who is like the beast? Who can make war against it?" (Revelation 13:4 NIV).

Therefore, God the Son, who deserves to be worshipped, will be worshipped. The man of sin, Antichrist, who does not deserve to be worshipped, will receive worship from a sinful, evil world.

6. HE MAY CLAIM A RESURRECTION

There is the possibility that the final Antichrist will pull off a fake or counterfeit resurrection. The Bible says the following event will transpire.

One of its heads seemed to have a mortal wound, but its mortal wound was healed, and the whole earth marveled as they followed the beast (Revelation 13:3 ESV).

In contrast, Jesus actually rose from the dead, never to die again. We have this wonderful account of what occurred on Easter Sunday.

And as they [the women] were frightened and bowed their faces to the ground, the men said to them, "Why do you seek the living among the dead? He is not here, but has risen. Remember how he told you, while he was still in Galilee (Luke 24:5-6 ESV).

Therefore, we have the contrast between a genuine resurrection, Jesus, and a phony, or counterfeit, resurrection that takes place with the man of sin.

Even if the first beast, the Antichrist, does actually die and then comes back to life, it will not be a resurrection like that of Jesus. Jesus came back in a glorified body. There is no indication whatsoever that the Antichrist will return in some type of indestructible body, as is the case in the body of Jesus.

Furthermore, Jesus' resurrected body cannot experience suffering. We know that whatever body the Antichrist has, he will suffer in it forever when he is cast alive into the lake of fire. Therefore, whatever does happen to him is certainly not the same thing as what happened to Jesus on Easter Sunday.

7. HE WILL PUT HIS MARK OR BRAND ON THE FOREHEAD OF HIS FOLLOWERS

Another way in which the final Antichrist will mimic the ministry of Jesus is by having a mark, or some type of branding, placed upon the forehead of his followers. We are told that the Lord marks 144,000 people out of the twelve tribes of Israel.

> Then I saw another angel ascending from the rising of the sun, with the seal of the living God, and he called with a loud voice to the four angels who had been given power to harm earth and sea, saying, "Do not harm the earth or the sea or the trees, until we have sealed the servants of our God on their foreheads." And I heard the number of the sealed, 144,000, sealed from every tribe of the sons of Israel (Revelation 7:2-4 ESV).

In the same way, the mark of the Antichrist will be placed upon all of those who dwell upon the face of the earth. His cohort, the false prophet will make this happen. The Bible explains it in this manner.

> The second beast was empowered to give life to the image of the first beast so that it could speak, and could cause all those who did not worship the image of the beast to be killed. He also caused everyone (small and great, rich and poor, free and slave) to obtain a mark on their right hand or on their forehead. Thus no one was allowed to buy or sell things unless he bore the mark of the beast-that is, his name or his number (Revelation 13:15-17 NET).

While this mark is actually facilitated by the false prophet, the second beast, it is another instance of the man of sin mimicking the "man of sorrows." Those who are marked belong to the beast.

These are some of the obvious ways in which the coming Antichrist will mimic Jesus, the genuine Christ.

SUMMARY TO QUESTION 41
HOW WILL A PERSONAL ANTICHRIST IMITATE JESUS?

The Antichrist will be an individual who will attempt of imitate or mimic Jesus Christ, the genuine Messiah, in every way possible. This is not surprising because the word *anti* can mean, among other things, "in place of" or "instead of." We find this personage mimicking Jesus in the following ways.

First, he will make a peace agreement with the Jews. Scripture says that Jesus also has an agreement of peace with Israel. Thus, by making his own agreement, the man of sin is imitating the Lord.

Antichrist is also pictured in Scripture as riding on a white horse. When Jesus returns to the earth with the believers He will be riding a white horse.

Jesus was a miracle worker. This was part of His credentials as the Messiah. Antichrist will also be a miracle worker of sorts with his own brand of miraculous deeds. Yet his miraculous deeds are called "lying wonders," or "lying miracles."

Jesus Christ is the eternal God. Therefore, He could rightly make claims that only God Himself can make. We find Jesus claiming to be God both directly and indirectly.

Antichrist will falsely claim Deity. In an act of defiance again the Lord, this man of sin will place himself in the Holy of Holies of a rebuilt temple and claim that he is God. Though his act will imitate the claims of the Lord, this man of lawlessness has no right to make any such claims.

As Christ Jesus rightfully received the worship of the people, the coming Antichrist will demand worship. It seems that while many will willingly worship this coming beast, the Antichrist, many will do so only because they will forfeit their lives if they do not. Therefore, not all of the worship that he receives will be heartfelt.

There is also the possibility that the final Antichrist will fake his own death and resurrection. In doing so, it would be a parody or counterfeit of the actual resurrection of Jesus.

We also have the possibility, even the likelihood that the Lord will allow this man of sin to die and come back to life. Yet this is not the same as the resurrection of Jesus. Jesus was raised in an eternal glorified body, one which is not subject to pain and suffering. The body of the final Antichrist, whatever the properties it may have, does not include indestructibility. Indeed, we are told that he will be consciously tormented day and night forever and ever. At the very best, he will be resuscitated, or re-animated, not resurrected.

Finally, we discover that Antichrist imitates Jesus in that his mark, or branding, is placed upon the forehead of his followers. The brand, 666, indicates ownership. Earlier in the Book of Revelation, we are told that Jesus places His mark on the foreheads of 144,000 people, twelve thousand men from each of the twelve tribes of Israel. Thus, we find another way in which the final Antichrist imitates Jesus.

Consequently, we see that in many ways, this coming man of sin, the false Messiah, will imitate Jesus Christ, the genuine Messiah.

Should We Try To Determine The Identity Of The Final Antichrist?

The Bible speaks of a personage coming on the scene of history known as the beast, the Antichrist. The evidence is clear that he has not yet appeared in history. This being the case, should we attempt to determine his identity? Are believers to look for this coming Antichrist?

1. THE PRE-TRIBULATION VIEW: THE CHURCH WILL NOT EXPERIENCE THE FINAL ANTICHRIST

There are many Bible believers who say that the Lord never intended the church, the true believers in Christ, to know the identity of the coming Antichrist because they will never experience him in person. While the spirit of Antichrist is certainly alive and well, and working in the world today, the final Antichrist has yet to come.

When he does come, the New Testament church will not be upon the earth. The church will first be taken out of the world at the rapture. The living believers will be caught up to meet the Lord in the air. It is only after this happens that the final Antichrist can be revealed.

2. ANTICHRIST DEALS PRIMARILY WITH ISRAEL

In addition, according to the pre-tribulation rapture position, the final Antichrist will primarily deal with the nation Israel. Indeed, the time of the appearance of Antichrist is known as the "seventieth week of Daniel." It is a period when the Lord once again deals with Israel as a nation. The church is not around at this time.

While Antichrist will indeed persecute the saints, these saints are not part of the New Testament church. The church is never pictured in the various predictions about the Antichrist. Therefore, this individual will not become prominent during this present age.

3. ALL ATTEMPTED IDENTIFICATIONS HAVE BEEN FUTILE

It is clear that the many past attempts to identify the final Antichrist have been mistaken. Though many sincere people were absolutely certain that they have correctly identified the coming man of sin with some contemporary personage, their identification has always been incorrect. This should teach us a lesson. It is not for us to know his identity!

4. ALL ATTEMPTED IDENTIFICATIONS WILL BE FUTILE

Indeed, if the pre-tribulation rapture view is correct, then all attempted identifications of the coming Antichrist, by definition, will be futile! His identity will remain unknown until the time the church is taken out of the world. It is only at that time that he will appear on the scene.

When he does appear, he will start as a relatively unknown person and then work his way up into a position of world leadership. This is further evidence that his identity will not be immediately apparent.

SUMMARY TO QUESTION 42
SHOULD WE TRY TO DETERMINE THE IDENTITY OF THE FINAL ANTICHRIST?

The final Antichrist, the man of sin who will rule over most, if not all of the world, is coming. This seems to be clear. This being the case, should Christians attempt to determine the identity of this future world ruler? What is our responsibility?

According to the pre-tribulation rapture position, the church will be taken out of the world before the appearance of this Antichrist. Thus, he will be unknown as far as the church is concerned. We will not be around to identify him.

This is because the future Antichrist will primarily deal with the nation of Israel, not the New Testament church. His coming on the scene of history has to do with fulfilling one final seven-year period of Israel's history, the seventieth week of Daniel. To this day, this time period remains unfulfilled.

This explains why all previous attempts to identify the coming Antichrist have been wrong. Well-meaning people have assumed they have determined the identity of the beast, the Antichrist. Yet all of them have been incorrect.

If the church is to be taken out of the world before the great tribulation period, then the identification of the coming man of sin is not only futile, it is not possible. His true identity is being held back until that moment the true church, the believers in Jesus, are removed from this world.

Christians, therefore, should not spend endless hours speculating on something to which they could never know the answer. Better use should be made of our time.

How Has Antichrist Been Misidentified In The Past?

The answer to this particular question could actually fill up several books! The predicted final Antichrist of Scripture has indeed been misidentified many times in the past. Furthermore, it seems fair to say that he will also be misidentified in the future.

However, it must be said that some of these people, who were misidentified as the final Antichrist, could rightly be called "Antichrist" since they have certain of the qualities of the coming man of sin. Yet, they were not the beast, the man of sin, the final Antichrist, the coming Caesar, which Scripture says will arrive upon the scene shortly before the return of Jesus Christ.

While not desiring to be exhaustive, we can list some of the more interesting identifications which have missed the mark. They include the following.

THE ROMAN GENERAL POMPEY: THE ANTI-MESSIAH

Even before the First Coming of Jesus Christ to the earth, there were identifications by the Jews of an "anti-Messiah." In a work written before the time of Christ, known as the "Psalms of Solomon," the Roman general Pompey is called the "adversary of God."

Pompey profaned the temple by entering the Holy of Hollies after his conquest of Jerusalem in 63 B.C. He, therefore, is called "the dragon" in this work written about 60 B.C. Scripture tells us that the final Antichrist will himself profane the temple in an act of defiance against the Lord.

CALIGULA: THE CRAZED ROMAN EMPEROR

During the first century, the Roman Emperor Caligula looked like a good candidate for the predicted Antichrist. Indeed, he ordered a statue of himself to be placed in the temple in Jerusalem. If this act would have been carried out, it would have fulfilled the prediction of Jesus. Indeed, the Lord warned the people to look for the following to take place.

> So when you see the abomination of desolation spoken of by the prophet Daniel, standing in the holy place (let the reader understand) (Matthew 24:15 ESV).

The temple is to be desecrated by the coming man of sin. Caligula attempted to fulfill this prediction. However, this crazed emperor died in A.D. 41, and his orders were never carried out. While for a time it looked like he may be the one Jesus spoke about, his premature death ended any chance of him being the predicted desolator.

NERO: THE EMPEROR WHO BLAMED CHRISTIANS FOR THE FIRE OF ROME

One of the most popular identifications of Antichrist was that of Caesar Nero. In many ways, his life mirrored that of the final Antichrist. For one thing, he blamed the Christians for the great fire of Rome. Nero then set out to specifically target them for persecution.

When he was condemned to death by the Roman Senate in A.D. 68, Nero committed suicide. Since he died alone, the rumors persisted that he was not really dead. While the return of Nero was expected for a number of years after his death, it was eventually realized that this man would not fulfill what the Scripture predicted about the final Antichrist.

DOMITIAN: THE EMPEROR WHO BANISHED THE APOSTLE JOHN TO PATMOS

The Roman Emperor Domitian was the person who banished John the Apostle to the Island of Patmos late in the first century A.D. Since he was the current Emperor at the time of the composition of the Book of Revelation, many saw him as the first beast, the Antichrist.

In fact, there are some interpreters of Revelation who still believe Domitian was the beast which John wrote about. This perspective holds that most of the events in the Book of Revelation were all fulfilled in the first century A.D., whether literally or figuratively.

DIOCLETIAN: THE EMPEROR WHO ORDERED EMPIRE-WIDE PERSECUTION OF CHRISTIANS

The Roman Emperor Diocletian had a number of qualities of the final Antichrist. In A.D. 303, Diocletian instituted the most thorough persecution of Christians to that date. The church historian Eusebius relates what happened in this manner.

> It was the nineteenth year of Diocletian's reign [A.D. 303] and the month Dystrus, called March by the Romans, and the festival of the Savior's Passion was approaching, when an imperial decree was published everywhere, ordering the churches to be razed to the ground and the Scriptures destroyed by fire, and giving notice that those in places of honor would lose their places, and domestic staff, if they continued to profess Christianity, would be deprived of their liberty. Such was the first edict against us. Soon afterwards other decrees arrived in rapid succession, ordering that the presidents of the churches in every place should all be first committed to prison and then coerced by every

possible means into offering sacrifice (Eusebius, *History of the Church* (VIII.2)

This edict concerned three things. Diocletian ordered all Christian churches to be destroyed, ordered all copies of Scripture to be burned, and deprived believers in Jesus Christ of their civil rights. These despicable acts made him a candidate for the predicted Antichrist.

JULIAN THE APOSTATE: HE WANTED TO REBUILD THE TEMPLE

After the rule of Constantine, there was the rise of an anti-Christian Emperor known as Julian the Apostate. This evil ruler attempted to rebuild the temple in Jerusalem in defiance of the words of Christ. In many ways, Julian was an Antichrist, but he was not the final Antichrist.

CHARLEMAGNE: THE MAN WHO WANTED TO REBUILD THE ROMAN EMPIRE

Charlemagne, Charles the Great, was the King of the Franks. He lived from A.D. 742-814. During his rule, he controlled a large portion of Europe. Indeed, he was the first ruler of an empire in Western Europe after the fall of the Roman Empire. He was viewed as a possible candidate for the final Antichrist because of his attempt to rebuild the fallen Roman Empire. This will ultimately occur when this future "man of sin" comes upon the scene. Charlemagne, however, died before achieving this lofty goal.

THE PROTESTANT REFORMERS BELIEVED THE POPE WAS ANTICHRIST

At the time of the Protestant Reformation, it almost became an article of faith that the pope and the papacy constituted the biblical Antichrist. In fact, the Protestant reformers were unified in their belief that Antichrist had appeared in the person of the pope in Rome.

Rome, of course, responded to those attacks. Interestingly, one of the arguments which Rome advanced to show that the pope could not be the predicted Antichrist was the fact that the coming man of sin had to be Jewish.

It was assumed that if the Jews accepted the Antichrist as their Messiah, then he would have to be a Jew. Otherwise it would be impossible for him to be embraced by the nation. Since there has never been a Jewish pope, the idea that the papacy was the predicted Antichrist was thoroughly rejected by Roman Catholics.

THE ROMAN CATHOLIC CHURCH BELIEVED PROTESTANTS WERE ANTICHRIST

The Roman Church turned the tables on the Protestants by claiming they were actually the biblical Antichrist! If the Roman Catholic Church was the sole work of Jesus Christ upon the earth, then to resist the church was to resist Christ. Therefore, Protestantism could rightly be called "Antichrist" by the Roman Catholic Church.

NAPOLEON BONAPARTE

During the French Revolution there was another popular candidate for Antichrist, Napoleon Bonaparte. As usual, the numbers which were attached to the name of Napoleon could be calculated to equal 666. While Napoleon seemed to have many of the characteristics of the predicted Antichrist, he too left the scene without fulfilling what the Scripture predicted.

THE SECOND WORLD WAR: MANY CANDIDATES FOR THE COMING ANTICHRIST ARISE

During the events leading up to the Second World War, as well as during the conflict, there were a number of books written which identified the final Antichrist as one of the leaders of the Axis powers. The main candidates were Adolph Hitler and Benito Mussolini, though some people suggested Joseph Stalin or even President Franklin Roosevelt!

PRESIDENT FRANKLIN DELANO ROOSEVELT

The numerical value of FDR's name was reported to add up to 666. Because of the Great Depression, FDR was the most autocratic United States President of the 20th century. Roosevelt was in office for 12 years. This was longer than any United States President.

HITLER: THE PERSECUTOR OF THE JEWS

Adolph Hitler was a favorite candidate for Antichrist during his rise to power. Indeed, there were many well-respected Bible interpreters who publicly came out and claimed Hitler was the biblical Antichrist.

As with others in the past, it was found that the letters of his name added up to 666. However, with the death of Hitler, and the end of the Second World War, the identification of him with the final Antichrist lost its momentum.

MUSSOLINI: THE ITALIAN ANTICHRIST

Benito Mussolini was also a popular choice among people who attempted to predict the identity of the first beast of the Book of Revelation. In fact, Mussolini seemed like a prime candidate. He wanted to re-establish the Holy Roman Empire, he was from Rome, and he had world domination in mind. Many booklets were written which depicted him as the coming beast, the man of sin.

Sad to say, some of these were composed by reputable Bible teachers. They, too, were caught up in the events surrounding the Second World War and therefore made the mistake of identifying a living person as the beast of Revelation. Like all of the interpreters before them, these godly people were wrong in their claim that Antichrist was alive and living among them.

JOSEPH STALIN: THE GREAT MASS MURDERER

Joseph Stalin, the Russian dictator, is believed to be the greatest mass murderer in history. He is said to have ordered the death of some

30 million people. While most rulers killed those of other nations, Stalin's victims were mostly his own people. He was a despicable human being and therefore seemingly a prime candidate for the biblical Antichrist. Yet, he was not the predicted one.

THE POST-WORLD WAR II ANTICHRISTS

World War II came and went. The final Antichrist had still not appeared. The embarrassments of the identifications of Hitler and Mussolini during the Second World War did not stop others from repeating their mistake.

Indeed, after the Second World War there were still candidates for the position of Antichrist among those who appeared on the world scene.

JOHN F. KENNEDY: THE MORTAL HEAD WOUND

For a while, a popular candidate was United States President John F. Kennedy (JFK). He was the first Roman Catholic who became President of the United States. This made him suspect to a number of people because it was believed that he would do whatever the pope asked.

In addition, at the 1956 Democratic convention, where he was not nominated for president, Kennedy received 666 votes. When President Kennedy was shot in the head in Dallas on November 22, 1963, it was thought that his deadly head wound would heal. Stories circulated that he was being kept alive in the Vatican. Eventually, the idea that John F. Kennedy would return and become this final Antichrist lost momentum.

HENRY KISSINGER: THE PEACEMAKER

Another popular candidate was the former Secretary of State Henry Kissinger. Because of Mr. Kissinger's peacemaking activity in the Middle East, he was labeled the Antichrist by some. However, he eventually withdrew from politics without fulfilling the biblical requirements of Antichrist.

ANWAR SADAT: THE MAN OF PEACE, MAN OF SIN?

Anwar Sadat, the leader of Egypt, was a popular choice for a while as being the biblical Antichrist. It was claimed that he was from the right geographical area, made a groundbreaking peace treaty with Israel and won the Nobel Prize as a "man of peace."

In fact, one Christian book named Anwar Sadat the Antichrist and claimed that this identification was by divine revelation! However, Sadat was soon assassinated and consequently the idea that he was the man of sin quickly faded.

This also illustrates the foolishness of people who claim that their own particular insight into the identity of the man of sin is somehow divinely given!

MIKHAIL GORBACHEV: THE MAN WHO DISMANTLED THE SOVIET UNION

Another favorite during the Cold War was the Soviet Leader Mikhail Gorbachev. He became a prime candidate because of his participation in dismantling the Soviet Union. Yet, this world leader fell from power and thus became a non-candidate.

PRESIDENT RONALD WILSON REAGAN: EACH OF HIS NAMES HAD SIX LETTERS

Strange as it may seem, during the 1980's, there was some speculation that President Ronald Reagan of the United States was the predicted Antichrist. The fact that he had six letters in all three of his names, Ronald Wilson Reagan, caused some to speculate that this popular president was actually the man of sin. As has been true with the other identifications in the past, this one turned out to be incorrect.

SADAAM HUSSEIN: THE BUTCHER OF BAGHDAD

Sadaam Hussein, the leader of Iraq, the butcher of Baghdad, was also highlighted as being a possible candidate for Antichrist in the early 1990's. For one thing, Hussein was going to rebuild the ancient city of Babylon whose location is in modern day Iraq.

Yet, like all previous candidates, this identification was incorrect. Hussein was eventually overthrown when Iraq was invaded by the United States and its allies. At the end of 2006, Hussein was executed for his murderous crimes.

The list goes on and on. This has merely been a sampling of the misidentifications of the past with respect to the identity of the final Antichrist.

THE MISIDENTIFICATIONS NEVER STOP

The misidentifications of the person of the Antichrist continue to this day. Indeed, it seems that anyone who becomes a public figure is sooner or later found to have the numbers of his name add up to 666.

LESSONS TO BE LEARNED FROM THESE MISTAKES

There are many lessons to be learned in these attempts to name the biblical Antichrist. Some of the more obvious ones are as follows.

1. WE SHOULD NOT ATTEMPT TO IDENTIFY ANTICHRIST AHEAD OF TIME

To begin with, we should not engage in such fruitless speculation. People will only know the identity of the final Antichrist when he arrives on the scene and performs certain predicted acts. Until that time, his identity will remain a mystery. To sum up, it is not possible to know who he is until then.

2. HIS NUMBER IS GIVEN TO CONFIRM HIS IDENTITY, NOT DISCOVER IT

Second, the number of his name, 666, is given to us to confirm his identity, not to discover it. In other words, it is to verify what is already believed about this man, that he is the beast, the man of sin, predicted in Scripture. We are not to know who he is ahead of time.

3. IT DOES NOT HONOR THE LORD WHEN PREDICTIONS ARE MADE

Finally, and most important, such public predictions of either the exact identity of Antichrist, or the precise timing of his coming, never honor the Lord. In fact, all they do is bring shame and ridicule to the Christian faith.

When unbelievers are told that they need to know that a particular person is the final Antichrist because the great tribulation is about to happen, and the coming of Jesus Christ is near, the message of Christ is shamed and held up to ridicule when the prediction does not come to pass.

In fact, who can blame unbelievers for this response when so-called Bible experts are telling them that they know, or they think they know, the identity of the coming man of sin?

If well-known Bible teachers are wrong about the identity of the final Antichrist, then unbelievers may conclude they are also wrong about Jesus Christ! Why trust anything which they say?

Therefore, hopefully one of the great lessons to be learned from the study of Antichrist concerns what we should not do. Indeed, we should not attempt to identify any living person as Antichrist. When Antichrist arrives on the scene, there will be no question about who he is. Indeed, when this political leader becomes the beast who dominates the world, there will be little doubt about his identity.

SUMMARY TO QUESTION 43
HOW HAS ANTICHRIST BEEN MISIDENTIFIED IN THE PAST?

The attempt to discover the identity of biblical Antichrist has been a favorite pastime throughout history. Indeed, even before the time of

Christ, there were identifications made of the coming anti-Messiah. We can list some of the false identifications which have been made in the past, as well as what lessons we should learn from these mistakes.

Before the time of Christ, General Pompey of Rome, took control of the city of Jerusalem in 63 B.C. and entered the Holy of Holies in the temple. He was deemed the Antichrist by a work called the *Psalms of Solomon*.

In the early years of the church, the Antichrist was thought to possibly be one of the first-century Roman Emperors. Caligula, Nero and Domitian were all thought to be candidates. Indeed each of these rulers had many qualities that are predicted of the coming man of sin, the beast of Revelation. Yet they passed from the scene without fulfilling the words of the Bible.

In A.D. 303 the Roman Emperor Diocletian instituted an empire wide persecution of Christians. His behavior mirrored that of the final Antichrist.

Another candidate from the Roman Empire was the Emperor Julian the Apostate. This man renounced Christianity and ordered persecution of Christians. He went so far as encouraging the Jews to rebuild the temple in Jerusalem. However, neither Diocletian nor Julian fulfilled the Scripture with respect to Antichrist.

Later in history, Charles the Great, Charlemagne, attempted to rebuild the fallen Roman Empire. This is something which Antichrist alone will accomplish. However, he died before fulfilling his goal.

During the Protestant Reformation, the pope and the papacy were assumed to be Antichrist by the Protestants. In fact, to call the pope the Antichrist almost became an article of faith.

Not to be outdone by the Protestants, the Roman Catholic Church claimed that the Protestantism was the actual Antichrist! They were thwarting God's unique work on earth, the Roman Church.

At the time of the French Revolution there were many who believed Napoleon was the predicted man of sin. It was found where his name could be added up to the number 666. Yet, this identification proved to be untrue.

The lead up to World War II, as well as during the War, saw a number of potential candidates for the final Antichrist. Many books and pamphlets were produced which named either Adolph Hitler or Benito Mussolini as the beast of Revelation. Joseph Stalin was also mentioned as a potential Antichrist. Even U.S. President Franklin Roosevelt was thought to be the beast by some!

Unhappily, a number of respected Bible teachers came out publicly designating either Hitler or Mussolini as the final Antichrist. When the War ended these identifications ceased.

In the 1960's, President John F. Kennedy was viewed as Antichrist because of his Roman Catholic beliefs, as well as his death by a head wound. When he did not return from the dead, the speculation ended.

In the 1970's, Anwar Sadat was considered to be Antichrist for his peacemaking efforts with Israel. His assassination ended that speculation.

In the 1980's, Mikhail Gorbachev was hailed as Antichrist for a time due to his efforts in ending the Soviet Union. Yet he soon fell from power. Even President Ronald Reagan was suggested as a possible candidate for the biblical Antichrist when it was discovered that his first, middle, and last name all have six letters!

During the Gulf War of 1992, Sadaam Hussein was thought to be the final Antichrist. It became especially alarming to many people when it was found he was rebuilding the ancient city of Babylon in Iraq. Yet when he was eventually deposed, such speculation ended. Later, he was executed.

What seems to be an undisputed fact is this: any new personage who comes on the world scene and makes some type of impact will sooner or later be designated the Antichrist by someone. Indeed, the number 666 will be somehow found in their name; no matter what type of mathematical gymnastics it takes to find it!

These examples should teach us many lessons. In fact, there are three lessons in particular which we should learn.

First, it seems that the Lord does not intend for us to know who this personage is until he arrives on the scene. Indeed, it is highly likely that we will not be able to know his identity until he appears and performs certain predicted acts. Therefore, we are not to engage in fruitless speculation of something which, by definition, we cannot know the answer.

Furthermore, the Lord gave us his number in Scripture, 666, as a means to confirm his identity, not to determine it. It has not been provided so that believers can continually engage in some guessing-game. Again, this teaches us not to be involved in speculating as to his identity. When this personage arrives and does what the Bible says he will do, the fact that the number of his name will equal 666 will only confirm what was already suspected of him.

Finally, it is not honoring the Lord to make such public speculation as to the identity of the coming Antichrist since each and every one of them turns out to be wrong! While it is certainly true that many if not most of these candidates are types of Antichrist, none of them is the final Antichrist predicted in Scripture.

Unfortunately, such speculation makes Bible-believers look like they do not know what they are talking about. If their interpretations cannot be trusted in one area of Scripture, then why should it be trusted in other areas? Unbelievers could logically come to this conclusion if the identity of a certain living person as Antichrist is presented as a fact of Scripture and then turns out to be false.

Therefore, we should learn a crucial lesson. Let us all be careful with our words when we proclaim what the Bible says about such and such a topic. To honor the Lord, we must continue to proclaim what the Bible tells us to say about Jesus Christ but we also must be careful not to say things which it does not say, especially about the topic of the final Antichrist.

Should We Be Looking For The Antichrist?

There is a question as to whether or not believers should be looking for the coming Antichrist. Will the New Testament church be around when he appears on the stage of history? Bible-believers are not in agreement on this particular issue. We can explain the situation as follows.

THE MID-TRIBULATION, PRE-WRATH AND POST-TRIBULATION VIEW: THE CHURCH WILL SEE ANTICHRIST

There are a number of Christians who do believe that we should be looking for the final Antichrist. Those who hold to a Mid-tribulation, Pre-wrath, or Post-tribulation rapture view, all believe that the church will live to see the final Antichrist. They believe the coming of Christ for the true believers will only take place sometime *after* this final Antichrist is revealed. The church will come face to face with this predicted man of sin.

Consequently, before we can look for Jesus Christ, we first must look for Antichrist. He will be a personage the New Testament church will eventually have to deal with.

PRE-TRIBULATIONISM: THE CHURCH WILL BE GONE BEFORE ANTICHRIST APPEARS

Those who hold the pre-tribulation rapture position, such as the author of this book, do not think this will be the case. We believe that the final Antichrist will only appear *after* the church has been removed from the world. Presently, the coming of the wicked one, the Antichrist, is being held back, restrained. Paul wrote.

> And you know what is restraining him now so that he may be revealed in his time. For the mystery of lawlessness is already at work. Only he who now restrains it will do so until he is out of the way (2 Thessalonians 2:6-7 ESV).

According to the pre-tribulation rapture position, the restrainer is usually identified with the Holy Spirit working through the members of the New Testament church, the true believers. While they are living on the earth and preaching the gospel of Jesus Christ, the coming of Antichrist is restrained. When the believers are removed from the world through the rapture of the church, the final Antichrist can then appear.

Consequently whether or not a Christian should be looking for the coming "man of sin" depends upon the one's view of what Scripture says about the timing of the rapture of the church. For those who hold any position other than the pre-tribulation rapture position, the church will have to face the predicted Antichrist.

However, if the pre-tribulation view is accurate, then the identity of Antichrist will not be known until the church has left the world (we have documented why we believe the Pre-Tribulation view is correct in our book "The Rapture").

SUMMARY TO QUESTION 44
SHOULD WE BE LOOKING FOR THE ANTICHRIST?

One of the questions which is often asked about the future Antichrist concerns whether or not the church, the true believers in Jesus Christ, should be looking for this personage. There are those which believe that the New Testament church will experience the persecutions which will be coming from the final Antichrist.

Before Christ returns to the earth, the church must go through a difficult period of time where the man of sin attempts to destroy all of those who believe in Jesus. The Lord returns before this evil beast, the Antichrist, can carry out his wicked plan.

Others do not think this is the right way of looking at it. Indeed, those who hold the pre-tribulation rapture position believe that the church will be caught up to meet the Lord in the air before the time the final Antichrist appears.

Therefore, we should not be looking for him at all. Instead, we should be looking for Jesus Christ. Antichrist will persecute believers but these saints come to trust in Christ *after* the church has been removed from the world.

Consequently, we should not spend any of our time looking for Antichrist since his appearing will not take place until the true believers in Jesus have been taken up in the rapture.

Therefore, whether or not Christians should be looking for the coming Antichrist basically depends upon what they believe is the biblical view of the timing of the rapture of the church.

QUESTION 45

What Are Some Of The Differences Between Jesus Christ And Antichrist?

There are many contrasts between Jesus, the genuine Messiah or Christ, and the final Antichrist, the one who opposes Jesus and attempts to usurp what is rightfully His. This coming Antichrist will be a counterfeit Messiah, a false Christ. Thus, the differences between the two are legion. We can note some of them as follows.

1. THEY HAVE A DIFFERENT ORIGIN

To begin with, Jesus came from heaven while the final Antichrist comes from beneath. Jesus said the following about His own origin.

> For I have come down from heaven, not to do my own will but the will of him who sent me (John 6:38 ESV).

On the other hand, the Book of Revelation describes Antichrist's origin as from the bottomless pit. Scripture says.

> And when they have finished their testimony, the beast that rises from the bottomless pit will make war on them and conquer them and kill them (Revelation 11:7 ESV).

The differences could not be more pronounced. Indeed, One is from above and the other from beneath.

2. JESUS CAME IN HIS FATHER'S NAME, ANTICHRIST WILL COME IN HIS OWN NAME

Jesus came in His Father's name while the Antichrist, when he arrives on the scene, will come in his own name. When speaking to those in His day who rejected Him, Jesus made it clear who the nation would accept and who they would not.

> I have come in my Father's name, and you do not accept me; but if someone else comes in his own name, you will accept him (John 5: 43 NIV).

Unfortunately the people will eventually accept a false Messiah instead of the genuine one. He is a person who comes in his own name, his own authority.

3. JESUS CAME TO SAVE, ANTICHRIST WILL COME TO DESTROY

Christ came to save sinners, while the Antichrist will come to destroy whomever he can. John wrote the following about the coming of Jesus Christ.

> For God did not send his Son into the world to condemn the world, but to save the world through him (John 3:17 NIV).

Jesus is the Savior. In another place, Jesus described His coming as follows.

FOR THE SON OF MAN CAME TO SEEK AND TO SAVE WHAT WAS LOST (LUKE 19:10 NIV).

Contrast this to the description of the coming man of sin.

> He will become very strong, but not by his own power. He will cause astounding devastation and will succeed in whatever he does. He will destroy the mighty warriors, the holy people (Daniel 8:24 NIV).

He is one who causes horrific devastation. What a contrast to the Lamb of God!

4. JESUS WAS HUMBLE ANTICHRIST WILL BE PROUD

When Jesus came to earth, He humbled Himself. In fact, The Bible says that He took upon Himself the form of a servant. Jesus described Himself in this manner.

> Take my yoke upon you and learn from me, for I am gentle and humble in heart, and you will find rest for your souls (Matthew 11:29 NIV).

Paul wrote the following about the humility of Jesus.

> He made himself nothing; he took the humble position of a slave and appeared in human form. And in human form he obediently humbled himself even further by dying a criminal's death on a cross (Philippians 2:7-8 NLT).

Jesus deliberately put Himself in a position of servant hood.

By contrast, the coming Antichrist will exalt himself. Paul wrote about the arrogance of this man of sin.

> He will exalt himself and defy everything that people call god and every object of worship. He will even sit in the temple of God, claiming that he himself is God (2 Thessalonians 2:4 NLT).

In an act of extreme arrogance, this man of sin exalts himself above everything and everyone.

5. JESUS WAS A LAMB ANTICHRIST WILL BE A BEAST

Christ was a lamb, while the final Antichrist is called a beast. John the Baptist identified Jesus as follows.

> The next day John saw Jesus coming toward him and said, "Look! The Lamb of God who takes away the sin of the world!" (John 1:29 NLT).

Jesus was the Lamb. However, this coming man of sin is described as a savage beast. The Book of Revelation says.

> Then I saw a beast rising up out of the sea. It had seven heads and ten horns, with ten crowns on its horns. And written on each head were names that blasphemed God (Revelation 13:1 NLT).

Again, we see the contrast between these two personages, the Lamb and the beast.

6. JESUS CAME TO DO THE FATHER'S WILL, ANTICHRIST WILL DO HIS OWN WILL

Jesus came to do the will of God the Father while the final Antichrist will come to do his own will. Jesus put it this way.

> For I have come down from heaven to do the will of God who sent me, not to do my own will (John 6:38 NLT).

In contrast, the Antichrist will do whatever he wishes to do. We read in Daniel.

> He will become very strong, but not by his own power. He will cause astounding devastation and will succeed in whatever he does. He will destroy the mighty warriors, the holy people (Daniel 8:24 NIV).

He demonstrates his arrogance in attempting to exert his own will.

7. JESUS IS THE TRUE GOD ANTICHRIST IS A FALSE DEITY

While Jesus Christ was God in human flesh, the final Antichrist, who has no claim to deity, will nevertheless claim to be God. John wrote the following about the true identity of Jesus.

In the beginning was the Word, and the Word was with God, and the Word was God (John 1:1 NIV).

The Antichrist, a false Christ, makes himself out to be deity, but he is not. Paul wrote about the blasphemous claims which he will make.

He will oppose and will exalt himself over everything that is called God or is worshiped, so that he sets himself up in God's temple, proclaiming himself to be God (2 Thessalonians 2:4 NIV).

Jesus is the true God. while this final Antichrist, the coming Caesar, is a false god.

8. JESUS DID GENUINE MIRACLES ANTICHRIST PERFORMS COUNTERFEIT MIRACLES

Jesus performed miracles when He was here upon the earth. They were part of the credentials of the predicted Messiah. The miracles of Christ advanced the kingdom of God. The Bible says the following.

When John heard in prison what the Messiah was doing, he sent his disciples to ask him, "Are you the one who was to come, or should we expect someone else?" Jesus replied, "Go back and report to John what you hear and see: The blind receive sight, the lame walk, those who have leprosy are cleansed, the deaf hear, the dead are raised, and the good news is proclaimed to the poor" (Matthew 11:2-5 NIV)

Jesus had the proper biblical credentials of the predicted Christ. His miracles testified that He was the One whom He claimed to be.

The Antichrist will also perform miracles, but his signs will advance the kingdom of Satan. The miracles of this final Antichrist are called deceptive or counterfeit. Paul described them as follows.

The coming of the lawless one is by the activity of Satan with all power and false signs and wonders, and with all wicked deception for those who are perishing, because they refused to love the truth and so be saved (2 Thessalonians 2:9,10 ESV).

These so-called miracles are "lying wonders," or "false signs."

9. CHRIST DESERVES WORSHIP ANTICHRIST DEMAND WORSHIP

Jesus, being God Almighty, deserved worship from the people. In fact, when He came into the world, the angels of God were commanded to worship Him.

> And again, when God brings his firstborn into the world, he says, "Let all God's angels worship him" (Hebrews 1:6 NIV).

In the same manner, those who follow Jesus Christ willingly worship Him. He certainly deserves our worship.

The Antichrist, being His counterfeit, will demand worship. Paul wrote the following to the Thessalonians about the undeserved worship the final Antichrist will demand.

> Who opposes and exalts himself against every so-called god or object of worship, so that he takes his seat in the temple of God, proclaiming himself to be God (2 Thessalonians 2:4 ESV).

On the one hand, Jesus receives His deserved worship by His loving followers, while on the other hand the final Antichrist demands worship he does not deserve.

10. JESUS WAS DESPISED AND REJECTED WHILE ANTICHRIST IS ADMIRED

At His First Coming Jesus was despised and rejected. However, the Antichrist will be admired when he comes on the scene. Scripture says of Jesus.

> He was despised and rejected by men; a man of sorrows, and acquainted with grief; and as one from whom men hide their faces he was despised, and we esteemed him not (Isaiah 53:3 ESV).

In the first chapter of the Gospel of John, there is one of the saddest verses in the entire Bible. It describes Jesus' entrance into our world as follows.

> He was in the world, and the world was made through him, yet the world did not know him (John 1:10 ESV).

In contrast, the final Antichrist will receive worldwide praise from a sinful world. The Book of Revelation says.

> One of its heads seemed to have a mortal wound, but its mortal wound was healed, and the whole earth marveled as they followed the beast. And they worshiped the dragon, for he had given his authority to the beast, and they worshiped the beast, saying, "Who is like the beast, and who can fight against it?" (Revelation 13:3,4 ESV).

The dissimilarity between the man of sin and the Lord Jesus is obvious. The godly One is despised while the ungodly one is admired.

11. ANTICHRIST WILL DO WHAT JESUS REFUSED TO DO IN HIS TEMPTATION

Interestingly, we find that the final Antichrist will do the three things that Jesus would not do when He was tempted by the devil.

For example, Satan tempted Jesus to turn stones into bread. This was a temptation for Jesus to perform a miracle to meet His own immediate needs instead of doing the will of God. Jesus refused.

However, the man of sin will perform miracles to further his own self-centered agenda. This is something Jesus would not do. He came to do the will of the Father.

In another instance, Jesus refused the temptation to jump from the pinnacle of the temple to the ground. He was not about to perform some supernatural sideshow just to gather a crowd.

Yet, the final Antichrist will do such things to get the attention of the unbelieving world. Indeed, he will do whatever it takes to get himself noticed.

Thirdly, Satan wanted Jesus to bow down and worship him. Jesus refused. In fact, He made it clear that worship belonged to God, and to Him alone.

The final Antichrist, along with the false prophet, will cause the entire world to bow down to Satan. What Jesus refused to do, the Antichrist will willingly do.

Therefore, in the three areas in which Jesus refused to give in to the devil, we find that the beast, the final Antichrist, will indeed succumb.

12. CHRIST IS DESTINED TO RULE, ANTICHRIST IS DESTINED FOR DESTRUCTION

We also find that the destiny of Jesus Christ and the final Antichrist is different. The Lord Jesus is destined to rule the world as King of Kings and Lord of Lords. He will assume the rule which is rightfully His. The Book of Revelation gives the following description of Christ at His return.

> Then I saw heaven opened, and a white horse was standing there. Its rider was named Faithful and True, for he judges fairly and wages a righteous war. His eyes were like flames of fire, and on his head were many crowns. A name was written on him that no one understood except himself. He wore a robe dipped in blood, and his title was the Word of God. The armies of heaven, dressed in the finest of pure white linen, followed him on white horses. From his mouth came

a sharp sword to strike down the nations. He will rule them with an iron rod. He will release the fierce wrath of God, the Almighty, like juice flowing from a winepress. On his robe at his thigh was written this title: King of all kings and Lord of all lords (Revelation 19:11-16 NLT).

The King will return to rule.

In complete contrast to this, the final Antichrist is destined for oblivion. He will be cast into the lake of fire along with the false prophet.

Then the beast was captured, and with him the false prophet who worked signs in his presence, by which he deceived those who received the mark of the beast and those who worshiped his image. These two were cast alive into the lake of fire burning with brimstone (Revelation 19:20 NLT).

The devil will eventually join them in this place of punishment. Again, we have the contrast of the destinies of Jesus and of the coming man of sin. They could not be more different.

CONCLUSION: THEY ARE DIFFERENT IN EVERY WAY

This sums up some of the major differences between Jesus Christ, God the Son, and the coming Antichrist, the man of sin. Obviously the differences between them are profound. Indeed, they are different in every conceivable way.

SUMMARY TO QUESTION 45

WHAT ARE SOME OF THE DIFFERENCES BETWEEN JESUS CHRIST AND ANTICHRIST?

The final Antichrist is a person who not only opposes Jesus Christ, he also attempts to usurp the things which rightfully belong to Jesus. The Bible gives us a number of specific differences between Jesus Christ and the coming Antichrist. We can sum them up as follows.

Jesus Christ came from above while the Antichrist is from below. In other words, they have different origins, heaven and the pit. The points of origin could not be more further apart.

In addition, Jesus came in his Father's name, in His authority. Antichrist will come in his own name to do his will, as well as the desires of his father, the devil. Thus, we have humility on one hand as opposed to self-promotion on the other hand.

Jesus came to save the world. That was the main purpose of His coming. Antichrist will come to destroy. Hence, the contrast is clear. Christ is the Savior of the world while Antichrist will attempt to obliterate everything sacred.

Jesus was humble in character while Antichrist will be proud. Jesus' goal was to meet the needs of others while Antichrist will only think about himself. Therefore, we have selflessness contrasted to selfishness.

Jesus is pictured in Scripture as a lamb, the Lamb of God. On the other hand, the coming Antichrist is described as a savage beast. The contrast here could not be greater.

Jesus came to the earth to do the will of God the Father while Antichrist does his own will. Indeed, one of his titles is "the willful king" or the "king who does according to his own will." Therefore, one person submits to God, while the other submits himself to the devil.

Jesus is God Almighty while Antichrist will falsely claim to be Deity. Accordingly, we have the true God versus the false God.

Jesus was a genuine miracle worker while Antichrist works phony or counterfeit miracles. Jesus' miracles were performed to glorify God the Father while the false signs of Antichrist will call attention to his father, the devil.

Jesus Christ deserves worship but was not rightly worshipped at His First Coming. The final Antichrist will demand worship though he does not deserve to be worshipped. Many people will willingly worship this foul character.

Jesus was despised and rejected by humanity when He came into the world. The people of Israel made it clear that they did not want Him to rule over them. In contrast, Antichrist will be admired when he arrives upon the scene. He will be warmly received by an unbelieving, ungodly world.

We also have the comparison between Christ and Antichrist in the temptations Jesus was given by the devil. Three times Jesus refused to give in to the devil's temptations. However, Antichrist will do the things Jesus refused to do.

This final Antichrist, along with the false prophet, will work miracles to further his own selfish purposes and he will perform a supernatural sideshow to get the attention of the unbelieving world. Also, he will cause the people to publicly worship the devil.

Finally, they each have a different destiny. When the Lord Jesus returns to the earth it will be as King of Kings and Lord of Lords. He will fulfill His destiny. Indeed, He will be ruler over everything.

Contrast to this the destiny of the final Antichrist. Though he will be the world ruler for a short period of time his destiny is punishment, the punishment of hell! Along with the false prophet, this man of sin will be thrown alive into the lake of fire. These two will be tormented there forever and ever. The devil will eventually join them.

These are some of contrasts between Jesus Christ and the final Antichrist. Clearly, the differences could not be greater.

Is It Possible The Antichrist Is Alive Today?

One of the questions which is continually asked about the biblical Antichrist concerns the possibility of him being alive today. Is this personage now among us? Is the final Antichrist alive? What do we know for certain?

1. WE DO NOT KNOW IF HE IS ALIVE NOW

The answer to this question is simple: we do not know. There are a number of reasons as to why this is the case.

If the final Antichrist appears after the rapture of the church, the pre-tribulation rapture view, then by definition *nobody* can know his identity until the church is out of the world.

Furthermore, he does not start out as a well-known figure but rather as a person who rises up out of obscurity. This is a further reason why he will be difficult, if not impossible, to identify until certain events unfold.

2. THE TIME OF THE LORD'S COMING IS UNKNOWN

Furthermore, the coming of the final Antichrist is linked to the time of the coming of the Lord. This personage will come immediately before the return of Christ. However, according to Jesus, nobody knows the timing of His coming. He said.

However, no one knows the day or hour when these things will happen, not even the angels in heaven or the Son himself. Only the Father knows (Matthew 24:36 NLT).

This being the case, we do not know the time of the coming of this final Antichrist.

WE ARE TOLD TO ALWAYS BE READY

In fact, it should not be our main concern whether or not this final Antichrist is alive today. Jesus commanded His followers to always be alert, to be ready for the coming of the Lord.

Be dressed for service and well prepared, as though you were waiting for your master to return from the wedding feast. Then you will be ready to open the door and let him in the moment he arrives and knocks (Luke 12:35-36 NLT).

No matter when the time of His coming may be, we need to be ready. Our Lord could come at any moment for us.

3. THERE ARE SIGNS SETTING THE STAGE

There are a number of factors which do show that the coming of Jesus Christ could be soon. They include the following.

ISRAEL IS AGAIN A FUNCTIONING STATE

The nation of Israel is back in their land as a modern state after some two thousand years of wandering the planet without a homeland. This is of the utmost significance. Indeed, the final seven year period, the great tribulation, does not begin until the Antichrist makes a seven year agreement with the state of Israel.

Of course, a state of Israel has to exist before this agreement can take place. There is now a functioning state of Israel.

THERE ARE PREPARATIONS TO BUILD THE THIRD TEMPLE

There are also preparations being made right now to construct a Third Temple upon the Temple Mount in the city of Jerusalem. Indeed there is so much happening with respect to the rebuilding of the temple that we have dedicated an entire book to this topic (*The Jews, Jerusalem, and the Coming Temple*).

THE EUROPEAN UNION

There is also the fact that Europe is now bound together with one central currency, the Euro. The fact that the European Union now exists as a powerful political and economic entity sets the stage for the coming man of sin to rule over a revived Roman Empire.

A GLOBAL IDENTIFICATION SYSTEM IS NOW POSSIBLE

With the rise of modern technology, the worldwide system of identifying each person who buys and sells is no longer a seeming fairy tale. Indeed, it is a reality. This is something all of us are painfully aware of.

These are four of the many factors which set the stage for the coming of the Lord. While this does not mean that the Lord must come back soon, the stage is being set for His return.

4. THERE IS "AN" ANTICHRIST WHO PRESENTLY EXISTS

Whether or not the "final" Antichrist is alive at this moment is unknown. One thing we do know for certain, there are people which are alive today who could fit the requirements of this man of sin. John wrote about Antichrists having already come in his day. He said.

> Dear children, the last hour is here. You have heard that the Antichrist is coming, and already many such antichrists have appeared. From this we know that the last hour has come (1 John 2:18 NLT).

John also wrote about the spirit of Antichrist which was already in the world.

> But if someone claims to be a prophet and does not acknowledge the truth about Jesus, that person is not from God. Such a person has the spirit of the Antichrist, which you heard is coming into the world and indeed is already here (1 John 4:3 NLT).

Paul wrote something similar to the Thessalonians. He put it this way.

> And you know what is holding him back, for he can be revealed only when his time comes. For this lawlessness is already at work secretly, and it will remain secret until the one who is holding it back steps out of the way (2 Thessalonians 2:6-7 NLT).

The spirit of Antichrist is presently with us. Many antichrists have come and gone and many now exist. In other words, there is always a living candidate who could fit the biblical description of this personage. The spirit of Antichrist is working and has worked from the beginning.

When the final Antichrist will appear is ultimately up to the Lord Himself. The world is running on His program, His schedule. Nothing can slow it down, nor speed it up. When He gives the Word these final events will be set in motion.

SUMMARY TO QUESTION 46
IS IT POSSIBLE THE ANTICHRIST IS ALIVE TODAY?

Yes, it is certainly possible that the predicted Antichrist is alive today. In fact, if the Lord's return will take place in the next forty years or so, then almost without doubt this personage is alive today.

Yet all we can say for certain is that the Antichrist may be alive; for only the Lord knows whether he is or is not. Nobody else knows the answer to this question; whether it be an angel, another type of created being, or a human being.

The coming of the man of sin is linked to the coming of the Lord. Scripture makes this very clear. Since the time of the Lord's coming is unknown, the time of the coming of the Antichrist is also unknown. This means nobody can say with any degree of certainty that the beast, the final Antichrist, is alive today.

Anyone who claims they can know is contradicting the teaching of Scripture. Though we do not know the time of His coming, we are commanded to always be ready. Indeed, His coming for us may be today!

While we do not know for certain when Christ will return, there are signs setting the stage for His coming and the appearance of Antichrist. There are four which clearly stand out.

First, Israel is back in their ancient homeland as a functioning state. This has not happened in two thousand years. For the great tribulation to start, an agreement must be made with the man of sin and the state of Israel. This is now a possibility because a state of Israel presently exists.

Second, there are preparations being made to construct a Third Temple upon the Temple Mount. Certain events during the career of Antichrist must take place around this rebuilt temple. These events which have been predicted so long ago are beginning to come to pass in our day.

Third, Europe is now united under a common currency. The European Union seems to be a forerunner of the final confederation predicted in Scripture, the revival of the ancient Roman Empire.

Fourth, the technology is in place for a worldwide system of monitoring what people buy and sell. Again, this ability has only been a recent phenomenon.

Each of these sets the stage for the coming of Christ which is preceded by the appearance of the final Antichrist.

Finally, there is also the fact that there are Antichrists which presently do exist. Indeed, in John's day he said many Antichrists had already come and others were present. Thus, whenever the time is right there will be a candidate for Antichrist.

Therefore, while it is indeed possible that Antichrist is presently living among us, we cannot know whether or not this is the case. The answer to this question is not known. What we do know for certain is that he is coming.

What Are Some Of The Unresolved Issues About The Antichrist?

While there are a number of things which we know for certain about Antichrist, there are other issues that are still under discussion. The following matters have been debated by Bible-believers, and are still being debated.

1. IS ANTICHRIST A PERSON, INSTITUTION OF EVIL FORCE?

While it seems evident from the Bible that Antichrist will be a final person who comes upon the stage of history, there are those who argue that Antichrist is more of an evil force in the world, or some type of wicked institution. Those who interpret prophecy allegorically or symbolically hold this view.

Though this is still debated, many Bible students see Scripture predicting that a final Antichrist will eventually arrive in our world. The Bible is speaking of a person, not an institution or an evil force. The spirit of Antichrist has been around for every generation and many institutions can rightly be designated "Antichrist" in their actions. Yet the Bible literally predicts the coming of a personal Antichrist.

2.HAS ANTICHRIST ALREADY COME OR IS HE STILL TO COME?

Some Bible students, who believe Antichrist is an actual person rather than some type of force or institution, think that the predicted man of sin has already appeared. In other words, we should not look for the coming of Antichrist in the future because he has already appeared in the past.

Those who hold the "preterist" view of the Book of Revelation see the Antichrist as an issue which was limited to the first century Christians. It is a personage they had to deal with. Therefore, there is no Antichrist to come.

However, this view is soundly rejected by those who believe Bible prophecy should be interpreted in a literal manner. Indeed, there is no possible way to see the fulfillment of these predictions as having happened in the past. They are still future.

3. IF HE HAS COME IN THE PAST, WHO WAS HE?

This point relates to the last question. If Antichrist has come in the past, as some people believe, then who was he? Again, there is no agreement among those who argue for his past appearing.

Some say it was Caesar Nero, others Caligula, or the Roman Emperor Domitian. It has also been popular to equate Antichrist with the Roman Empire itself and the Emperor. While this position is still held, it seems difficult if not impossible to maintain when one reads the entire Book of Revelation. To hold to this viewpoint, Revelation must be interpreted allegorically or symbolically. Otherwise, it is clear that what was written remains to be fulfilled.

Furthermore, the Book of Revelation clearly claims to be a prophecy of future events. These events have not yet taken place. Antichrist is still to come.

4. WILL A COMING ANTICHRIST CLAIM TO BE THE MESSIAH?

One of the seemingly accepted truths concerning this subject is that when Antichrist comes he will claim to be the long-awaited Jewish

Messiah. Since he allows the Jews to rebuild their temple, and re-institute their sacrificial system, he will be received as the Messiah. This, it is argued, is why he is designated the Antichrist; he is a faker, a counterfeit, of the real Christ.

Yet this is something which is still debated. There is the view that the beast of Revelation will be Antichrist in the sense that he attempts to usurp the rightful authority, worship, and rule which belong to Jesus the genuine Messiah. However, he will not claim to be the Messiah of the Jews. For one thing, he may be a Gentile, and not Jewish.

5. WILL A FINAL ANTICHRIST BE A JEW OR GENTILE?

This brings us to our next point. There is also the issue of whether Antichrist will be a Jew, or whether he will be a Gentile. If he is going to claim to be the Messiah of the Jews, then it seems undeniable that he must be Jewish. It is difficult if not impossible to imagine the Jews accepting a Gentile as their promised Messiah.

On the other hand, if Antichrist does not claim to be the Messiah of the Jews, and is not received as such, then he could be a Gentile. In this case, he is an "Antichrist" in the sense that he usurps certain things which belong to Jesus alone. His nationality is an issue which is still debated among Bible-believers.

6. WHICH BEAST IS THE ANTICHRIST, THE FIRST OR SECOND?

One of the little-known debates, in the various issues concerning Antichrist, is about his identification. It is almost universally believed that the final Antichrist is the "first beast" mentioned in Revelation chapter thirteen. He is the person who makes, or confirms, a covenant with the Jews, breaks it, and then declares himself to be God. He is a distinct personage from the second beast, the false prophet.

A minority view believes the second beast, the false prophet, is actu-ally the Antichrist. While the first beast is the person who makes the covenant, etc., he should not be understood to be the final Antichrist which John was writing about.

John's Antichrist, it is argued, is that false prophet who promotes the worship of the first beast. Therefore, Antichrist should be equated with the false prophet, the religious leader, rather than with the political leader. The fact that the false prophet may be a Jew, while the first beast may be a Gentile, gives further support for this argument.

7. IS HIS NUMBER 666 OR 616?

The number of the beast is given to us in Scripture. Traditionally it is believed to be 666. However, there are some ancient manuscripts of the Book of Revelation which read 616 rather than 666. We know that the reading 616 existed in manuscripts of the Book of Revelation before the year A.D. 200. While most textual scholars believe 666 is what John originally wrote in the passage, there are some who argue that 616 is more likely the original reading.

Of course, this will have implications at the time Antichrist comes on the scene since the number of his name, either 666 or 616, is given to confirm his identity. It will be an issue for those living at that time to sort out.

8. DOES ANTICHRIST COME FROM WESTERN EUROPE OR THE MIDDLE EAST?

There is also the question of the geographical origin of Antichrist. Most people believe his origin is from Western Europe since he heads up a confederation of nations from the revived Roman Empire. However, there is a minority view which sees him coming from the Middle East. He will be an Assyrian, of Middle Eastern origin, not someone from Western Europe.

9. WILL THE CHURCH SEE ANTICHRIST?

When Antichrist does appear, will the New Testament church be around to experience him? Again, this is debated among Bible-believing Christians. Those who believe the rapture of the church will occur before the great tribulation, the pre-tribulation rapture theory, insist the church will not be around to see Antichrist. His will not be revealed until the believers are caught up to be with the Lord. Consequently, it is impossible to confirm his identity until the rapture of the church takes place.

Those who hold a different view of the timing of the rapture insist that the church will be around for at least part of the time of Antichrist's appearance.

10. WHAT IS PRESENTLY RESTRAINING ANTICHRIST?

Finally, there is the issue of what is keeping Antichrist from appearing. According to the Apostle Paul, something is presently restraining him from arriving upon the scene. Usually, those who hold the pre-tribulation rapture position argue that the Holy Spirit, indwelling the members of the true church, is what will be removed before the man of sin is revealed. Until that time, the Spirit of God, working through the believers, is the restraining force.

Others argue for a different restrainer. Some believe it to be human governments. Still others believe it is Satan himself who is keeping the final Antichrist from appearing.

Again, there are differences of opinion among Bible-believers as to whom or what is holding back Antichrist.

THESE ISSUES WILL CONTINUE TO BE DEBATED

Each of these issues continues to be debated among Bible-believing Christians. Since we are dealing with prophetic issues dealing with the unknown future, it may not be possible to resolve some of them until the Lord Himself returns.

Therefore, as we discuss these matters, we should exercise grace toward others and humility for ourselves. There is much we all can learn.

SUMMARY TO QUESTION 47
WHAT ARE SOME OF THE UNRESOLVED ISSUES ABOUT THE ANTICHRIST?

As we have examined the subject of the Antichrist from a biblical perspective we have discovered that there remain a number of unresolved matters. These issues continue to be debated among Bible-believing Christians. We can sum up some of the main disputes as follows.

To begin with, there remains the issue as to whether Antichrist is a person, an evil spirit, or an institution. Christians still debate this point. However, many Bible believers assume that the Scripture says that a particular person will come upon the scene of history, a personal Antichrist.

For those who believe Antichrist is a person, the question is whether he has already come and gone, or whether his coming is still in the future. This point is also debated among Christians.

There are those who insist that he has already come and gone in history. Candidates such as the Roman Emperors Caligula, Domitian and Caesar Nero are often offered as the biblical man of sin. Others think the Roman Empire itself, with the one of its emperors, was the beast mentioned in the Book of Revelation.

Those who understand Bible prophecy in a literal manner insist the personal Antichrist is still to come. They are adamant that the words of the Book of Revelation, coupled with other passages in Scripture, makes the coming of the man of sin something which is still to occur.

There is also the issue as to the claims the coming Antichrist will make. Will he claim to be the Messiah of the Jews? Will he be received as such?

Again, Christians are divided. Some believe he will claim to be the Jewish Messiah, while others, believing him to be a Gentile, assume that he will claim to be much more than that. He will exalt himself above Jesus, the genuine Messiah. He is the "anti" Christ in the sense that he usurps the things which rightly belong to Jesus. This includes worship due to Christ alone.

The nationality of the Antichrist is also debated. Those who believe he will claim to be the Messiah of the Jews conclude that he must be Jewish. There is no possibility the Jews would accept a Gentile Messiah. However, if the Antichrist does not claim to be the Messiah of the Jews, but rather usurps the things which rightly belong to Jesus, then he could be a Gentile.

While most people believe the first beast of the Book of Revelation is the predicted Antichrist, there are those who think that the second beast, the false prophet, is the coming man of sin. This issue, though not often discussed, is still a matter of debate among some Christians. The false prophet, being the religious leader is seen to have more in common with the description of Antichrist than the political leader, the first beast. However, both of these evil personages are "anti" Christ in their character and behavior.

The unique number of this coming "man of sin" is also debated. While the number 666 is generally assumed to be his number, there are a few manuscripts, including the earliest in the Book of Revelation, which read 616. Some textual scholars believe this is the true number of the beast. This will be an issue for those living at that time when he appears.

The place of origin of Antichrist is also a matter which has not been resolved. Though usually it is thought that Antichrist arises out of

Western Europe, and must be European, there are others who think the evidence that Antichrist will come from the Middle East, possibly from the area of ancient Assyria.

Whether or not the church will see Antichrist is another issue which is discussed among Christians. If the church is taken out of the world before the great tribulation, then they will not see the final Antichrist. However, if the church will go through the seventieth week of Daniel, the great tribulation, then the church will see Antichrist. Christians continue to debate this issue.

Finally, there is the matter of whom or what is presently restraining Antichrist from appearing. Those who hold the pre-tribulation rapture position usually see the Holy Spirit, living in the members of the New Testament church, as the restraining force.

Others believe it to be human governments, while still others think it is the devil himself who is restraining the coming man of sin. As is true with these other issues, there are good Bible-believing Christians who hold these different positions.

This briefly sums up some of the main areas of disagreement about the coming Antichrist from the perspective of those who believe the Bible is God's divinely inspired Word. Until these events eventually unfold, the discussions and disagreements will continue. Hopefully, Bible-believers can disagree agreeably with each other on these matters.

QUESTION 48

What Should We Conclude About The Idea Of A Coming Antichrist?

We have looked at the subject of the biblical Antichrist in some detail. Many things were learned, while a number of questions remain unanswered. After our investigation as to what the Bible has to say about the coming Antichrist, we can make a number of observations and conclusions. They are as follows.

1. WE NEED TO KNOW CERTAIN THINGS ABOUT THIS PERSONAGE

While the subject of Antichrist should not be our main theme of study as we look at the Scriptures, it is important that we know certain things about this individual. Indeed, since this personage occupies a great deal of space in Scripture with respect to coming events, it is essential that we have some idea of who he is, as well as what he will be trying to accomplish. After all, there are reasons as to why the Lord gave so much space in Scripture to this coming personage.

2. MANY ANTICHRISTS HAVE COME: A FINAL ANTICHRIST IS COMING

While still debated, it seems clear that a final personal Antichrist is coming. However, each generation has had its own antichrists. This is important for us to understand. There will always be people who have characteristics of the final Antichrist.

While many of the more famous ones such as Nero and Hitler were not the biblical man of sin, they did exhibit many of the traits that this predicted man of sin will possess.

3. THERE IS A MESSAGE OF HOPE IN THE STUDY OF ANTICHRIST

Strange as it may seem, the study of Antichrist brings a message of hope to Christians. Through all the terrible events which will occur in the earth's future, at the end of the day, there will be triumph for the believers. Jesus Christ will defeat this final Antichrist, hurl him into the lake of fire, and then set up His righteous kingdom upon the earth.

Furthermore, the coming of the predicted Antichrist signals the coming of Jesus Christ. This man of sin will appear immediately before the return of the Lord. Therefore, as terrible as his coming may be, the appearance of the beast, this Antichrist, will actually be a sign of hope that the world will soon forever change.

4. WE SHOULD BE LOOKING FOR JESUS CHRIST, NOT ANTICHRIST

Finally, we should be putting our complete attention on the coming of Jesus Christ, not the final Antichrist. This is where our study of Scripture should focus. Paul wrote about the hope of Christians to Titus.

> While we wait for the blessed hope—the appearing of the glory of our great God and Savior, Jesus Christ (Titus 2:13 NIV).

The hope of believers is the return of Christ to the earth. This is where our eyes should be fixating upon. As Jesus has taught, we need to be ready. He said.

> Be dressed for service and keep your lamps burning, as though you were waiting for your master to return from the wedding

feast. Then you will be ready to open the door and let him in the moment he arrives and knocks (Luke 12:35-36 NLT).

Let us then fix our personal hope on the coming of Christ. In doing so, we must be ready for Him to return at any moment. That time could be today!

SUMMARY TO QUESTION 48
WHAT SHOULD WE CONCLUDE ABOUT THE IDEA OF A COMING ANTICHRIST?

As we sift through the Bible in an attempt to discover what it teaches about this subject of the final Antichrist, we learn a number of significant things. They include the following.

For one thing, we find that we do need to know certain things about this personage. Since Scripture highlights him in many passages, as well as in types, it tells us that this subject is important for us to understand. Indeed, he is the key player on the earth before the Second Coming of Jesus Christ. For this reason alone the topic of Antichrist should be given serious study.

We have also found that many Antichrists have already come and gone. While certain people have mistakenly identified these individuals as "the" Antichrist of Scripture, they are not entirely wrong in their assessment of these people.

Indeed, people like Nero and Hitler were Antichrists in the sense they opposed Christ and His kingdom, as well as persecuting God's chosen people, the Jews.

However, they were not the predicted "final" Antichrist. He is still to come. In point of fact, anyone who denies that God became a human being in the Person of Jesus Christ is an Antichrist. Yet, there is one final Antichrist which will arrive immediately before the Second Coming of Christ. He will be the evilest of them all.

In our study of the subject of Antichrist we have found that there is a message of hope. The coming of Antichrist will directly precede the return of Jesus Christ to the earth. Though the world will experience its worst period of suffering in its entire history, this time frame will be relatively short.

At the end of the great tribulation is the return of Jesus. Therefore, even in the midst of all the havoc Antichrist will bring upon the earth, there is still hope for the believer and for our planet. A better world is coming.

Above all, our goal should be the daily looking for Jesus Christ, not Antichrist. The return of Christ is the "blessed hope" of the church. This is what we should be fixing our attention upon.

Therefore, anything which we learn about the coming Antichrist should be placed in the overall context of Scripture. The Bible is not about Antichrist, it is about Jesus Christ! He is the One whom our hearts should be fixated upon.

Is The Final Antichrist The Same Character As Gog In Ezekiel 38,39?

In Scripture, there are two personages who are highlighted as major players in the last days.

First, there is the leader of the invasion of Israel in as recorded in Ezekiel 38,39. His title is "Gog." He comes from the land of MaGog.

Second, there is a coming world leader. Through the help of his cohort, the false prophet, the entire world will be forced to worship him and his image. Among other titles, he is known as the Antichrist.

Since these two individuals have certain things in common, some assume they are the same person. Is this what the Bible teaches? Is Gog the predicted Antichrist of Scripture?

THEY ARE NOT THE SAME PERSON

There are a number of reasons as to why Gog and the final Antichrist are not the same person. They can be listed as follows.

1. THEY ARE FROM DIFFERENT GEOGRAPHICAL AREAS

The last days coalition of nations against Israel is led by a leader with the title of Gog. He is said to come to Israel from the "far north." The farthest point north from both Israel and Babylon (where Ezekiel was prophesying from) is modern day Russia.

On the other hand, the final Antichrist will arise from the revived Roman Empire. This is a geographical description of western Europe.

In other words, these two "last days" personages arise from two different geographical areas.

2. GOG IS A MAN OF WAR, ANTICHRIST STARTS OUT AS A MAN OF PEACE

When we are introduced to these two characters we find completely different descriptions of them.

Antichrist rises out of obscurity. Eventually he becomes known as "a man of peace." It is only after three and one half years in the limelight that his true nature is revealed, he is a beast.

Gog, on the other hand, is an established warrior, a man of war. When we are introduced to him it is in the context of invading Israel. He wants to take something from the chosen people that he, as well as the other invading countries, both want and need.

3. GOG RULES A COUNTY, ANTICHRIST THE ENTIRE WORLD

Gog is a leader of a particular country. Most likely, it is modern day Russia.

On the other hand, the final Antichrist will never be the leader of only one country. Indeed, he will rise up to head up a ten nation confederation. Eventually he will become a worldwide dictator while Gog's influence will be localized to one country.

4. GOG SEEMINGLY APPEARS BEFORE THE RISE OF ANTICHRIST

The timing is also different. One of the last days scenarios, though certainly not the only one, has Gog arising before Antichrist. In other words, the invasion of Ezekiel 38 and 39 takes place before the Antichrist rises to prominence. In other words, they do not appear on the stage of history at the same time.

5. THE ARMY OF GOG IS STOPPED WHEN ENTERING THE HOLY LAND, ANTICHRIST SETS UP HIS HEADQUARTERS THERE

Gog is destroyed when he enters the Promised Land. The final Antichrist, on the other hand, establishes his headquarters in the Holy Land. This is another indication that they cannot be the same person.

6. GOG IS DESTROYED BY GOD WHEN HE ENTERS THE HOLY LAND, ANTICHRIST IS THROWN INTO THE LAKE OF FIRE AT THE RETURN OF CHRIST

While not specifically stated, it seems Gog is destroyed, along with his coalition, the moment they set foot in the Promised Land.

Antichrist will rule the world for some three and one half years. He will only be stopped at the Second Coming of Christ.

While more points could be added the conclusion is clear; we are looking at two different persons when we consider Gog and the final Antichrist.

SUMMARY TO APPENDIX 1
IS THE FINAL ANTICHRIST THE SAME CHARACTER AS GOG IN EZEKIEL 38,39?

At the time of the end, there are two personages who stand out. They are Gog, the leader of a "last days" invasion of Israel, and the final Antichrist, the coming Caesar, the man who will rule the world. Since there are some similarities between the two it is often thought they are the same personage.

However, there are a number of differences between them which illustrates that they cannot be the same person. These dissimilarities can be summed up as follows.

When we are introduced to Gog we discover that he is the warlike leader of a huge invasion force. In other words, he is already an established leader.

As we have documented in this book, the final Antichrist rises up out of obscurity. Furthermore, when he does rise in popularity, for a number of years, he is seen as a man of peace. His evil intentions are only manifested a number of years later.

Gog is the leader of one particular country. This final Antichrist, will never lead one country but rather a coalition of ten countries. Eventually he will become the leader of the entire world. This makes it clear that they are two different personages.

The geography is also different. Gog invades Israel from the far north, likely modern day Russia, while this Antichrist will actually make his headquarters in Israel and rule from there.

While Gog and his armies are stopped when they enter Israel, Antichrist actually sets up his headquarters there.

Gog will be destroyed at this invasion of Israel. Antichrist will receive a heavenly judgment. Indeed at the Second Coming of Christ, He will be taken by Jesus Christ and thrown into the lake of fire.

The conclusion seems obvious. Gog and the final Antichrist are two different persons who will arise in the "last days."

What Is The Theory Of The Assyrian Antichrist? Could He Be A Muslim?

While the majority of Bible commentators believe a future Antichrist will arise from Western Europe, the revived Roman Empire, a minority hold a different perspective. Instead Antichrist will arise from the Middle East. This is known as the theory of the "Assyrian Antichrist."

THE CASE FOR THE ASSYRIAN ANTICHRIST

Those who argue for an Assyrian Antichrist, rather than one from Western Europe, make the following case from the Scripture.

1. HE IS CALLED AN ASSYRIAN

To begin with, the final Antichrist is specifically called an Assyrian. We read in Micah.

> And he shall be their peace. When the Assyrian comes into our land and treads in our palaces, then we will raise against him seven shepherds and eight princes of men (Micah 5:5 ESV).

While some view this passage as referring to the past invasions of the Assyrian nation, others believe it refers to the coming "man of sin."

2. HE IS THE KING OF THE NORTH

Antichrist is also introduced to us as the "King of the North." We read of this in the Book of Daniel. It says.

> At the time of the end, the king of the south shall attack him, but the king of the north shall rush upon him like a whirlwind, with chariots and horsemen, and with many ships. And he shall come into countries and shall overflow and pass through (Daniel 11:40 ESV).

Assyria was located north of Israel. This is another clue that Antichrist will be an Assyrian.

3. HIS HEADQUARTERS IS IN THE HOLY LAND, NOT EUROPE

We also find that the headquarters of this coming man of sin will be in the Holy Land and not in Western Europe. Daniel wrote.

> He will pitch his royal tents between the seas at the beautiful holy mountain. Yet he will come to his end, and no one will help him (Daniel 11:45 NIV).

His tents will be "between the seas." This indicates there are bodies of water on either side of his headquarters. The seas are most often understood to be the Mediterranean Sea on the west, and the Dead Sea on the east.

The exact location of the "beautiful holy mountain" is usually believed to refer to Mt. Zion. This is another name for Jerusalem, the location of the Holy Temple. This fits with the specified geographical location. Jerusalem is located "between the seas."

Therefore, this passage seems to teach that the final Antichrist will use the rebuilt temple in Jerusalem as his headquarters while the battles he will fight will be elsewhere.

Some believe that the location of his camp is not in Jerusalem proper but rather at some location between the Mediterranean Sea and Jerusalem. Whatever the case may be, this King of the North will set up his headquarters in the Holy Land.

4. ANTIOCHUS WAS FROM THAT REGION

A further reason why the coming Antichrist may be from the region of ancient Assyria is found in the clearest pre-figurement, or type, of this coming man of sin, Antiochus IV.

The Book of Daniel compares the rule of Antiochus to that of the coming Antichrist. Since Antiochus, the clearest type of Antichrist, was from that geographical region, the final Antichrist may also come from that area.

These facts have caused a minority of Bible students to claim that the final Antichrist will be from a geographical area north of Israel, in the Middle East, rather than from Western Europe.

COULD HE BE A MUSLIM?

If the final Antichrist will arise from the Middle East, rather than western Europe, the question is often asked about his religion. Could he be a Muslim? In fact, in recent years a number of books have come out with the claim that the final Antichrist, the coming Caesar, will actually be a Muslim.

Rather than go into great detail in a point by point refutation of this theory, we will make a few basic observations.

OBSERVATION 1: THE KINGDOM OF ANTICHRIST IS WORLDWIDE, NOT LIMITED TO THE MIDDLE EAST

From Scripture, we know that the rule of Antichrist will be worldwide, it will not be a regional kingdom limited to the Middle East as the theory of a Muslim Antichrist usually claims.

OBSERVATION 2: ISRAEL WOULD NEVER PUT THEIR SECURITY IN THE HANDS OF A MUSLIM

We also know that this final Antichrist will make a pact with Israel in which he will guarantee their security. It seems rather obvious that Israel would never agree to place the security of their nation into the hands of a Muslim. This is a non-starter. In addition, any Muslim who would guarantee the security of Israel would immediately lose any status that he had in the Islamic world.

OBSERVATION 3: NO MUSLIM WOULD HELP ISRAEL BUILD THEIR NEXT TEMPLE

There is every indication that the final Antichrist will help Israel in the construction of the Third Temple. Any Muslim who even suggested such a thing would be signing his death warrant.

OBSERVATION 4: NO MUSLIM WOULD CLAIM TO BE GOD

The fact that the final Antichrist claims to be God rules him out as being a Muslim. In fact, stating that there is another God would be bad enough, claiming to be God would be the ultimate of blasphemy as far as Muslims are concerned.

OBSERVATION 5: THE IDENTITY OF THE FINAL ANTICHRIST WILL ONLY BE KNOWN AFTER THE CHURCH IS GONE

There is one final thing that we should note. The identity of the final Antichrist will only be known after the church, the true believers in Jesus Christ, are taken from the earth in the rapture of the church. It is only after this event occurs that the final Antichrist will be revealed.

Therefore, attempting to discover his exact identity is fruitless. Indeed, since we will not be around to see him we should spend our time studying more beneficial things.

SUMMARY TO APPENDIX 2
WHAT IS THE VIEW OF THE ASSYRIAN ANTICHRIST? COULD HE BE A
MUSLIM?

There is a minority view among commentators of the Bible that the Antichrist will actually arise out of the Middle East and not from Rome or Western Europe. This theory is known, among other things, as the "Assyrian Antichrist." There are a number of reasons as to why this view is held.

In the Book of Micah, this coming man of sin is called an Assyrian. Consequently, it can be argued that this is where he arises, from the people, or the geographical area, of ancient Assyria.

He is called the "King of the North." Assyria was located north of Israel. This is another indication of his Middle Eastern origin.

We also find that the headquarters of this king is in the Middle East, not Western Europe. In fact, we are told it is somewhere between the seas at the beautiful holy mountain. This means that it is somewhere in Israel between the Mediterranean and the Dead Sea. The beautiful holy mountain is Jerusalem. These facts give further evidence that Antichrist will come from this part of the world.

There is also the pre-figurement of Antichrist in the person of Antiochus IV. He is the clearest type of Antichrist in Scripture. He was from the Seleucid Empire which was also located in the Middle East, he was not from Western Europe.

These things have led certain scholars to hold to the Assyrian Antichrist theory.

If it is possible for the this coming man of sin to be an "Assyrian," then is it also possible that he will be a Muslim? While there have been those who have advocated the theory of a "Muslim Antichrist" the following points make this idea highly unlikely, if not impossible.

First, the rule of Antichrist is worldwide. It is not a regional empire as the Muslim Antichrist theory holds.

Second, Israel would never put their security in the hands of a Muslim. Yet we know they will trust the final Antichrist to protect them.

Third, Antichrist seems to have a prominent part in helping the Jews build a Third Temple. No Muslim would suggest such a thing, let alone be at the forefront of accomplishing it.

Fourth, the man of sin will sit in the temple and claim to be God. Muslim believe there is only one God, Allah. Any Muslim who suggested to the contrary would be put to death. Any Muslim who personally claimed to be God would not live out the day. This certainly precludes Antichrist from being a Muslim.

Finally, since the appearance of Antichrist will only take place after the true believers in Jesus Christ, the church, have left the earth, it is fruitless to try to speculate about his identity.

About The Author

Don Stewart is a graduate of Biola University and Talbot Theological Seminary (with the highest honors).

Don is a best-selling and award-winning author having authored, or co-authored, over seventy books. This includes the best-selling *Answers to Tough Questions*, with Josh McDowell, as well as the award-winning book *Family Handbook of Christian Knowledge: The Bible*. His various writings have been translated into over thirty different languages and have sold over a million copies.

Don has traveled around the world proclaiming and defending the historic Christian faith. He has also taught both Hebrew and Greek at the undergraduate level and Greek at the graduate level.

Made in the USA
Monee, IL
23 May 2020

31711795R00226